Computational Nonlinear Morphology

By the late 1970s, phonologists, and later morphologists, had departed from a linear approach for describing morphophonological operations to a nonlinear one. Computational models, however, remain faithful to the linear model, making it very difficult, if not impossible, to implement the morphology of languages whose morphology is nonconcatanative. *Computational Nonlinear Morphology* aims at presenting a computational system that counters the development in linguistics. It provides a detailed computational analysis of the complex morphophonological phenomena found in Semitic languages that is based on linguistically motivated models.

The book outlines a new generalized regular rewrite rule system that uses multitape finite-state automata to cater for root-and-pattern morphology, infixation, circumfixation, and other complex operations such as the broken plural derivation problem found in Arabic and Ethiopic.

George Anton Kiraz is the founder and director of Beth Mardutho: The Syriac Institute. Previously he was a technical manager at Nuance Communications in New York. Earlier, he worked as a research scientist in Bell Laboratories' Language Modeling Department, where he developed language modeling for text-to-speech applications by using finite-state methods. He is the author of the six-volume *Concordance to the Syriac New Testament* (1993) and the four-volume *Comparative Edition of the Syriac Gospels* (1996). He has also published various pedagogical textbooks on Syriac and numerous scientific papers on computational linguistics in international journals and conference proceedings. In his free time, he serves as the general editor of *Hugoye: Journal of Syriac Studies* and on the editorial board of *Journal of the Aramaic Bible.*

STUDIES IN NATURAL LANGUAGE PROCESSING

Also in the series

Douglas E. Appelt, *Planning English Sentences*
Madeleine Bates and Ralph M. Weischedel (eds.), *Challenges in Natural Language Processing*
Steven Bird, *Computational Phonology*
Peter Bosch and Rob van der Sandt, *Focus*
Pierette Bouillon and Federica Busa (eds.), *The Language of Word Meaning*
T. Briscoe, Ann Copestake, and Valeria Paiva (eds.), *Inheritance, Defaults and the Lexicon*
Ronald Cole, Joseph Mariani, Hans Uszkoreit, Giovanni Varile, Annie Zaenen, Antonio Zampolli, and Victor Zue (eds.), *Survey of the State of the Art in Human Language Technology*
David R. Dowty, Lauri Karttunen, and Arnold M. Zwicky (eds.), *Natural Language Parsing*
Ralph Grishman, *Computational Linguistics*
Graeme Hirst, *Semantic Interpretation and the Resolution of Ambiguity*
András Kornai, *Extended Finite State Models of Language*
Kathleen R. McKeown, *Text Generation*
Martha Stone Palmer, *Semantic Processing for Finite Domains*
Terry Patten, *Systemic Text Generation as Problem Solving*
Ehud Reiter and Robert Dale, *Building Natural Language Generation Systems*
Manny Rayner, David Carter, Pierette Bouillon, Vassilis Digalakis, and Matis Wiren (eds.), *The Spoken Language Translator*
Michael Rosner and Roderick Johnson (eds.), *Computational Linguistics and Formal Semantics*
Patrick Saint-Dizier and Evelyn Viegas (eds.), *Computational Lexical Semantics*
Richard Sproat, *A Computational Theory of Writing Systems*

Computational Nonlinear Morphology

With Emphasis on Semitic Languages

George Anton Kiraz
Beth Mardutho: The Syriac Institute

CAMBRIDGE
UNIVERSITY PRESS

PUBLISHED BY THE PRESS SYNDICATE OF THE UNIVERSITY OF CAMBRIDGE
The Pitt Building, Trumpington Street, Cambridge, United Kingdom

CAMBRIDGE UNIVERSITY PRESS
The Edinburgh Building, Cambridge CB2 2RU, UK
40 West 20th Street, New York, NY 10011-4211, USA
477 Williamstown Road, Port Melbourne, VIC 3207, Australia
Ruiz de Alarcón 13, 28014 Madrid, Spain
Dock House, The Waterfront, Cape Town 8001, South Africa

http://www.cambridge.org

First published 2001

Printed in the United Kingdom at the University Press, Cambridge

Typeface Times Roman 10/12 pt.   *System* LaTeX 2ε [TB]

A catalog record for this book is available from the British Library.

Library of Congress Cataloging in Publication Data
Kiraz, George Anton.
Computational nonlinear morphology : with emphasis on Semitic languages/George Anton Kiraz.
p. cm. – (Studies in natural language processing)
Includes bibliographical references and index.
ISBN 0-521-63196-3
1. Grammar, Comparative and general – Morphology – Data processing. 2. Semitic languages – Morphology – Data processing. I. Title. II. Series.
P241 .K538 2001
492′.045′0285 – dc21
2001022304

ISBN 0 521 63196 3 hardback

In loving memory of my father

Anton *bar* Artin *bar* Daoud *bar* Barṣoum *d'beth* Kiraz
of Kharput
may the Lord rest his soul,

And to my mother

Nijmeh *bath* Abd el-Aḥad *d'beth* Khamis
of Beth Zabday
may He prolong her life.

رَحِمَ اللّٰهُ مَن قَرٰى
وَغَفَرَ لِمَن كَتَب

God be merciful to him who reads,
And forgive him who wrote.

Marginal note in a Garšûnî Syriac manuscript
on the works of Aphrahaṭ († *c.* 350?)

Contents

Preface

The emergence of two-level morphology by Koskenniemi (1983) – based on earlier work on computational phonology by Kay and Kaplan (1983) – marked a milestone in the field of computational morphology. Its finite-state approach meant that morphology could be implemented with the simplest computational devices, that is, finite-state automata, whose computational power is lesser by far than that of Turing machines. Additionally, the implementation of two-level morphology in the form of finite-state transducers made it possible to use the same automata for analysis and generation, which provides for bidirectionality. As a result, two-level systems were implemented for a large number of languages, some of which are morphologically rich. Yet the two-level model fell short of providing elegant means for handling complex morphological operations labeled as being "nonlinear" or "nonconcatenative," in which the lexical description of a word is not simply the concatenation of the morphemes that constitute the word in question.

Nonlinear computational morphology is of interest for theoretical and practical reasons. Theoretically, since the late 1970s, phonologists (and later morphologists) have departed from the linear approach of *The Sound Pattern of English* (Chomsky and Halle, 1968) to a nonlinear framework, under which concatenation does not lie at the heart of morphophonological operations. A corresponding computational morphophonological model is indeed needed to counter this development in linguistics. Practically, nonlinear operations lie at the heart of the morphological description of many languages, most of which are either commercially important or of scholarly interest. Languages that exhibit nonlinearity in their morphology include Amharic (Ethiopia), Arabic (Middle East and North Africa), Dakota (Central North America), Hebrew (Israel and the Jewish diaspora), Syriac (Middle East and the diaspora, also with a large corpus of literary tradition), Tagalog (Philippines), Terena (Brazil), Tiv (Nigeria), and Ulwa (Nicaragua), to name a few.

The objective of this work is twofold: First, to present a tractable computational model that can cope with complex morphological operations, especially in Semitic languages, as well as less complex morphological systems present in Western languages. Second, to provide the computational linguistics community with a monograph on computational morphology, especially because the last two (and only) monographs on this topic – Ritchie et al. (1992) and Sproat (1992) – appeared more than five years ago. This work is closer to the former in that it presents one particular model. Sproat's work continues to be the primary textbook on the topic.

The choice of Semitic stems from a personal interest in Syriac, the most attested literary dialect of Aramaic that is still in use and, to a lesser extent, spoken by followers of the various ancient Syriac Churches in the Middle East, the Malabar Coast of Southwest India, and the Syriac diaspora in the West. Regardless of this personal interest, Semitic seems to be the perfect choice for at least two reasons. First, Semitic (in the form of Arabic) ubiquitously exemplifies nonlinear morphology in the linguistics and computational linguistics literature: In fact, Semitic (in the form of Hebrew) features in the very first work within generative phonology (Chomsky, 1951). Second, it seems only appropriate that modern research pay a tribute to the long history of the Semitic grammatical tradition. Many of the notions and technical terms that the classical grammarians used appear, directly or indirectly, in modern linguistics. The term *schwa*, for instance, originates from the Hebrew and Syriac grammatical traditions, where it is represented by two vertical dots under or over a consonant that is followed by a *very* short [e]; the term was used as early as the seventh century by the Syriac grammarian Jacob of Edessa, albeit to mark accentation in Bible reciting. The terms *surface* and *underlying* are analogous to Arabic *ẓaahir* "outer, manifest" and *baaṭin* "inner, hidden," which started as two theological schools of thought but developed into distinct linguistic theories; hence, one speaks of the Ẓaahirite school of grammar. Even the modern theory of *government and binding* has a counterpart in classical Arabic syntax: the *ʕaamil* "governor" and *ʕamal* "governance" (Versteegh, 1997b). But most importantly, at least for our purposes, the Semitic grammatical tradition may have been the first to recognize what we now call *morphemic analysis*. Unlike their ancient Greek and Roman counterparts whose morphological models did not venture below the word level (Robins, 1979), classical Semitic grammarians were not only well aware of the root-and-pattern phenomenon of their tongues, but also recognized the root as being an abstract (morphemic) entity. As Mark Aronoff notes, "It may thus well be that all Western linguistic morphology is directly rooted in the Semitic grammatical tradition" (Aronoff, 1994, p. 3).

Qualifying the subtitle of the book, this work by no means covers the morphology of all Semitic languages. Arabic largely receives attention for two simple reasons: First, it is used in the linguistic models on which this book relies (see Chapter 2). Second, it is also used in previous computational linguistic models that deal with nonlinear morphology (see Chapter 4). Syriac examples appear throughout because of a personal interest in that language. Having said that, the underlying morphological system of Semitic languages hardly varies in terms of the root-and-pattern nature of stem formation (which is our main concern here). The concepts developed in this work should apply to the entire Semitic family.

Outline of Presentation

This book is divided into eight chapters. The first four chapters are introductory: Chapter 1 provides linguistics, computational, and Semitic preliminaries for the nonspecialist. Chapter 2 introduces Semitic root-and-pattern (or templatic) morphology, with emphasis on Arabic. Chapter 3 provides a brief survey of finite-state morphology, especially two-level morphology. Chapter 4 describes previous proposals for handling Semitic morphology computationally.

Chapter 5 outlines a new computational morphology model made of three components: (1) a lexicon that consists of sublexica, with each sublexicon corresponding to a lexical representation: (2) rewrite rules that allow the mapping of multiple lexical representations to one surface representation; and (3) a morphotactic word grammar in two versions – the first is based on regular relations, and the second is in the form of context-free relations.

Chapter 6 is dedicated to modeling Semitic morphology. It demonstrates how the nonlinear morphological problems, discussed in Chapter 2, can be handled under the new model. It also discusses practical issues that arise when developing Semitic morphology.

Chapter 7 shows how lexica and rules are compiled into multitape finite-state automata or transducers. Finally, Chapter 8 provides concluding remarks and outlines some outstanding issues.

It must be stressed that the research behind this work was completed between 1992 and 1996 and hence covers that period.

Acknowledgments

The current work represents, for the most part, my doctoral research at the Computer Laboratory, University of Cambridge.[1] Aḥmad Shawqi (1868–1932), the Egyptian Prince of Poets, once said,

قف للمعلم وافه التبجيلا كاد المعلم أن يكون رسولا

Rise in front of the teacher in honor
For the teacher is almost a prophet

I thank Dr. Stephen Pulman (University of Cambridge), my Ph.D. supervisor, whose constant feedback and comments were invaluable throughout my research. The constructive criticism of my examiners, Dr. Graeme Ritchie (University of Edinburgh) and Dr. Geoffrey Khan (University of Cambridge), contributed in shaping this work into a more accurate account. I give them all my utmost and sincere gratitude.

A number of people provided valuable comments on various versions of this work, in full or in part. During my doctoral research, John McCarthy kindly

[1] Some of the material presented here appeared elsewhere in other forms. Solo works include Kiraz (1994, 1996a, 1996b, 1996c, 1997a, 1997b, 1998). Collaborative works include Bowden and Kiraz (1995), Grimley-Evans, Kiraz, and Pulman (1996), and Kiraz and Grimley-Evans (1997).

checked the Arabic linguistic material of Chapter 2. My former colleagues at Cambridge, Edmund Grimley-Evans and Richard Tucker, and my hostel-mate and friend Daniel Delbourgo were subjected to many a formal definition. Earlier versions of parts of the thesis were proofread at various stages by Nancy Chang, Ruth Glassock, and Daniel Ponsford. As for the production of this book, Elisabeth Maier and Daniel Ponsford kindly reviewed the entire manuscript and gave many invaluable comments. Richard Sproat and Jo Calder read the penultimate version. Steven Bird, acting as editor on behalf of Cambridge University Press, helped immensely in pointing out areas that needed further clarification. Bob Carpenter answered questions regarding unification-based grammars. I give them all my utmost and sincere appreciation. Mistakes, as always, remain mine and only mine.

I am also grateful to the Master, President, and Fellows of St John's College, Cambridge, for offering me a Benefactors' Studentship, Scholarship, and various grants. The Computer Laboratory generously financed a number of conference trips; its staff have always been most helpful.

Dedication

This work is dedicated to the memory of my father Anton, may the Lord rest his soul, who passed away during the second year of my doctoral research, and to my mother Nijmeh, may He prolong her life and grant her a long and healthy life. I would not have achieved my goals if it were not for their encouragement and zeal toward education and learning, which, at times, was out of the ordinary. On many occasions, my father would take me from Bethlehem to the book shop of al-Muḥtasib in Jerusalem, where I – a high school kid at the time – would choose the voluminous masterpieces of the Arabic linguistic tradition: The *'Alfiyya* of Ibn Mâlik (d. 1273), a grammatical treatise in one thousand verses; *Lisân al-'Arab* "Language of the Arabs" of Ibn Manẓûr (d. 1311), probably the most popular classical Arabic lexicon; and *Taĵ al-'arûs* "The Bride's Crown" of Murtaḍa az-Zabîdî (d. 1791), a monumental lexicon with more than 120,000 entries in 10 huge volumes. All this was paid for by the little income my mother provided while sitting behind her 1940s Singer sewing machine for more than half a century. I am proud to say that all her customers – from the wives of politicians and ambassadors of British-mandate Palestine to the ladies of modern-day Bethlehem – would vouch that she was the best seamstress in town!

Last, but most definitely not least, to my *'arûs* "bride" Christine... I can truly and honestly say that had she not entered my life, this book would have appeared much earlier – a most delightful delay!

Piscataway, New Jersey
Commemoration of the Syriac Mathematician and Grammarian
Mor Gregorious bar Ebroyo (1226–1286)
30 July 1998

George Anton Kiraz

Abbreviations and Acronyms

Abbreviations

C consonant
H high tone, heavy syllable
L low tone, light syllable
Lex lexical expression (in rewrite rules)
M mid tone
Surf surface expression (in rewrite rules)
V vowel

Acronyms

CR context restriction
FSA finite-state automaton
FST finite-state transducer
LLC left lexical context
LSC left surface context
NPG number, person, gender
PC prosodic circumscription
PT pattern tape
RLC right lexical context
RSC right surface context
RT root tape
SC surface coercion
ST surface tape
TT tone tape
VIM verbal inflectional marker
VT vocalism tape

Grammatical Features

ACT active
CAUS causative
COM common
DU dual

FEM	feminine
IMPF	imperfect
MASC	masculine
PASS	passive
PERF	perfect
PL	plural
REFL	reflexive
SING	singular

Greek Symbols

β	morpheme boundary
ϵ	empty string
μ	mora
σ	syllable
σ_μ	monomoraic syllable
$\sigma_{\mu\mu}$	bimoraic syllable
σ_x	extra syllable

Sigla

{ }	morpheme, set
/ /	phonological string
$\langle\ \rangle$	*n*-tuple of elements
[ ]	phoneme, character
" "	string
' '	symbol, letter, character
$*$	theoretical word, Kleene Closure, uninstantiated context (in rewrite rules)
+	Kleene Plus
#	word boundary

Transliteration of Semitic

From the mouth of an-Nûĵašân bin Abd il-Masîḥ, from the mouth of the student of al-Kindî: When he [al-Kindî] needed to use the languages of the various nations, Persians, Syriacs, Romans and Greeks, he devised for himself a system of writing composed of forty symbols of various shapes and forms, and there was nothing he could not transcribe or recite.

Ḥamzah bin al-Ḥasan al-Iṣfahânî (fl. 904-961)
kitâb at-tenbîh ʿalā ḥudûth at-taṣḥîf

Tables 0.1 and 0.2 (on the following page) provide the transliteration used in this work. Parenthesized symbols indicate emphatic consonants. Unless otherwise specified, Syriac spirantization is ignored; for a discussion, see Kiraz (1995).

Arabic long vowels are indicated by the repetition of the corresponding short vowel; for example, long *a* is *aa*, according to current practice. Unlike Arabic, the Syriac vowel system indicates vowel quality, rather than quantity. A circumflex over a vowel, for example, *â*, indicates that the vowel is followed by *matres lectionis* (ʔ, *w*, and *y*). A macron indicates Syriac long vowels, for example, *ē*.

Table 0.1. *Consonants*

	Plosive		Fricative				
	−*V*	+*V*	−*V*	+*V*	Nasal	Liquid	Glide
Bilabial	p	b			m		w
Labiodental			f	v			
Interdental			θ	ð (ð̣)			
Dental	t (ṭ)	d (ḍ)			n	l/r	
Alveolar			s (ṣ)	z			
Palatal							y
"-alveolar			š	ĵ			
Velar	k	g	x	ğ			
Uvular	q						
Pharyngeal			ħ	ʕ			
Glottal	ʔ		h				

Table 0.2. *Vowels*

	Front	Back
Close	i	u
Mid	e	o
Open		a å

Note: Arabic employs [a], [i], and [u]. Syriac employs the six phonemes (in addition to a long [e], which does not occur in this book), albeit with dialectical variants between East and West Syriac. For example, West Syriac collapses [o] and [u] together. Hebrew makes use of [ə] in addition to other vowels that do not feature here.

Errata and Corrigenda

The careful scholar loves to look
Where faults are marked and variants collected;
Only a fool prefers a book
Where not one single letter is corrected.

Isaac of Antioch († *c.* 460)
Mimrê, Bickell's Edition (ii, 348)

Despite all the care given in preparing this work, the attentive reader might find some (hopefully small) slip-ups. An errata sheet will be available on the Internet at

`www.BethMardutho.org/gkiraz`

and will be periodically updated. I shall be most grateful to those who will take the trouble to communicate errors to me via the above Web page.

1 Introduction

aṣ-ṣarf *of words* the deriving of words one from another, *of winds* shifting from one direction to another, *of wine* drinking it.

al-Fayrûz Abâdî (1329–1414)
al-qâmûs al-muḥîṭ

aṣ-ṣarf The shifting a thing from one state, or condition, to another.

Lane's *Arabic-English Lexicon*

Morphology The science of form.

Oxford English Dictionary

mor·phol·o·gy A study and description of word formation in a language including inflection, derivation, and compounding.

Webster's Third

This book might have a wide audience: computational linguists, theoretical and applied linguists, Semitists, and – who knows – maybe Biblical scholars with interest in Semitic. This is a mixed blessing. While it may serve as an interdisciplinary text, it makes introducing the matter at hand an arduous task. Nevertheless, this chapter attempts to introduce linguistic preliminaries to the nonlinguist, some computational prerequisites to the noncomputer specialist, and the basics of Semitic morphology to the nonsemitist. (To amuse the disappointed reader, I resorted to using quotations at the beginning of each chapter and elsewhere, mostly from the classical Semitic grammatical tradition. I hope this does not prove to be a further disappointment!)

In the definition of terms below, use was made of Trask (1993) and Crystal (1994). It must be noted that what follows is not intended to be an exhaustive coverage of the topics at hand. It must also be stressed that linguists may not necessarily, and often would not, agree with many of the definitions given here (the day is still to come when linguists agree on a definition for what the term "word" denotes). Definitions are given here in the context of the current work.

1.1 Linguistic Preliminaries

It has long been claimed that the morphology of many languages lies within the expressiveness of a class of formal languages known as "regular languages," and computational morphologists have taken up this claim. This section is an introduction to morphology (Section 1.1.1) and regular languages (Section 1.1.2). Another class of formal languages, the class of context-free languages on which some morphotactic models rely, is introduced as well (Section 1.1.3).

1.1.1 Morphology

1.1.1.1 Basic Definitions

Morphology is the branch of grammar that deals with the internal structure of words (Matthews, 1974). Although linguists may argue for other definitions of morphology, they mostly agree that morphology is the study of meaningful parts of words (McCarthy, 1991). In the English word /boys/, for example, there are two meaningful units: {boy} and the plural marker {s}. Such units, called *morphemes*, are the smallest units of morphological analysis. (Morphemes are shown in braces, { }; and the phonological word in solidi, / /.)

Sometimes, morphemes are not easily detected. Like /boys/, the English word /men/ is also a plural noun, but the plural morpheme in this case is embedded in the vowel [e], as opposed to [a] in singular /man/. In fact, morphemes are considered to be abstract units such as {PLURAL}. The {PLURAL} morpheme is realized in various forms called *morphs*: [s] in /boys/ and the vowel [e] in /men/.

Morphs in turn are made of *segments*. For example, {boy} consists of the segments: [b], [o], and [y]. Unless it constitutes a morph, a segment is meaningless. (Segments are shown in brackets, [ ].)

The morpheme that gives the main meaning of the word, for example, {boy} in /boys/, is called the *stem* or *root*. A *free morpheme* can stand on its own. In such a case, the morpheme and the word will be one and the same, for example, the word /boy/ and the morpheme {boy}. A *bound morpheme* requires additional morphemes to form a word, for example, the plural morpheme {s}.

Morphemes that precede the stem or root are called *prefixes*, such as {un} in English /unusual/. Those that follow are called *suffixes*, such as {s} in /boys/. In some languages, a morpheme may consist of two portions, neither of which is meaningful on its own. The first portion acts as a prefix and the second as a suffix. Such morphemes are called *circumfixes*. For example, in the Syriac word /neqṭlūn/ "to kill – IMPF PL 3RD MASC," the circumfix is {ne-ūn} "PL 3RD MASC."

The inventory of all morphs in a language constitutes the morphological lexicon. A lexicon of English need not have entries for /move/, /moved/, /moving/, /cook/, /cooked/, /cooking/, and so on. It only needs to list the unique morphs {move}, {cook}, {ed}, and {ing}. The suffixes apply to {move}, {cook}, and other verbs as well.

The sequence of lexical entries that make up a word is the *lexical form* of the word. For example, the lexical form of /moved/ is {move}β{ed}, where β denotes a *boundary symbol* that separates lexical entries. The word itself as one sees it on paper (or as one hears it), for example, /moved/, is called the *surface form*.

One important issue in morphology is conditional changes in morphemes. As noted above, the English word /moved/ contains two morphemes: {move} and {ed}. However, the [e] in {move} is deleted once the two morphemes are joined together. In this case, the change is merely orthographic. In other cases, the change might be phonologically motivated. For example, the nasal [n] in the negative morpheme prefix {in} becomes [m] when followed by a labial such as [p]. Hence, English /inactive/ from {in}β{active}, but /impractical/ from {in}β{practical}. Such changes are expressed by *rewrite rules*, also called *productions*. The [n] to [m] change in the above case may be expressed by the rule

$$\text{n} \rightarrow \text{m} \ / \ \_\_\_ \ \text{p}$$

which reads: [n] rewrites as [m] before [p].

How does one know that */edkill/, as oppose to /killed/, from the morphemes {kill} and {ed}, is invalid? The licit combinations of morphemes are expressed by another form of rewrite rules, which we shall call here *morphotactic rules* such as

$$\text{word} \rightarrow \text{stem suffix}$$

which reads: "word" rewrites as "root" followed by "suffix." Rewrite rules will be introduced further in Section 1.1.2.3.

1.1.1.2 Linear versus Nonlinear Morphology

Apart from Syriac /neqṭlūn/, the examples given above share one characteristic. The lexical form of a particular word is a sequence of morphemes from the lexicon. For example, the analysis of English /unsuccessful/ produces the lexical form {un}β{success}β{ful}. Because the surface form is generated by the concatenation of the lexical morphemes in question, this type of morphology is called *concatenative* or *linear* morphology.

In many languages, linearity does not hold. Consider the Arabic verb /kutib/ "to write – PERF PASS." This verb consists of at least two morphemes: the root {ktb} "notion of writing" and the vocalic sequence {ui} "PERF PASS." The concatenation of the two morphemes, */ktbui/ or */uiktb/, does not produce the desired result. In this case, the morphemes are combined in a *nonconcatenative*, or *nonlinear*, manner. (It will be shown in the next chapter how a third somewhat abstract morpheme dictates the manner in which the root and vocalic sequence are joined.)

The most ubiquitous linguistic framework for describing nonlinear morphology is based on the autosegmental model as applied to phonology (Goldsmith, 1976). *Autosegmental phonology* offers a framework under which nonlinear phonological (and morphological) phenomena can be described. Tense in Ngbaka, a language

Table 1.1. *Ngbaka tense is marked by tone*

Verb	Tone
kpòlò	low
kpōlō	mid
kpòló	low-high
kpóló	high

of Zaire (the modern Republic of Congo), for example, is indicated by tone, which is considered a morpheme in its own right. Consider the data in Table 1.1 (Nida, 1949). Each verb consists of two autonomous morphemes: {kpolo} "to return" and the respective tense morpheme, which is indicated by a specific tone.

Under the autosegmental model, autonomous morphemes are graphically represented on separate *tiers* as shown in Fig. 1.1. Each morpheme sits on its own autonomous tier: The morpheme {kpolo} sits on the lower tier, while the various tone morphemes, {L} "low," {M} "mid," {LH} "low-high," and {H} "high," sit on the upper tier. *Association lines* link segments from one tier to another. A pair of tiers, linked by some association line, is called a *chart*.[1]

Association lines follow specific rules of association according to two stipulations. The first stipulation is the *Well-Formedness Condition*: All vowels are associated with at least one tone segment and all tone segments are associated with at least one vowel segment, and association lines must not cross. The autosegmental representations in Fig. 1.1 meet this condition. However, the ill-formed representations in Fig. 1.2 violate the Well-Formedness Condition: In Fig. 1.2(a), the last vowel segment is not associated with a tone segment. In Fig. 1.2(b), the first tone segment is not associated with a vowel. In Fig. 1.2(c), association lines cross.

The second stipulation is the language-specific *Association Convention*, which states: Only the rightmost member of a tier can be associated with more than one member of another tier. The association of one member of a tier to more than one member of another tier is called *spreading*, for example, the spreading of the tone morphemes {L}, {M}, and {H} in Fig. 1.1.

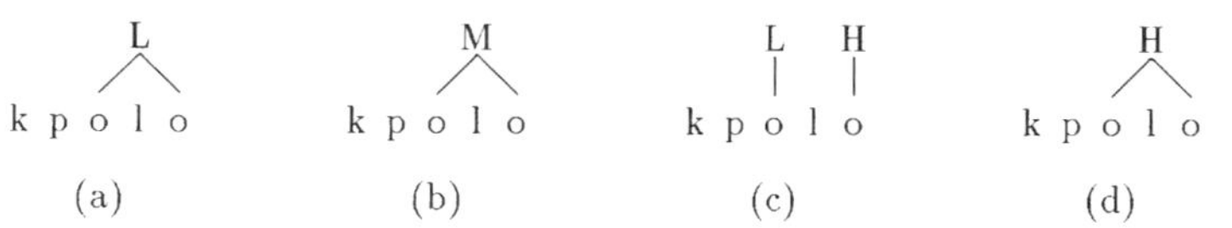

Fig. 1.1. Autosegmental representation of the Ngbaka tense in graphical form: (a) /kpòlò/, (b) /kpōlō/, (c) /kpòló/, (d) /kpóló/. Each morpheme sits on its own autonomous tier, with the stem on the lower tier and the respective tense tone morpheme on the upper tier.

[1] The term "chart" is mostly used in the computational linguistics literature, but not in the linguistic literature.

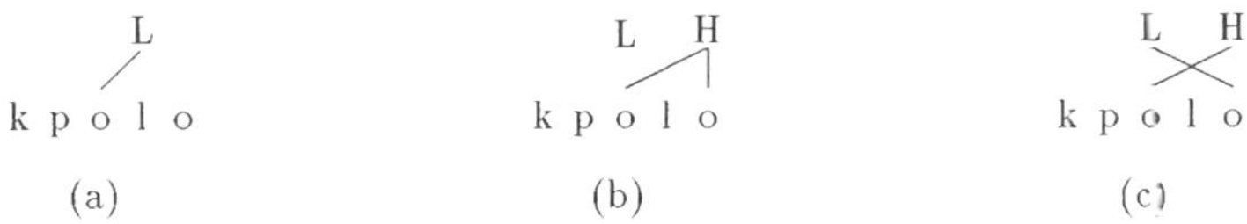

Fig. 1.2. Ill-formed autosegmental representations (a) the last [o] segment is not linked; (b) the [L] tone segment is not linked; (c) association lines cross.

1.1.1.3 Between Phonology and Syntax

It was mentioned above that morphology is the branch of grammar that deals with the internal structure of words. Two other branches of grammar interact with morphology: phonology and syntax. The former concerns itself with the study of the sound system of languages, while the latter deals with the rules under which words combine to make sentences. Hence, phonology deals with units smaller than morphemes, while syntax describes units larger than words.

One rarely speaks of morphology without reference to phonology. (The term *morphophonology* denotes the phonological structure of morphemes.) One important aspect of phonology, which can hardly be separated from any morphological analysis of words, is *phonological processes*. These are conditional changes that alter segments. Some of the processes mentioned in this book are as follows: *assimilation*, in which one segment becomes identical to, or more like, another as in [n] → [m] above (see p. 3); *syncope*, or *deletion*, as the deletion of the first [a] in Syriac */qaṭal/ → /qṭal/[2] "to kill"; *epenthesis*, or *insertion*, as the insertion of / ʔi/ in Arabic /nkatab/ → / ʔinkatab/[3] "to write – REFL"; and *gemination*, or *doubling*, which involves the repetition of a segment (usually consonant) as in Arabic /katab/ → /kattab/[4] "to write – CAUS"; in this case, the gemination of [t] is morphologically motivated.

Another phonological phenomenon that concerns us is syllabification. The English word /morphology/, for example, consists of the syllables (separated by dots): mor·pho·lo·gy. *Open* syllables end in a vowel, for example, /lo/, while *closed* syllables end in a consonant, for example, /mor/. The components of a syllable can be represented by a smaller unit, the mora, for example, /lo/ consists of one mora while /mor/ consists of two morae; syllabic weight is defined by the number of morae in a syllable: *light* syllables contain one mora, while *heavy* syllables contain two morae.

One also rarely speaks of morphology without reference to syntax. It is not uncommon for an orthographic word in one language to represent a sentence in another. For example, Syriac /baytå/ "the house," /bbaytå/ "in the house," /dabbaytå/ "he who is in the house," /ldabbaytå/ "to him who is in the house," /waldabbaytå/ "and to him who is in the house" (Robinson, 1978). Syntax (apart from what is

[2] Syriac does not allow unstressed short vowels in open syllables, apart from few diachronic cases, for which see p. 115.

[3] Arabic is devoid of initial consonantal clusters.

[4] The Arabic causative is derived by the gemination of the second consonant.

required by morphotactics) is beyond the scope of this work. It suffices to note that for many languages, such as Semitic, the analysis of the orthographic word ventures into the realm of morphosyntax. In practical computational systems, a morphology module must account for phonology and – to some extent – syntax.

1.1.2 Regular Languages

Formal language theory establishes a hierarchy of formal languages based on their complexity and expressiveness. The class of regular languages is the most basic in the hierarchy.

Formal languages are defined in terms of *strings*, strings in terms of *alphabets*, and alphabets in terms of *sets*. These terms are introduced below.

1.1.2.1 Sets

A *set* is a collection of objects without repetition. A set can be specified by listing its objects. The following set represents the days of the week:

{ Monday, Tuesday, Wednesday, Thursday, Saturday, Sunday, Friday }

Each object in the set is called an *element* of the set. Elements are separated by a comma and are placed in braces, { }. No two elements can be the same; however, the order of the elements is not important. For instance, in the above set, Friday appears after Sunday. When the elements in the set are too long to list, one can use a *defining property* instead. The above set can be rewritten as follows:

$\{ x \mid x \text{ is a weekday} \}$

Read: x where x is a weekday.

If an element x is a member of a set A, we say $x \in A$ (read: x in A). If an element x is not a member of a set A, we say $x \notin A$ (read: x not in A). For example, given the set $A = \{ 1, 2, 5 \}$, we say $2 \in A$, but $3 \notin A$.

The set containing no elements, usually denoted by { } or Ø, is called the *empty set*.

A set A is a *subset* of another set B, designated by $A \subset B$, if every element in A is an element in B. For example, { 1,2 } is a subset of { 1,2,3,4 }; however, { 1,5 } is not a subset of { 1,2,3,4 } because the latter does not include the element 5. If A is a subset of B but may also be equal to B, we say $A \subseteq B$.

There are several operations that can be applied to sets: The *union* of sets A and B, denoted by $A \cup B$, is the set that consists of all the elements in either A or B. For example, let $A = \{ 1, 2, 3 \}$ and $B = \{ 3, 4, 5 \}$, then $A \cup B = \{ 1, 2, 3, 4, 5 \}$. Note that since a set cannot have duplicates, the union contains only one instance of the element 3. We write

$$\bigcup_{i=1}^{n} A_i$$

to denote $A_1 \cup A_2 \cup \cdots \cup A_n$.

The *intersection* of sets A and B, denoted by $A \cap B$, is the set that consists of all the common elements in A and B. For example, let $A = \{1, 2, 3\}$ and $B = \{3, 4, 5\}$; then $A \cap B = \{3\}$. We write

$$\bigcap_{i=1}^{n} A_i$$

to denote $A_1 \cap A_2 \cap \cdots \cap A_n$.

The *difference* of sets A and B, denoted by $A - B$, is the set that consists of all the elements in A that are not in B. For example, let $A = \{1, 2, 3\}$ and $B = \{3, 4, 5\}$; then $A - B = \{1, 2\}$.

The *complement* of a set A, denoted by $\overline{A}$, is the set that consists of all the elements in the universe that are not in A. The *universe* set contains all elements under consideration. If we assume that the universe set contains all the days of the week and

$$A = \{\text{Monday, Wednesday, Friday}\}$$

then

$$\overline{A} = \{\text{Tuesday, Thursday, Saturday, Sunday}\}$$

The *cross product* of sets A and B, denoted by $A \times B$, is a set consisting of all the pairs (a_1, a_2) where the first element, a_1, is in A_1 and the second element, a_2, is in A_2. For example, let $A = \{1, 2\}$ and $B = \{3, 4, 5\}$; then $A \times B = \{(1, 3), (1, 4), (1, 5), (2, 3), (2, 4), (2, 5)\}$. We write

$$\prod_{i=1}^{n} A_i$$

to denote $A_1 \times A_2 \times \cdots \times A_n$. We also write B^n to denote the cross product of B by itself n times; that is, $\underbrace{B \times B \times \cdots \times B}_{n \text{ times}}$.

With the use of defining properties, the above operations can be defined as follows:

$$\begin{aligned}
A \cup B &= \{x \mid x \in A \text{ or } x \in B\} \\
A \cap B &= \{x \mid x \in A \text{ and } x \in B\} \\
A - B &= \{x \mid x \in A \text{ but } x \notin B\} \\
\overline{A} &= \{x \mid x \notin A\} \\
A \times B &= \{(a_1, a_2) \mid a_1 \in A_1, a_2 \in A_2\}
\end{aligned}$$

A *finite* set contains a finite number of elements. For instance, the set $\{n \mid 1 \le n \le 10\}$ is a finite set of 10 elements, that is, the integers 1 to 10. An *infinite* set contains an infinite number of elements. For example, $\{n \mid 1 \le n\}$ represents all positive integers, from 1 to infinity.

Any subset of the cross product $A_1 \times A_2$ is called a *binary relation*. A_1 is called the *domain* of the relation and A_2 is called the *range* of the relation. It is possible to have a relation on one set, for example, a relation on $A \times A$.

1.1.2.2 Alphabets and Strings

An *alphabet* is a finite set of symbols. *Symbols* are usually letters or characters. The English alphabet is the set

$$\{ \text{A,B}, \ldots, \text{Y,Z,a,b}, \ldots, \text{y,z} \}$$

A *string over* some alphabet is a finite sequence of elements drawn from that alphabet. If $A = \{\text{a,b,c}\}$ is an alphabet, then the following sequences, *inter alia*, are strings over A: "a," "aa," "aab," "aac," "caa," and "cbbba." However, the string "aad" is not a string over A since the element 'd' is not in A. (Strings are shown in double quotes when they appear in text; characters or symbols are shown in single quotes.)

The number of elements in a string x determines the *length* of the string, denoted by $|x|$. The length of the string "ab" is two and the length of "cbba" is four. A string of length zero is called the *empty string* and is denoted by ϵ.

The terms prefix and suffix apply to strings as they apply to natural languages (see p. 2).

The *concatenation* of two strings x and y, denoted by xy, is the string formed by appending y to x. For example, if x is "may" and y is "be," then xy is "maybe."

Concatenation is used to define *exponentiation*. If x is a string, we write x^2 to denote the concatenation of x with itself twice, that is, xx. Similarly, x^3 denotes the concatenation of x with itself thrice, that is, xxx. In this vein, $x^1 = x$ and x^0 is the empty string ϵ. For example, let x be the string "ha;" we say x^0 is ϵ, x^1 is "ha," x^2 is "haha," x^3 is "hahaha," and so on.

The *Kleene star*, denoted by x^*, denotes zero or more concatenations of x with itself: ϵ, x, xx, xxx, and so on. To exclude the empty string, we use the Kleene plus notation, x^+, which denotes one or more concatenations of x with itself.

1.1.2.3 Languages, Expressions, and Grammars

The term *language*, or *formal language*, denotes any set of strings over some alphabet. For example, let $A = \{ \text{a,b,c} \}$ be some alphabet. All of the following sets of strings are languages over A:

$$L_1 = \{ \text{b,ab,aab,aaab,aaaab}, \ldots \}$$
$$L_2 = \{ \text{b} \}$$
$$L_3 = \{ \text{abcc,abca,aaba,ccca,caba}, \ldots \}$$

L_1 is an infinite language over A where each string consists of zero or more instances of 'a' followed by one instance of 'b'. L_2 is a finite language over A, and it consists of only one string, the string being a symbol from the alphabet. L_3 is a finite language over A whose strings are of length four. The language { abc, add }, however, is not a language over A since "add" is not a string over A; this is so because 'd' is not in A.

Expressions are used to describe the strings of a language. The strings in L_1, for example, can be expressed by the expression a*b: zero or more instances of 'a' followed by one 'b'. The language L_2 can be expressed by the expression b since it contains only that element. Expression may contain other operators such as disjunction, | (read 'or'). For instance, the strings in L_3 begin with either an 'a' or a 'c', followed by three arbitrary symbols from A; this can be described by the expression $(\mathrm{a} \mid \mathrm{c})A^3$.

Given two alphabets, one can use expressions to describe languages over the two alphabets. Consider the following two alphabets, which represent capital and small letters, respectively:

$$C = \{\, \mathrm{A,B}, \ldots, \mathrm{Y,Z} \,\}$$
$$S = \{\, \mathrm{a,b}, \ldots, \mathrm{y,z} \,\}$$

The language CS^* consists of all strings that start with one capital letter followed by zero or more small letters, e.g. "I," "Good," "Bed." The language

$$(C \mid S)S^3\,\mathrm{ing}$$

consists of all strings that start with either a capital or small letter, followed by three small letters, followed by "ing," for example, "booking," and "Writing."

Languages are described by grammars. A *formal grammar* consists of an alphabet and a set of rewrite rules. Generally, a *rewrite rule* consists of a left-hand-side and a right-hand side separated by an arrow, for example,

$$\mathrm{y} \rightarrow \mathrm{i\,e}$$

Read: 'y' rewrites as 'i' followed by 'e'. Applying the rule on the string "entrys," which consists of the stem {entry} concatenated with the plural morpheme {s}, results in "entries," after replacing 'y' by "ie." This is the rule that applies to English plurals ending in a 'y.' However, there is nothing preventing the rule from applying to any 'y.' Applying the rule on "may" results in the undesired "maie."

To restrict the application of rules, one specifies *left* and *right contexts*, separated by an environment bar ___ . The rule only applies when the contexts are satisfied. The above rule can be rewritten as

$$\mathrm{y} \rightarrow \mathrm{i\,e} \,/\, \underline{\quad}\ \mathrm{s}$$

Read: 'y' rewrites as 'i' followed by 'e' before 's.' Here, the left context is not specified. (The slash, /, separates the contexts from the right-hand side.) The above

S → the A
A → old B
B → man
B → woman

Fig. 1.3. A set of rewrite rules that generate the sentences *the old man* and *the old woman*. Nonterminal symbols start with a capital letters.

rule only applies when there is an ‘s’ to the right of ‘y;’ hence, it does not apply to “may.”

So far, *terminal symbols* were used in rules; that is, symbols drawn from the alphabet in question. It is also possible to use *nonterminal symbols*; that is, symbols that are derived from other symbols. These are designated with capital letters. Consider the following alphabet whose symbols are actual words, {man, old, the, very, woman}, and the rules in Fig. 1.3. The first rule states that a sentence S rewrites as the word “the” followed by A. According to the second rule, the symbol A in turn, rewrites as the word “old” followed by B. Now B rewrites as either “man” or “woman” according to the third and fourth rules, respectively. This grammar generates the two sentences: “the old man” and “the old woman”. The derivations can be illustrated graphically by *parse trees* as in Fig. 1.4.

Grammars, and hence languages derived from them, are of various complexities. The least complex are *regular languages*. These can be generated by rewrite rules of the form

$$\mathrm{A} \rightarrow a\ \mathrm{B}$$

or

$$\mathrm{A} \rightarrow a$$

Here A and B are nonterminal symbols and a is a terminal symbol. The formal definition of regular languages over an alphabet Σ is as follows:

(i) The empty set is a regular language.
(ii) For each a in Σ, $\{ a \}$ is a regular language.

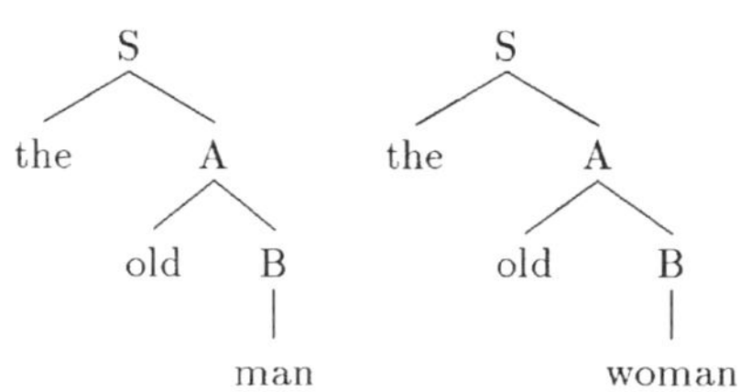

Fig. 1.4. Parse trees for the sentences generated by the rules in Fig. 1.3.

(iii) If L_1, L_2, and L are regular languages, then so are

$$L_1L_2 = \{ xy \mid x \in L_1, y \in L_2 \} \quad \text{(concatenation)}$$
$$L_1 \cup L_2 = \{ x \mid x \in L_1 \text{ or } x \in L_2 \} \quad \text{(union)}$$
$$L^* = \bigcup_{i=0}^{\infty} L^i \quad \text{(Kleene star)}$$

(iv) There are no other regular languages.

Every regular language is described by a regular expression. A *regular expression* over some alphabet is an expression consisting of a sequence of symbols from the alphabet constructed by means of concatenation, union, or Kleene star. For example, let { a,b,c } be an alphabet; then "ab" (concatenation), a ∪ b (union), and a* (Kleene star) are regular expressions. More formally, a regular expression over an alphabet Σ is defined as follows:

(i) ∅ is a regular expression and denotes the empty set.
(ii) ϵ is a regular expression and denotes the set $\{ \epsilon \}$.
(iii) For each a in Σ, a is a regular expression and denotes the set $\{ a \}$.
(iv) If r_1, r_2, and r are regular expressions denoting the languages R_1, R_2, and R, respectively, then so are
 $r_1 r_2$, denoting $R_1 R_2$ (concatenation)
 $r_1 \mid r_2$, denoting $R_1 \cup R_2$ (union)
 r^*, denoting R^* (Kleene star)
(v) There are no other regular expressions.

Some languages cannot be expressed by regular grammars. Let 'a' and 'b' be two symbols in an alphabet. It is possible to express a language that contains a *specified* number of 'a's followed by the same number of 'b's, say a^3b^3, which denotes the language { aaabbb }. However, it is not possible to express a language that contains an *unspecified* number of 'a's followed by the same number of 'b's such as the expression a^nb^n, that is, n 'a's followed by n 'b's.

1.1.3 Context-Free Languages

A more expressive class of languages is the *context-free* family of languages, which can cope with a^nb^n languages. Context-free languages are generated by context-free grammars.

1.1.3.1 Context-Free Grammars

Context-free languages are generated by rewrite rules called *context-free rules*. These may not contain left or right contexts as their name implies. However, unlike regular grammars, context-free rewrite rules may contain any number of nonterminals on the right-hand side of rules.

Consider the rules in Fig. 1.5, which generates the sentences "the book," "the books," "a book," and "some books." Figure 1.6 gives the parse trees of the generated sentences.

$$
\begin{array}{rcl}
\text{NP} & \rightarrow & \text{Det SingNoun} \\
\text{NP} & \rightarrow & \text{Det PlNoun} \\
\text{NP} & \rightarrow & \text{SingDet SingNoun} \\
\text{NP} & \rightarrow & \text{PlDet PlNoun} \\
\text{Det} & \rightarrow & \text{the} \\
\text{SingDet} & \rightarrow & \text{a} \\
\text{PlDet} & \rightarrow & \text{some} \\
\text{SingNoun} & \rightarrow & \text{book} \\
\text{PlNoun} & \rightarrow & \text{books}
\end{array}
$$

Fig. 1.5. A context-free grammar. Nonterminals start with a capital letter.

The first four rules in Fig. 1.5 actually describe one linguistic phenomenon: a noun phrase (NP) rewrites as a determiner (Det) followed by a noun. The duplication in rules (with the prefixes 'Sing' and 'Pl' to indicate singular and plural, respectively) are necessary in order to ensure that the determiner and noun agree in number. Unification provides a mechanism by which such duplications can be avoided.

1.1.3.2 Unification

A *feature* represents a characteristic. For example, NUMBER is a feature of nouns. Similarly, PERSON is a feature of verbs. Typically, a feature has a *value*. The feature NUMBER, for example, takes the values sing and pl for singular and plural, respectively. (Features are shown in SMALL CAPS, while values are shown in small type.)

A matrix of features constitutes a *category*, for example,

$$
\begin{bmatrix}
\text{NUMBER} = \text{sing} \\
\text{PERSON} = \text{2nd} \\
\text{GENDER} = \text{masc}
\end{bmatrix}
$$

Unification is an operation that combines two categories into one as long as the two initial categories do not contain conflicting information. The resulting category

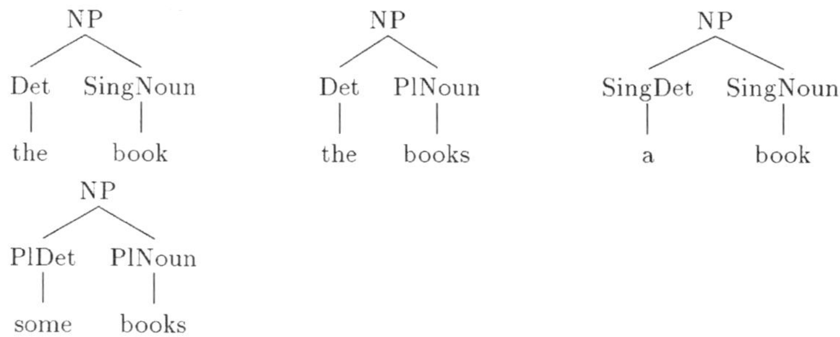

Fig. 1.6. Parse trees for the sentences generated by the rules in Fig. 1.5.

contains all the information in the two initial categories. As a way of illustration, let

$$A = \begin{bmatrix} \text{NUMBER} = \text{sing} \\ \text{PERSON} = \text{2nd} \end{bmatrix}, B = \begin{bmatrix} \text{PERSON} = \text{2nd} \\ \text{GENDER} = \text{masc} \end{bmatrix}$$

The unification of A and B produces a new category C,

$$C = \begin{bmatrix} \text{NUMBER} = \text{sing} \\ \text{PERSON} = \text{2nd} \\ \text{GENDER} = \text{masc} \end{bmatrix}$$

which combines all the information in A and B. Boxed indices, e.g. $\boxed{1}$, $\boxed{2}$, and so on, are used to avoid writing the same value again and again in different categories. For example, A and B above can be rewritten as

$$A = \begin{bmatrix} \text{NUMBER} = \text{sing} \\ \text{PERSON} = \text{2nd}\,\boxed{1} \end{bmatrix}, B = \begin{bmatrix} \text{PERSON} = \boxed{1} \\ \text{GENDER} = \text{masc} \end{bmatrix}$$

If the value of PERSON is unknown, but both A and B must have the same value, then the following can be written

$$A = \begin{bmatrix} \text{NUMBER} = \text{sing} \\ \text{PERSON} = \boxed{1} \end{bmatrix}, B = \begin{bmatrix} \text{PERSON} = \boxed{1} \\ \text{GENDER} = \text{masc} \end{bmatrix}$$

Now let

$$D = \begin{bmatrix} \text{NUMBER} = \text{sing} \\ \text{PERSON} = \text{2nd} \end{bmatrix}, E = \begin{bmatrix} \text{PERSON} = \text{1st} \\ \text{GENDER} = \text{masc} \end{bmatrix}$$

The unification of D and E fails since they contain contradicting information, that is, the value of the feature PERSON.

Unification is more powerful than the above examples show. The value of a feature may be a variable. Let

$$F = \begin{bmatrix} \text{NUMBER} = \text{sing} \\ \text{PERSON} = \text{X} \end{bmatrix}, G = \begin{bmatrix} \text{PERSON} = \text{1st} \\ \text{GENDER} = \text{Y} \end{bmatrix}$$

where X and Y are variables. The unification of F and G produces the following new category H,

$$H = \begin{bmatrix} \text{NUMBER} = \text{sing} \\ \text{PERSON} = \text{1st} \\ \text{GENDER} = \text{Y} \end{bmatrix}$$

where the value of PERSON was *instantiated* from G. The value of GENDER, however, remains uninstantiated.

When a feature can possibly take more than one value, set notation is used, for example,

$$I = \begin{bmatrix} \text{NUMBER} = \{\text{sing,plural}\} \\ \text{PERSON} = \text{1st} \\ \text{GENDER} = \text{Y} \end{bmatrix}$$

Unification allows the passing of information from one category to another. It is used in grammars, which gives rise to the term "unification-based" grammars.

1.1.3.3 Unification-Based Context-Free Grammars

The rules in Fig. 1.5 are repeated in Fig. 1.7, using unification. Here, all nonterminals are associated with a category indicating number. All categories present in a rule must unify. The first rule states that a noun phrase rewrites as a determiner followed by a noun, both of which must have the same value for NUMBER, that is, X. Hence, "a book" and "some books" are valid, while *"a books" is invalid. Since the determiner "the" can take singular and plural nouns, its NUMBER value is

$$\text{NP}\begin{bmatrix}\text{NUMBER} = \text{X}\end{bmatrix} \rightarrow \text{Det}\begin{bmatrix}\text{NUMBER} = \text{X}\end{bmatrix}\ \text{Noun}\begin{bmatrix}\text{NUMBER} = \text{X}\end{bmatrix}$$

$$\text{Det}\begin{bmatrix}\text{NUMBER} = \text{X}\end{bmatrix} \rightarrow \text{the}$$

$$\text{Det}\begin{bmatrix}\text{NUMBER} = \text{sing}\end{bmatrix} \rightarrow \text{a}$$

$$\text{Det}\begin{bmatrix}\text{NUMBER} = \text{pl}\end{bmatrix} \rightarrow \text{some}$$

$$\text{Noun}\begin{bmatrix}\text{NUMBER} = \text{sing}\end{bmatrix} \rightarrow \text{book}$$

$$\text{Noun}\begin{bmatrix}\text{NUMBER} = \text{pl}\end{bmatrix} \rightarrow \text{books}$$

Fig. 1.7. A repetition of the rules in Fig. 1.5, using unification-based context-free rules. Nonterminals are associated with a category indicating number.

a variable X. The value is instantiated from noun entries: sing in "the book" and pl in "the books."

1.2 Computational Preliminaries

It was mentioned that the claim that the morphology of many languages lies within the expressiveness of regular languages was adopted by computational morphologists. The main attraction of regular languages is the ease of modeling them by the simplest computational devices, known as "finite-state automata." This section introduces computational morphology and topics related to finite-state automata.

1.2.1 Computational Morphology

Computational morphology is a subfield of computational linguistics (also called "natural language processing" or "language engineering"). Computational morphology concerns itself with computer applications that analyze words in a given text, such as determining whether a given word is a verb or a noun. Consider, for example, a spelling checker. To find if a word is spelled correctly, the program searches a lexicon (a list of the words in that language) for the word in question. In order for the spelling checker to work, the lexicon must contain all the forms and inflections of each word (e.g., book, books, booked, booking, etc.), resulting in a huge lexicon with a few hundred thousand entries. This is even more dramatic in morphologically rich languages: some of the Arabic spelling checkers have a lexicon with over 10 million entries!

A more efficient and elegant spelling checker can be achieved by listing in the lexicon unique stems and morphemes, and having a morphological component of the program derive words. An Arabic spelling checker that makes heavy use of morphology should not contain more than 10,000 lexical entries[5] to cover Modern Standard Arabic, of course excluding personal names, foreign loans, and so on.

Almost all practical applications that deal with natural language must have a morphological component. After all, an application must first recognize the word in question before analyzing it syntactically, semantically, or whatever the case may be.

The typical morphological analyzer tackles three issues: the morphological lexicon, rewrite rules, and morphotactic rules. The lexicon encodes all the morphemes in a given language. Rewrite rules handle orthographic changes, phonological processes, and the like. Morphotactic rules determine which morphemes can be combined to form grammatical words.

[5] Wehr's dictionary of Modern Standard Arabic (Wehr, 1971) contains 6167 roots, 3014 of which are used in the derivation of both verb and noun stems (Daniel Ponsford, personal communication).

The state-of-the-art methodology in computational morphology for handling the lexicon and rewrite rules makes use of devices called finite-state automata. Morphotactic grammars can be described in two ways: either by using finite-state automata, especially for most purely concatenative languages, or unification-based context-free grammars for more complex languages. The rest of this section introduces finite-state automata and demonstrates their application in computational morphology.

1.2.2 Finite-State Automata

A finite-state automaton (FSA) is usually modeled by a program. The program receives a string from an input *tape*. It reads one character at a time from left to right. After reading the last character, it either accepts or rejects the string. An automaton that accepts English strings would accept the input /receive/ but would reject */recieve/. The terms "automaton" and "machine" will be used interchangeably.

A FSA consists of a finite number of *states*. Before scanning the first character from the input tape, the machine will be in a special *initial state*. At any point while scanning the input, the FSA will be in one particular state, called the *current state*. One or more states will be marked as *final states*. The FSA in Fig. 1.8(a),

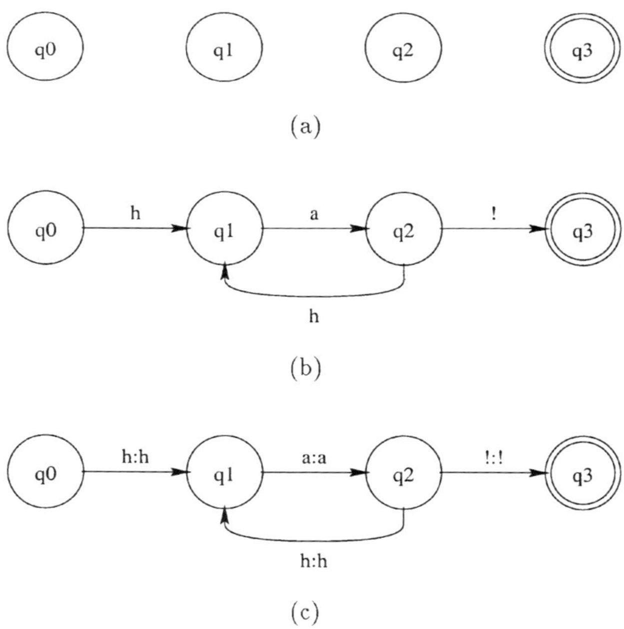

Fig. 1.8. A laughing automaton: (a) gives the states of the machine with final states marked by double circles; (b) adds transitions; (c) is the identity transducer of the automaton in (b) where each symbol is mapped to itself.

for example, consists of four states (represented by circles), labeled q_0, q_1, q_2, and q_3. By default we always assume that state q_0 is the initial state. Final states are indicated by double circles (e.g. q_3).

The program that represents the FSA consists of a set of instructions of the form (q_0, h, q_1), which is interpreted as follows: if the machine is currently in state q_0 and the next character to scan from the input tape is 'h,' then move to state q_1. Graphically, such an instruction is represented by a *transition*, an arrow labeled 'h' that goes from state q_0 to state q_1. The FSA in Fig. 1.8(a) is repeated in Fig. 1.8(b) with the following transitions: (q_0, h, q_1), (q_1, a, q_2), (q_2, h, q_1), $(q_2, !, q_3)$.

A *deterministic* finite-state automaton does not have more than one transition leaving a state on the same label. An *ϵ-free automaton* does not contain any transitions labeled with the empty string ϵ.

After the last character of the input is scanned, if the automaton is in a final state, the input is *accepted*; otherwise, it is *rejected*. Consider the input string "ha!" and the automaton in Fig. 1.8(b). After reading the 'h,' the automaton moves from state q_0 to q_1. After reading the 'a,' it moves to state q_2. After reading the last character '!,' it moves to state q_3. Since there are no more characters in the input string and the machine is in a final state, the input "ha!" is accepted. In fact, the machine is a laughing machine, which accepts the strings "ha!," "haha!," "hahaha!," and so on (after Gazdar and Mellish, 1989). Now consider the input string "ha" (without the exclamation mark). After reading the first 'h' and the 'a,' the machine will be in state q_2. There are no more characters in the input string; however, state q_2 is *not* a final state. Hence, the string "ha" is rejected.

The set of strings that an automaton accepts is the *language* accepted by that machine. The language accepted by the above laughing machine is $L = \{\text{ha!, haha!, hahaha!, \ldots}\}$. Languages that can be described by an FSA belong to the class of regular languages, as opposed to the more powerful class of context-free languages (see Sections 1.1.2 and 1.1.3).

The result given by a FSA is limited: either the string is accepted, or it is rejected. Another form of FSAs is finite-state *transducers* (FSTs). An FST is a FSA, but instead of scanning one tape, it scans two tapes simultaneously. One string is usually designated as input and the other as output. Each transition is labeled with a pair: the first denotes the character on the first tape, and the second denotes the character on the second tape. Consider the FST in Fig. 1.9(a). It *transduces* (or maps) English laughter into French laughter. If we consider the first tape to be the input and the second the output, then the machine will transduce English 'ha!' into French 'ah!' as follows: after reading an 'h' on the first tape, it writes an 'a' on the second tape and enters state q_1. Similarly, reading 'a' from the first tape, it writes 'h' on the second tape ending in state q_2. Finally, the machines reads '!' from the first tape and writes the same character on the second tape. The transitions for transducing English "haha!" into French "ahah!" are shown schematically in Fig. 1.9(b). The numbers between the two tapes indicate the current state after scanning the input symbol in question.

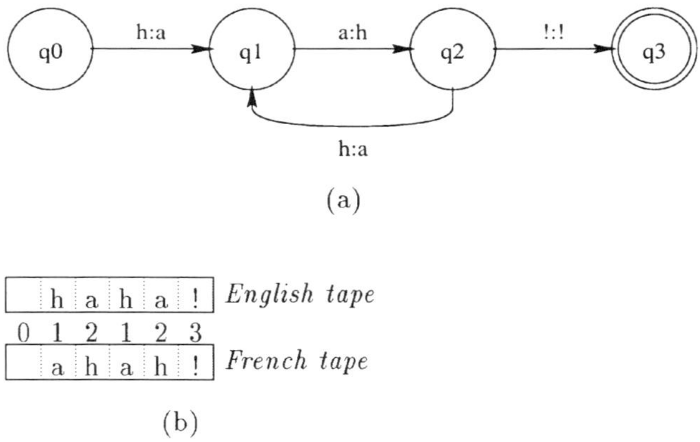

Fig. 1.9. An English–French laughing transducer: (a) gives the transition diagram that maps English laughter into French; (b) shows the transitions for the input "haha!," with the numbers between the two tapes indicating the current state after the input symbol in question is scanned.

The transducer that maps every symbol to itself is called the *identity transducer*. For example, the identity of the automaton in Fig. 1.8(b) is the transducer in Fig. 1.8(c). We denote the identity transducer of a machine A by $Id(A)$.

It was mentioned above (see p. 11) that every regular language is described by a regular expression. It was also mentioned in this section that languages that are described by FSAs are regular. The *Kleene correspondence theorem* shows the equivalence among regular languages, regular expressions, and finite-state automata as follows:

(i) Every regular expression describes a regular language.
(ii) Every regular language is described by a regular expression.
(iii) Every finite-state automaton accepts a regular language.
(iv) Every regular language is accepted by a finite-state automaton.

FSAa and FSTs are interesting for a few reasons. First, they are simple to model. The transitions in Fig. 1.8(b), for example, can be represented by a simple matrix as shown in Table 1.2.[6] Second, transducers are bidirectional. There is nothing stopping us from using the second tape as input and the first as output. In the case of the transducer in Fig. 1.9(a), this results in a French–English laughing transducer. Third, their closure properties (discussed next) allow the combination

[6] Representing an automaton with n states using a matrix, however, requires n^2 space, regardless of the number of transitions. A more efficient way would be to store transitions. For an example in C++, see Budd (1994, Section 16.5); for an example in Prolog, see Kiraz and Grimley-Evans (1997). Compression methods for large and sparse automata can be found in Aho, Sethi, and Ullman (1986, p. 144 ff.).

Table 1.2. *Transitions for Fig. 1.9(a)*

	q_0	q_1	q_2	q_3
q_0		h:a		
q_1			a:h	
q_2		h:a		!:!
q_3				

of various machines using operations such as concatenation, union, and so on to create more complex machines.

1.2.3 Regular Operations and Closure Properties

One performs operations on automata in the same manner by which one performs operations on sets, for example; union, intersection, and so on. Since FSAs represent regular languages and a language is merely a set of strings, one can intuitively deduce the result of such operations. The union of two automata A and B, for example, produces an automaton that accepts strings that are accepted by either A or B.

In addition to the operations mentioned in the formal definition of regular languages (i.e., concatenation, union, and Kleene star; see p. 10), one can define other operations that may be applied to FSAs or FSTs. Like the intersection of sets (see p. 7), the *intersection* of automata A and B, denoted by $A \cap B$, is the automaton that accepts strings that are accepted by both A and B. For example, if A describes the regular language $a \mid b \mid c^*$ and B describes the regular language $a^2 \mid b \mid c^+$, then $A \cap B$ accepts the language $b \mid c^+$.

The *difference* of automata A and B, denoted by $A - B$, is the automaton that accepts strings that are accepted by A, but not by B. For example, considering automata A and B from the previous example, then $A - B$ accepts the language $a \mid \epsilon$ (note that $c^* - c^+$ gives ϵ).

The *complement* of an automaton A, denoted by $\overline{A}$, is the automaton that accepts all strings (over some alphabet) apart from those in A. For example, let Σ be an alphabet and let A be an automaton; then $\overline{A} = \Sigma^* - A$.

Like the cross product of sets (see p. 7), the *cross product* of automata A and B, denoted by $A \times B$, is the transducer that maps the strings accepted by A into the strings that are accepted by B. For example, if A describes the regular language $ab \mid c$ and B describes the regular language $de \mid f$, then $A \times B$ produces the regular relation

$$\big((ab){:}(de)\big) \mid \big((ab){:}f\big) \mid \big(c{:}(de)\big) \mid \big(c{:}f\big)$$

One additional operation we shall encounter is *composition*, which is confined to FSTs. When two transducers are composed, the output of the first transducer is used as input to the second. For example, if T_1 is a transducer that maps a to b, and T_2 is another transducer that maps b to c, then their composition, denoted by $T_1 \circ T_2$, is the transducer that maps a to c.

A regular language is said to be *closed under* a specific operation if the application of the operation to any regular language results in another regular language. From the definition of regular languages (see p. 10), we say that regular languages, and their corresponding FSAs, are closed under concatenation, union, and Kleene star. This is so because the concatenation of any two regular languages – by definition – results in a regular language. The same holds for union and Kleene star.

FSAs and ϵ-free transducers are closed under intersection, difference, and complement. However, ϵ-containing transducers are not closed under these operations (Kaplan and Kay, 1994, p. 342). Transducers are closed under composition.

1.2.4 Finite-State Morphology

This section demonstrates how computational morphology makes use of regular languages, regular expressions, and finite-state automata. A typical morphological analyser handles lexica, rewrite rules, and morphotactic rules.

1.2.4.1 The Lexica

The morphological lexicon is the set of stems and morphemes in a language. Being a set of strings, it is usually represented with an automaton (Sproat, 1992, p. 128 ff.). Figure 1.10(a) gives an automaton for a small English lexicon representing the words /book/ (with transitions through states q_0–q_4), /hook/ (with transitions through the same states but with a different path), /move/ (states q_0, q_5–q_9), and /model/ (states q_0, q_5–q_{12}). Final states mark the end of a lexical entry. Note that entries that share prefixes (in the formal sense), such as "mo" in /move/ and /model/, share the same transitions for the prefix. Figure 1.10(b) gives another automaton for the suffixes {ed} and {ing}.

One way to combine the two machines in Fig. 1.10 is by concatenation, yielding a machine that accepts /booked/, /booking/, /hooked/, /hooking/, and so on. Usually however, one would want to separate the morphemes by a special boundary symbol, say β. A two-state machine that accepts this symbol is created and is concatenated between the two machines in Fig. 1.10, that is, $L_1 \beta L_2$. This machine accepts /bookβed/, /bookβing/, /hookβed/, /hookβing/, and the like.

1.2.4.2 Rewrite Rules

The finite-state approach is the most common method in computational morphology and phonology for modeling rewrite rules. Each rule is compiled, by some algorithm, into a finite-state transducer that performs the mapping desired by the rule. As a way of illustration, consider the derivation of /moving/ from the lexical

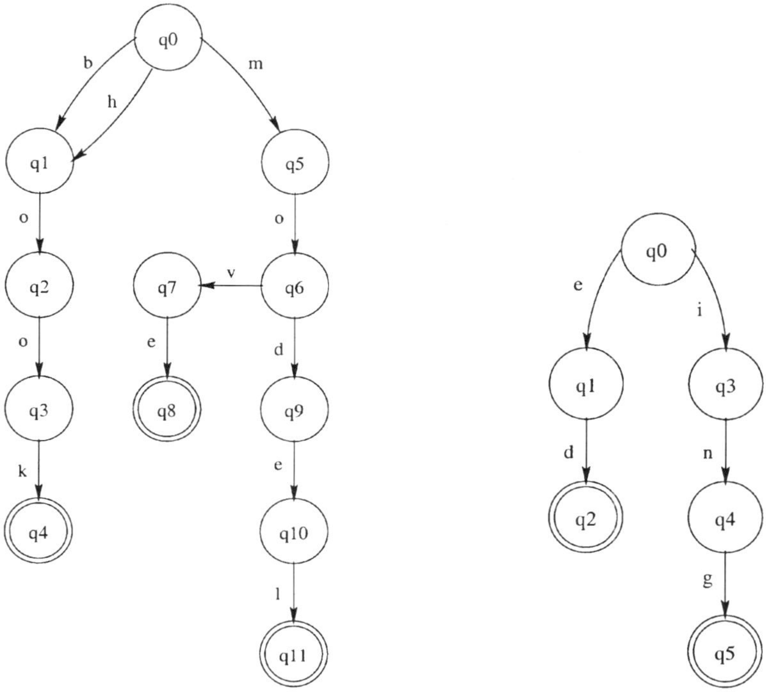

(a) L_1 (b) L_2

Fig. 1.10. Lexical representation by automata: (a) FSA that accepts the words *book*, *hook*, *move*, *mode*, and *model*; (b) FSA that accepts the suffixes {ed} and {ing}.

morphemes {move} and {ing}, separated by the boundary symbol β. Note that the [e] in {move} is deleted once the two morphemes join. This final-*e*-deletion rule takes place following a consonant, [v] is this case, and preceding β, which is followed by a vowel, [i] of {ing} in this example. The rule can be expressed as follows:

$$\text{e} \rightarrow \epsilon \; / \; \text{v} \; \_\_\_ \; \beta \; \text{i}$$

The rule states that [e] maps to ϵ (i.e., deleted) when it is preceded by a 'v' and followed by the sequence "βi."

The corresponding FST is depicted in Fig. 1.11. The transition *:* from a particular state represents any mapping other than those explicitly shown to be leaving that state. Given a particular input, the transducer remains in state q_0 until it scans a 'v' on its input tape, upon which it will output 'v' and move to state q_1. Once in state q_1, the left context of the rule has been detected.

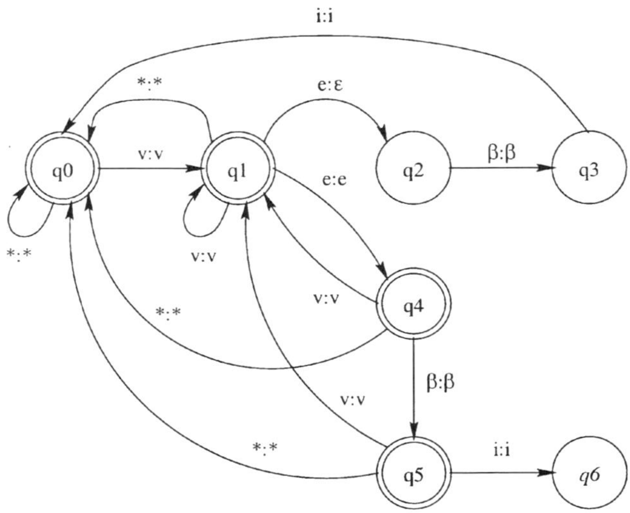

Fig. 1.11. Final-*e*-deletion rule in transducer form. Transitions marked with *:* from a particular state represent mappings other than those explicitly shown from that state. State q_6, shown in italic, is a dead state.

When in state q_1 and faced with an 'e' (the symbol in question for this rule), the transducer has two options: (i) to map the 'e' to an ϵ, that is, apply the rule, and move to state q_2, or (ii) retain the 'e' on the output and move to state q_4. In the former case, one expects to see the right context since the rule was applied; the transition on $\beta{:}\beta$ to q_3 and the subsequent transition on i:i back to state q_0 fulfill this task. In the latter case, one expects to see anything *except* the right context since the rule was not applied. If the right context is scanned on the input tape, the transducer moves from state q_4 to state q_6 and halts there since state q_6 is not a final state and no transition leaves it. In order to succeed, the transducer has no choice but to take the correct path by deleting the 'e'.

After processing /mov/ of /moveβing/ ending up in state q_1, say that the machine takes the wrong path and moves to state q_4 without deleting the 'e'. The next input symbol, β, takes the machine to state q_5. The next symbol, 'i' leads to state q_6, a nonfinal state without any output transitions. We say that the machine halts, backtracks to q_1, and takes the correct path moving to state q_2. In this manner, the deletion of 'e' is enforced.

Context expressions can be more complex. For example, the final-*e*-deletion rule also applies with the suffix {ed} as well. To cater for this, the rule becomes

$$\text{e} \rightarrow \epsilon \,/\, \text{v} \_\_\_ \beta \; (\text{i} \,|\, \text{e})$$

The affect of this on the corresponding FST would be two additional transitions on e:e – one from q_3 to q_0, and the other from q_5 to q_6.

1.2.4.3 Morphotactic Rules

The lexicon defines the set of morphemes in a language, while rewrite rules state conditional changes when the morphemes are put together. One more specification is required in a morphology system: morphotactics, that is, the set of licit combinations of lexical forms. For example, the morpheme {ed} may be suffixed to {move}, but not prefixed to the same stem.

As to how morphotactics works in a computational system, there are two schools of thought of concern to us: The first implements morphotactics in the finite-state description, while the second makes use of context-free grammars (see Section 1.1.3).

Finite-state morphotactics puts morphemes together by using regular operations. For example, suffixing the strings of lexicon L_2 to the stems of lexicon L_1 in Fig. 1.10 can be achieved by simply concatenating the former with the latter. The regular expression for doing so is

$$L = L_1 L_2$$

It is usually desirable to separate morphemes with a boundary symbol, say β. The above regular expression becomes

$$L = L_1 \beta L_2$$

which is depicted in Fig. 1.12(a). Note that this machine accepts the stems followed by suffixes, but it does not accept the stems on their own. To remedy this, one performs the following operations:

$$L = (L_1 \beta L_2) \cup L_1$$

which is depicted in Fig. 1.12(b). The only difference here is that the states marking the end of a stem are final, which allows for the stems to be accepted on their own as well.

Context-free morphotactics makes use of (unification-based) context-free grammars, whose expressiveness and computational power exceeds that of regular languages. These cater for rich description of morphotactics, especially in the case of long-distance dependencies, when a particular morpheme has common features with a morpheme that is not adjacent to it. Here, there is a trade-off: more elegant description for additional computational power. For example, the strings of the previous example can be generated by the rules in Fig. 1.13.

1.2.4.4 Putting Things Together

The machines in Fig. 1.12 have one problem: the [e] of /move/ has to be deleted when the suffixes {ed} and {ing} are attached.

Applying rules to lexica may be done by means of the composition operator (see p. 19). However, this operator is defined on transducers. Hence, one takes

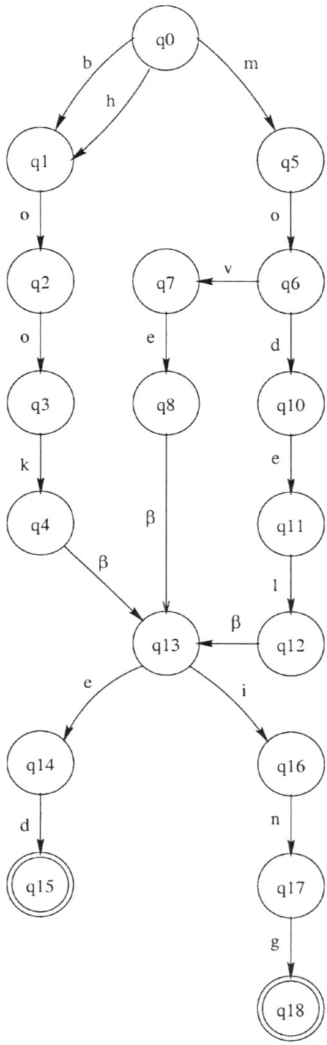

(a) $L = L_1 \beta L_2$

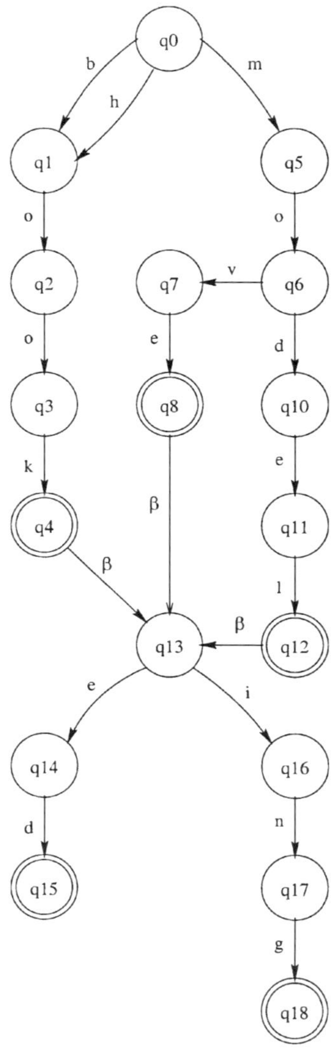

(b) $L = (L_1 \beta L_2) \cup L_1$

Fig. 1.12. Finite-state morphotactics: (a) gives the machine that concatenates suffixes to stem; (b) gives the same machine that accepts the stems on their own as well.

the identity transducer (see p. 18) of the machine in Fig. 1.12(b) and composes the result with the rule in Fig. 1.11, which we shall denote by R. The expression for this procedure is $Id(L) \circ R$, whose result is depicted in Fig. 1.14. Note the deletion of [e] between states q_8 and q_9.

$$
\begin{aligned}
\text{S} &\rightarrow \text{Stem} \\
\text{S} &\rightarrow \text{Stem Suffix} \\
\text{Stem} &\rightarrow \text{book} \\
\text{Stem} &\rightarrow \text{hook} \\
\text{Stem} &\rightarrow \text{move} \\
\text{Stem} &\rightarrow \text{mode} \\
\text{Stem} &\rightarrow \text{model} \\
\text{Suffix} &\rightarrow \text{ed} \\
\text{Suffix} &\rightarrow \text{ing}
\end{aligned}
$$

Fig. 1.13. Context-free morphotactics for the strings that appear in Fig. 1.12.

A more detailed description of finite-state morphology is given in Chapter 3.

1.3 Semitic Preliminaries

Semitic covers a wide range of languages and dialects spoken in Western Asia, many of which have been classified as dead languages for centuries, even millennia. These languages and dialects exhibit common characteristics in their lexica and grammars, that is, phonology, morphology, vocabulary, and syntax.

The term "Semitic" is borrowed from the Bible (Gene. x.21 and xi.10–26). It was first used by the Orientalist A. L. Schlözer in 1781 to designate the languages spoken by the Aramæans, Hebrews, Arabs, and other peoples of the Near East (Moscati et al., 1969, Sect. 1.2). Before Schlözer, these languages and dialects were known as *Oriental languages*.

1.3.1 The Semitic Family

Semitic languages are usually classified in groups according to geographical areas, rather than linguistic characteristics; their linguistic classification is still under much debate. Northeast Semitic (Mesopotamia) is represented by Akkadian in all its phases. Northwest Semitic (Syria–Palestine) includes Canaanite, Aramaic, Hebrew, Ugaritic, and other languages from the second millennium B.C. South Semitic (Arabia and Ethiopia) includes Nabatæan, Palmyrene, South Arabic, Modern Arabic, and Amharic.

A number of Semitic languages and dialects survive. Arabic is the widest and is spoken all over the Arab World. Hebrew (including Israeli Hebrew) is spoken in Israel and is the religious tongue of all Jewish communities worldwide. Amharic is spoken in Ethiopia. Aramaic is preserved as a written language in Syriac, originally the Aramaic dialect of Edessa (modern Urfa in Turkey), but later the language of the Christians in Syria and Mesopotamia. A number of spoken, but not written,[7]

[7] Some of the spoken Aramaic dialects have become recently written, most notably Literary Urmia Aramaic (Murre-van den Berg, 1995).

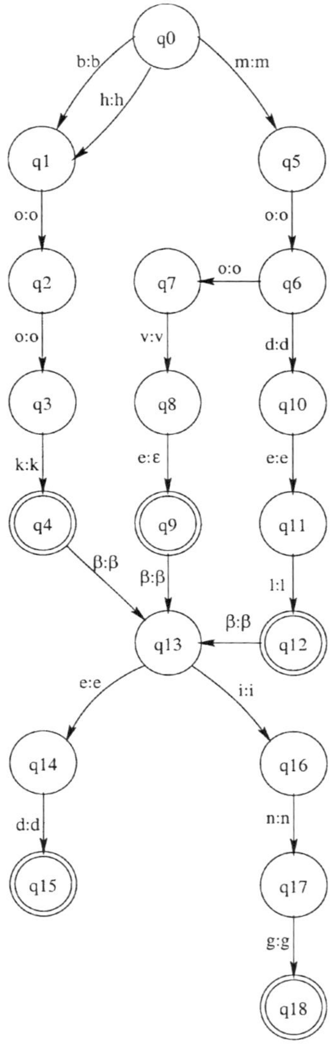

Fig. 1.14. The result of the composition of the identity transducer in Fig. 1.12(b) with the rule transducer in Fig. 1.11.

Aramaic dialects survive: Ṭūrōyô is spoken by the Syriac Orthodox Christians of Ṭūr ʻAḇdīn, South East Turkey. Jewish Aramaic was spoken in Kurdistan and is fighting for survival after the immigration of its speakers to Israel.[8] Swadaya Aramaic is spoken by the East Syrian Christians (modern Assyrians, Chaldæans)

[8] In an attempt to preserve their tongue, a group of the *Nashe Didan* "our people" – as they refer to themselves – Israeli Aramaic speakers has produced a CD of New Age-style songs in Aramaic (Krist, 1998)!

around lake Urmia, Mosul, and other districts in Turkey, Iraq, and Iran as well as the diaspora. Other dialects are spoken in three villages in Syria that, from time to time, make headlines in leading newspapers when a journalist "discovers" a living community speaking the language of Christ! (For the latest case, see Malula Journal in *The New York Times*, Sept. 4, 1999, and the corresponding Letter to the Editor by G. Kiraz, Sept. 11, 1999.)

1.3.2 Semitic Morphology

There are various linguistic models that describe the structure of the Semitic stem. These are described in more detail in Chapter 2. The following is a brief description of Semitic stem morphology, which aims at introducing the material present in the current work and is by no means exhaustive. This work makes use of data from Arabic and Syriac.

1.3.2.1 Templatic Nature

The main characteristic of Semitic derivational morphology is that of the root and pattern, which gave rise to the term *root-and-pattern* or *templatic* morphology. This term came into usage in the past few decades, but its origin goes back beyond medieval times. Classical grammarians of Arabic, Hebrew, and Syriac were well aware of the root-and-pattern phenomenon of their native tongues. The Arabic *ĵaðr* (Syriac *šeršâ*) "root" was the basic unit in classical lexicography. The Arabic *wazn* (Syriac *kaylâ*) "measure" determined the form of nominal and verbal words. This notion of *ĵaðr* and *wazn* was adopted by Western philologists in traditional Semitic grammars; hence, the terms "root" and "pattern" emerged.

Consider the Arabic words /kattab/ "caused to write" and /maktab/ "office." The *root* represents a morphemic abstraction, usually consisting of three consonants, for example, {ktb} "notion of writing," but may be of four consonants, for example, {dħrj} "notion of rolling," or more. A few roots are biliteral, for example, {ʔb} "notion of fatherhood." Stems are derived from the root by the superimposition of patterns. A *pattern* (or *template*, measure, binyan in the case of Hebrew) is a sequence of segments containing Cs that represent the root consonants, for example, $C_1aC_2C_2aC_3$ and $maC_1C_2aC_3$ (the indices refer to root consonants). Root consonants are slotted in place of the Cs to derive stems, for example, Arabic /kattab/ "caused to write" and /maktab/ "office" from the root {ktb} and the above two patterns, respectively. There are various linguistic models for representing patterns, some of which are described in the following chapter. For example, some models represent $C_1aC_2C_2aC_3$ with the more abstract pattern CVCCVC.

1.3.2.2 Verb Morphology

Each of the Semitic languages has a set of verbal *patterns* into which root consonants are slotted. In the native languages, these are identified by using the root {fʕl}; hence, the patterns of /katab/ and /kaatab/ are faʕal and faaʕal, respectively. In Western grammars, and in this work, the patterns are usually numbered. Hence, one speaks of patterns 1 and 3 for the two patterns mentioned in this example. (A list of Arabic measures is given in Table 2.1).

Each pattern is associated to a somewhat predictable semantic unit. The templates modify the root consonants by a combination of the following processes: lengthening (or doubling) the middle consonant, inserting vowels between the consonants, and adding consonantal affixes (Holes, 1995). Consider for example the root {ktb} "notion of writing" with some of the triliteral verbal patterns in Arabic. The first pattern, CVCVC, inserts vowels between the consonants, for example, /katab/. The second pattern is achieved by lengthening the middle consonant, that is, /kattab/, giving a more intensive–extensive or causative meaning. The third pattern lengthens the first vowel, that is, /kaatab/, giving a conative meaning. The fourth pattern prefixes the morpheme {ʔa}, that is, /ʔaktab/ (the vowel after [k] is deleted by a phonological rule in a CVC ___ CVC environment), giving a causative or factitive meaning, and so on.

Syriac is not as rich in verbal patterns. It only utilizes three main patterns. The first pattern corresponds to its Arabic counterpart, except that in Syriac a phonological vowel deletion rule deletes short vowels in open syllables; hence, Arabic /katab/ corresponds to Syriac /ktab/. The second pattern lengthens the middle consonant as in Arabic, for example, /katteb/ (the vowel sequence in Syriac is different from Arabic). The third and final pattern is similar to the Arabic fourth pattern in that it prefixes an {ʔa}, for example, /ʔakteb/, again with the deletion of the vowel after [k].

As for *mood*, the active is indicated in Arabic with the vowel morpheme {a} while the passive with {ui}, for example, /kattab/ and /kuttib/ for pattern two, respectively. In Syriac, the active vowel morpheme is {ae} while the passive one is {a} in conjunction with the passive prefix {ʔet}, for example, /katteb/ and /ʔetkattab/, respectively. It must be noted, however, that the active vowel in the first pattern differs from one root to another and is lexically marked (see below).

Concerning *tense*, Semitists have always referred to the past tense by the term "perfect" and the future tense by "imperfect." The perfect is indicated by verbal inflectional markers (VIMs) in the form of suffixes that are specific to number, person, and gender, for example, Arabic /kataba/ "he wrote," /katabat/ "she wrote" with the suffixes {a} and {at}, respectively. The imperfect is indicated by circumfixes, for example, Arabic /yaktubu/ "he writes," /taktubiin/ "you (FEM) write" with the circumfix {ya-u} and {ta-iin}, respectively (note the deletion of the vowel after a consonant, [k] in this case, in this phonological environment).

Roots do not take all verbal patterns; each root takes only a subset of the patterns. For example, out of 15 verbal patterns for triconsonantal roots, Arabic { ktb } occurs in patterns 1–4, 6–8, and 10, while {qtl} appears only in patterns 1–3, 6, 8, and 10 (Wehr, 1971). These idiosyncrasies are lexically marked.

Another lexical idiosyncrasy is the quality of the second vowel in the first pattern as it differs from one root to another, for example, /qatal/ "to kill," /samuħ/ "to be generous," and /samiʕ/ "to hear," from the roots {qtl}, {smħ}, and {smʕ}, respectively. These are marked in the lexicon as well.

1.3.2.3 Noun Morphology

Like verbs, nouns in Semitic are derived according to patterns, albeit semantically unpredictable in many places. Arabic employs *case*, which is marked by suffixation: {u} for nominative, {a} for accusative, and {i} for genitive, for example, /kitaaba/, /kitaabu/, /kitaabi/ "book." When indefinite, an {n} is added as well, for example, /kitaaban/, /kitaabun/, /kitaabin/.

Syriac does not employ case, but its nominals are marked with what philologists call *state*: absolute, emphatic, and construct (these terms derive from early Latin terminology of Semitic morphology). The absolute is the basic form and is the least frequent (but by no means rare as most grammars claim). The emphatic is marked with a suffix, for example, [å] in /ktåbå/ "book." Both absolute and emphatic are equivalent in meaning. The former is mostly used in idioms. Finally, the construct is marked by its own set of suffixes as well and is always followed by another noun, for example, /ktåbay qudšå/ "Holy Books, Bible."

Number is one of the attributes of nominals. While *sound plurals* are derived by suffixation (e.g., Arabic /kaatib/ "writer," /kaatibuun/ "writers"), *broken plurals*, a phenomenon of Arabic and Ethiopic, involve internal changes to the singular form by means of various morphological processes (e.g., Arabic /kitaab/ "book," /kutub/ "books"). In some cases, the broken plural also takes a suffix in addition to the internal changes (e.g., Tigre–Ethiopic /suq/ "shop," /ʔäswaqat/ "shops" with the {at} ending). The case of the broken plural is one of the main challenges in a computational system and is given due attention in the following chapters (see Sections 2.4 and 6.4).

1.3.3 The Writing System

Any real application of Semitic must take into account the writing system. There is ample documentation today on how to deal with Semitic languages, particularly in the Unicode coding scheme (The Unicode Consortium, 1997) and the OpenType font specification (Ballard and Kohen, 1996). It suffices here to give a brief description.

Unlike Western languages, Semitic languages, apart from Amharic, are written right to left. In addition, Arabic and Syriac can have up to four glyphs per consonant, depending on their position in a word: stand alone, initial, medial, and final. Further, short vowels – when given in the orthographic form (see below) – appear in the form of diacritical marks above and below letters. These issues, however, are not of concern here. The *visual representation* of strings is usually handled by an input–output component of the system in question and can be handled by finite-state devices (as will be discussed in Section 6.5.4). The *logical representation* of strings usually maintains one code per letter (regardless of its shape) and represents the string in memory left to right.

Leaving visual issues aside, the orthographic representation of Semitic does not include short vowels in most texts. This, indeed, is of concern. The orthographic form represents consonants. Three graphemes, which are used for consonants as well, are used to represent long vowels: ʔ, *w*, and *y* for the long vowels *aa*, *uu*, and *ii*, respectively, in the case of Arabic. These are called *matres lectionis*, "mothers of reading." Orthographically, Semitic texts appear in three forms. *Consonantal texts* do not incorporate any vowels but *matres lectionis*, for example, Arabic ⟨ktb⟩ for /katab/ "to write – ACT," /kutib/ "to write – PASS," and /kutub/ "books," but ⟨kʔtb⟩ for /kaatab/ "to write – MEASURE 3, ACT" and /kaatib/ "writer."[9] *Partially vocalized texts* incorporate some vowels to clarify syntactic and semantic ambiguity, for example, ⟨kutb⟩ for passive /kutib/ to distinguish it from its active counterpart /katab/. *Vocalized texts* incorporate full vocalization, for example, ⟨staktab⟩ for /staktab/ "to write – MEASURE 10, ACT." Consonantal texts are by far the most common, appearing in almost all kinds of documents. Partially vocalized words appear in consonantal texts to clarify ambiguity in the case of Arabic and Hebrew; in Syriac, however, quite a large number of texts are partially vocalized – though unfortunately in an unsystematized manner – to ease reading. Finally, fully vocalized texts are used only in religious texts and children's books. The exclusion of short vowels in the orthographic form is one of the challenges that a successful system must resolve, as will be shown in Section 6.5.2.

1.3.4 Transliteration

The system adopted here in the transliteration of Semitic is given on pp. xvii ff.

Computational morphology systems usually aim at processing texts in their orthographic form. The current work, however, uses transliteration instead, for a variety of reasons. First, transliteration, as opposed to transcription, is the norm in the linguistics and Semitic literature. Second, the reader may not be familiar with the various Semitic scripts. Third, the linguistically motivated transliteration scheme adopted here gives linguistic insights on the structure of stems. It is understood that working systems will be dealing with whatever coding the text is represented in.

1.4 Further Reading

A few books that may serve as introductory texts for the topics discussed in this chapter are given here to aid the reader. This is by no means an exhaustive bibliography.

[9] Additionally, these strings denote the various case endings {a}, {i}, and {u}, as well as their indefinite counterparts {an}, {un}, and {in}.

A good introduction to morphology is given by Spencer (1991). An important earlier monograph is that of Matthews (1974).

Any of Linz (1990), Rayward-Smith (1983), or Partee, ter Meulen, and Wall (1993, Sect. E) serves as an introduction to formal language theory. A more advanced account and the standard in the field is Hopcroft and Ullman (1979).

Computational morphology is discussed by Sproat (1992). A special system for English is described by Ritchie et al. (1992). Other applications of finite-state methods to language problems are published in collection edited by Roche and Schabes (1997).

A comparative grammar of Semitic is given by Moscati et al. (1969). Modern Arabic is described by Holes (1995), and Syriac by Robinson (1978) and Muraoka (1997). The Semitic writing system is discussed in Daniels and Bright (1996). Implementational aspects are found in the Unicode Standard (The Unicode Consortium, 2000).

2 Survey of Semitic Nonlinear Morphology

> Indeed a single word, or one syllable only of a noun or a verb, gives no pleasure to the soul because it shows no meaning . . . but when we add nouns to verbs, and noun and verb have thus been joined together, then the soul is pleased.
>
> Job of Edessa (760–835?)
> *Book of Treasures*

Until the mid-1970s, phonologists took a linear approach to generative phonology along the lines of *The Sound Pattern of English* (Chomsky and Halle, 1968). Under this framework, a word is analyzed as a series of one or more segments. The concatenation of these segments makes up the word in question. When the linear concatenation model is applied to morphology, the English word /unsuccessful/ results from the concatenation of the morphemes {un}, {success}, and {ful}. By the late 1970s, however, phonologists had departed from this linear approach to a nonlinear framework under which concatenation does not lie at the heart of phonological operations. This approach was later adopted by morphologists; hence, one speaks of *linear* versus *nonlinear* morphology.

Nonlinear morphology covers a wide range of morphophonological phenomena. Some of these are *root-and-pattern* (*templatic*) *morphology*, in which the structure of a word relies on a pattern–template and a root; *infixation*, in which a morpheme is inserted within a stem; and *circumfixation*, in which a morpheme is split into two parts, one acting as a prefix and the other as a suffix. This chapter provides an overview of these phenomena as they appear in Semitic languages, with a great deal of emphasis on Arabic, which appears ubiquitously in the linguistics literature.

There is no place here for reviewing the structure of Semitic words from the point of view of classical and traditional grammarians.[1] Briefly, early grammarians invented a notation for describing root-and-pattern morphology. They represented the three radicals of the root with the consonants [f], [ʕ], and [l], respectively, to which they added any vowels and auxiliary consonants. The pattern for /kaatib/ "writer" from the root {ktb}, for example, is represented by /faaʕil/. Likewise, the pattern for /maktab/ "office" from the same root is /mafʕal/ (Versteegh 1997a).

[1] For a study on the Arabic linguistic tradition, see Versteegh (1997b).

The first linguistic analysis to appear that is of relevance to the current work is that of Harris (1941). In his work on the structure of the Hebrew current in Jerusalem and in official circles of Judah around 600 B.C., Harris classified morphemes into *root morphemes*, consisting of a sequence of consonants, and *pattern morphemes*, consisting of a sequence of vowels and affixes. Morphemes that fall out of the domain of the root-and-pattern system, such as particles and prepositions, are classified under a third class, consisting of successions of consonants and vowels. According to this taxonomy, the Arabic verb /kuttib/ "to write – CAUS PERF PASS" consists of two morphemes: the root {ktb} "notion of writing" and the pattern { _u_:i_ } "CAUS PERF PASS" (where the underbar indicates a consonant slot, and the colon indicates gemination, or doubling). The Arabic verb /kuttib/ is formed by filling the slots in the pattern morpheme with the root consonants.

Chomsky (1951) developed a formal account of Semitic morphology using transformational rules. In this vein, forms like /kuttib/ are generated by the rule

$$C_1C_2C_3 + V_1V_2 \rightarrow C_1V_1C_2C_2V_2C_3$$

where the Cs represent the three root consonants, respectively, and the Vs represent the two vowels, respectively.

John McCarthy and Alan Prince presented a series of studies describing Arabic morphology that have become influential in the field. What follows is a description of their work.

2.1 The CV Approach

The CV approach argues for a pattern morpheme that consists of sequences of Cs (representing consonants) and Vs (representing vowels); hence, a *CV pattern*. To illustrate this, consider the Arabic verbal system in the perfect tense for the roots {ktb} and {dħrĵ} in Table 2.1. Verbs in Arabic are classified according to 15 triliteral and four quadriliteral measures.[2] Glancing over the table horizontally, one notes the same pattern of consonants and vowels per measure; the only difference is that the vowels are invariably [a]s in active stems, but [u]s in passive stems, with the last vowel being an [i].

McCarthy (1981) proposed a linguistic model for describing such data under the framework of autosegmental phonology (see p. 3). In this model, a stem is represented by three types of morphemes: *root morphemes* consist of consonants, *vocalism* (or vowel melody) *morphemes* consist of vowels, and *pattern morphemes* consist of Cs and Vs. For example, the analysis of /katab/ (measure 1) produces three morphemes: the root morpheme {ktb} "notion of writing," the vocalism morpheme {a} "PERF ACT," and the pattern morpheme {CVCVC} "measure 1."

[2] Some grammars use the term "form" or "conjugation." We prefer to use the term "measure," which was employed by native classical grammarians; it is a translation of Arabic *wazn* and Syriac *kaylâ* (see p. 27).

Table 2.1. *Arabic verbal stems with the roots {ktb} (triliteral measures 1–15) and {dȟrĵ} (quadriliteral measures Q1–Q4)*

Measure	Active	Passive	Measure	Active	Passive
1	katab	kutib	8	ktatab	ktutib
2	kattab	kuttib	9	ktabab	
3	kaatab	kuutib	10	staktab	stuktib
4	ʔaktab	ʔuktib	11	ktaabab	
5	takattab	tukuttib	12	ktawtab	
6	takaatab	tukuutib	13	ktawwab	
7	nkatab	nkutib	14	ktanbab	
			15	ktanbay	
Q1	daȟraĵ	duȟriĵ	Q3	dȟanraĵ	dȟunriĵ
Q2	tadaȟraĵ	tuduȟriĵ	Q4	dȟarĵaĵ	dȟurĵiĵ

Note: The data provide stems in underlying morphological forms. Hence, the following should be noted: (i) mood, case, gender, and number marking is not shown (see Section 2.5.1); (ii) some stems experience phonological processing to give surface forms (see Section 2.5.2); and (iii) measures 9, 11–15 do not occur in the passive.

Some stems include *affix morphemes*, for example, the prefix {st} in /staktab/ (measure 10).

Each morpheme sits on its own autonomous tier in the autosegmental representation as in Fig. 2.1: The middle tier represents the pattern morpheme, while the lower and upper tiers represent the root and vocalism morphemes, respectively. The morphemes are coordinated under the principles of autosegmental phonology according to the following version of the Well-Formedness Condition (cf. p. 4): Every CV skeletal slot must be associated with at least one melody element, every consonantal melody element must be associated with at least one C slot, every vocalic melody element must be associated with at least one V slot, and association lines must not cross. The Association Convention on p. 4 holds.

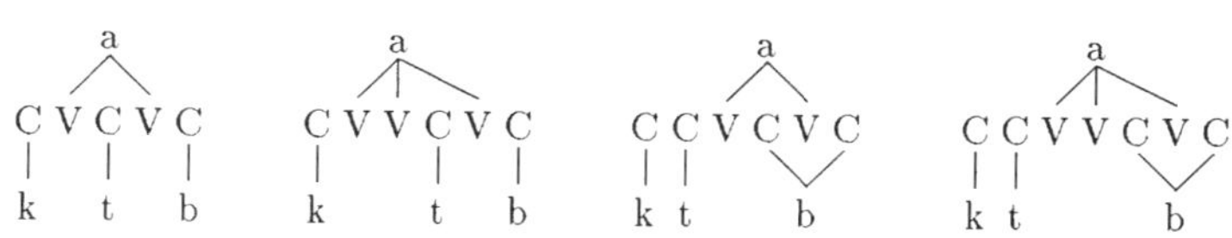

(a) /katab/ (b) /kaatab/ (c) /ktabab/ (d) /ktaabab/

Fig. 2.1. Derivation of measures 1, 3, 9, and 11. Every CV skeletal slot must be associated with at least one melody element, every consonantal melody element must be associated with at least one C slot, every vocalic melody element must be associated with at least one V slot, and association lines must not cross.

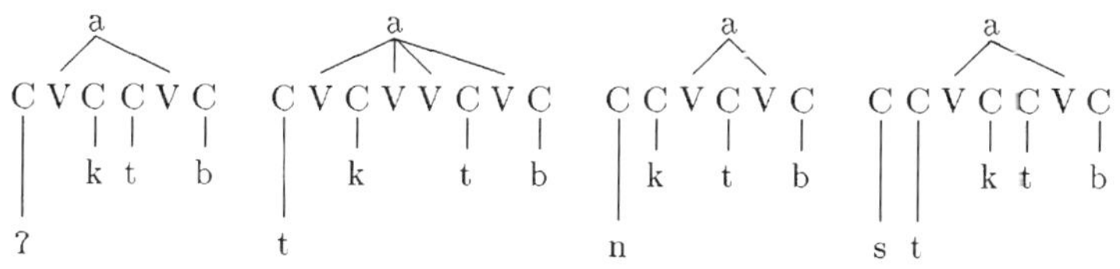

(a) /ʔaktab/ (b) /takaatab/ (c) /nkatab/ (d) /staktab/

Fig. 2.2. Derivation of measures 4, 6–7, and 10. First, the affix material is linked to the pattern and then to the rest of the morphemes' segments. Affixes sit on an autonomous tier.

Measures with affixes are derived in a similar manner, but with association of the affix material first. The derivations of measures 4, 6, 7, and 10 are given in Fig. 2.2. Note that affix morphemes sit on an autonomous tier.

The same procedure applies to measures 14 and 15, but with prelinking affixes in the initial configuration as in Fig. 2.3.

Recall (see p. 4) that the Association Convention states that only the rightmost member of a tier can be associated with more than one member of another tier. This is problematic for measures 2, 5, 12, and 13, as the representations in Fig. 2.4(a) show. For example, in measure 2, the spreading of [b] results in the incorrect form */katbab/, rather than /kattab/ with the spreading of the [t]. A special erasure rule that deletes the link between the penultimate C and a root consonant is used to fix the problem in the following manner: After conventional association, the incorrect forms */katbab/, */takatbab/, and */ktawbab/ are produced as shown in Fig. 2.4(a).

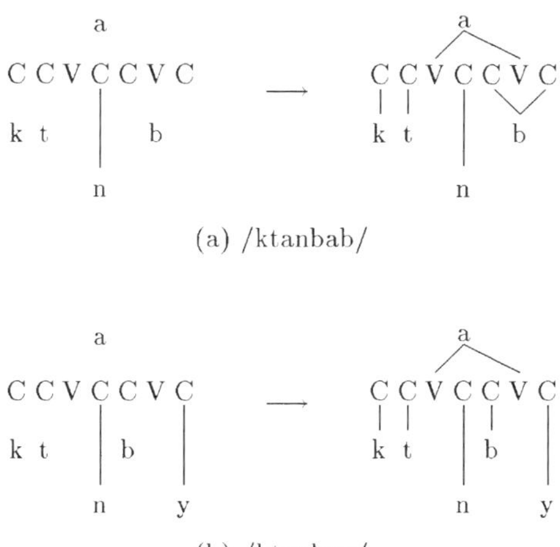

(a) /ktanbab/

(b) /ktanbay/

Fig. 2.3. Derivation of measures 14 and 15. The affix segments are prelinked before the usual association takes place.

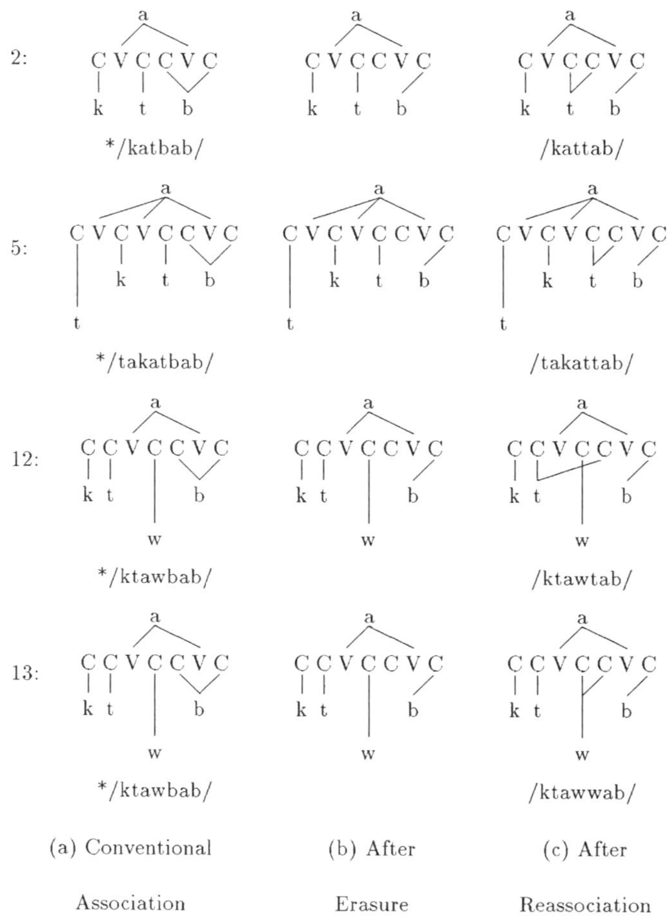

Fig. 2.4. Derivation of measures 2, 5, 12 and 13. First, conventional association takes place as in column (a). This is followed by applying the erasure rule, which deletes the association line between the penultimate C slot and [b] as in column (b). Finally, the unlinked C slot is reassociated with the nearest consonant slot to the left as in column (c). Note that in the autosegmental representation of /ktawtab/, since {ktb} and {w} are on different tiers, the two lines linking the third C slot with [w] and the fourth C slot with [t] do not cross. Imagine the graph in three dimensions, where one of the lines is on top of the other.

To fix the error, the erasure rule is invoked, deleting the association line between the penultimate C slot and [b] as in Fig. 2.4(b). Finally, the unlinked C slot is reassociated with the nearest consonant slot to the left as shown in Fig. 2.4(c). Note that the only difference between measures 12 and 13 is that while the second radical spreads after erasure in the former, the affix spreads in the latter.

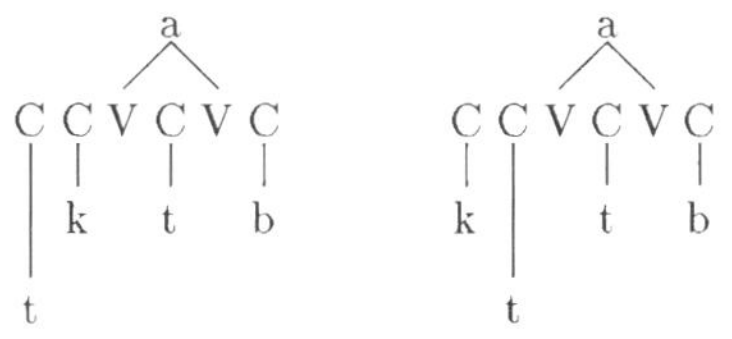

(a) (b)

Fig. 2.5. Derivation of measure 8. A flopping rule unlinks the reflexive {t} infix from the first C slot and links it to the second C slot; (a) shows the configuration before flopping and (b) shows it after flopping.

The Association Convention also fails in producing measure 8. This measure requires a flopping rule that unlinks the reflexive {t} infix morpheme from the first C slot and links it to the second C slot as illustrated in Fig. 2.5. The first C slot takes the first root consonant [k].

Quadriliteral measures do not pose any complications. Their derivation is shown in Fig. 2.6. Note that the [n] affix in /dħanraĵ/ is prelinked to the template.

Passive forms pose additional problems. The vocalism of the passive is {ui}, but with the spreading of [u], instead of [i], which is against the Association Convention (see p. 4). In such cases, a language-specific vowel association rule that links the last V segment of the pattern to the [i] segment of the vocalism has precedence over universal (or default) association. Such derivations are illustrated in Fig. 2.7.

2.2 The Moraic Approach

While the above CV approach describes pattern morphemes in terms of Cs and Vs, the moraic approach argues for a different vocabulary motivated by prosody. To illustrate this model, consider the Arabic nominal stems in Table 2.2.[3]

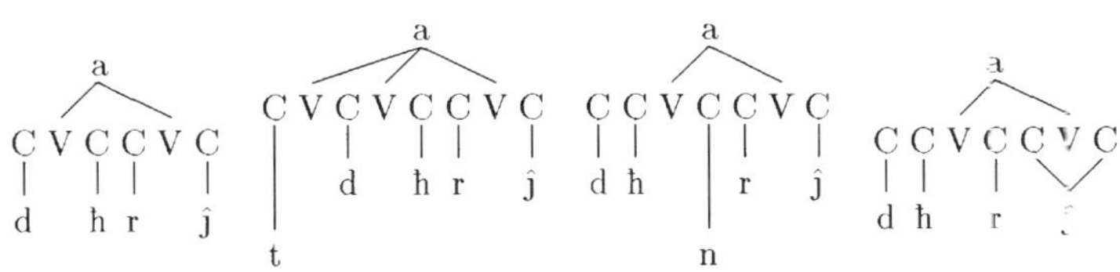

(a) /daħraĵ/ (b) /tadaħraĵ/ (c) /dħanraĵ/ (d) /dħarĵaĵ/

Fig. 2.6. Derivation of quadriliteral measures. The [n] affix in /dħanraĵ/ (c) is prelinked to the template.

[3] Some entries are taken from McCarthy and Prince (1990a) to match the plural data in Section 2.4 (Table 2.3).

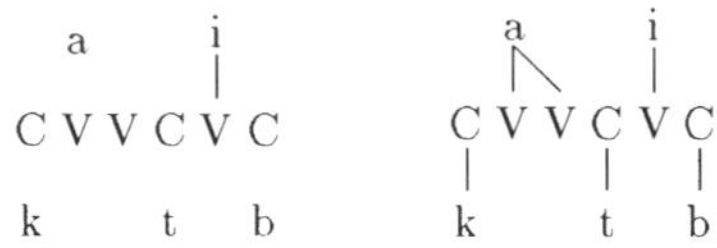

(a) (b)

Fig. 2.7. Derivation of passive forms. A vowel association rule links the last V segment of the pattern to the [i] segment of the vocalism (a). This is followed by conventional association (b).

McCarthy and Prince (1990b) argue for representing the pattern morpheme in terms of the authentic units of prosody. Moraic theory states that the phonological word is made up of feet; the foot is composed of at least one stressed syllable (σ) and may have unstressed syllables, and the syllable weight is measured by the unit *mora* (μ). A light (L) syllable is monomoraic, denoted by σ_μ, while a heavy (H) syllable is bimoraic, denoted by $\sigma_{\mu\mu}$.

Arabic syllables are of three kinds: open light consisting of a consonant followed by a short vowel (CV), open heavy consisting of a consonant followed by a long vowel (CVV), and closed heavy consisting of two consonants separated by a vowel (CVC). This typology is illustrated in Fig. 2.8. Association of consonants and vowels to patterns takes the following form: in monomoraic syllables, a node σ always takes a consonant, and its mora μ takes a vowel as in Fig. 2.8(a). In bimoraic syllables, the second μ may be associated with either a consonant or a vowel as in Fig. 2.8(b and c).[4] Hence, a bimoraic syllable does not distinguish between open heavy (CVV) and closed heavy (CVC) syllables.

Table 2.2. *Arabic nominal stems classified by their CV pattern*

	CV Pattern	Noun	Gloss
(a)	CVCC	nafs	soul
(b)	CVCVC	raĵul	man
(c)	CVCVVC	ĵaziir	island
(d)	CVVCVVC	ĵaamuus	buffalo
(e)	CVCCVVC	sulṭaan	sultan
(f)	CVVCVC	xaatam	signet-ring
(g)	CVCCVC	ĵundub	locust

Note: Other nouns may appear with different lexically marked vocalic melodies.

[4] Other conventions associate consonant melodies left-to-right to the moraic nodes, followed by associating vowel melodies with syllable-initial morae (Moore, 1990, pp. 61–62).

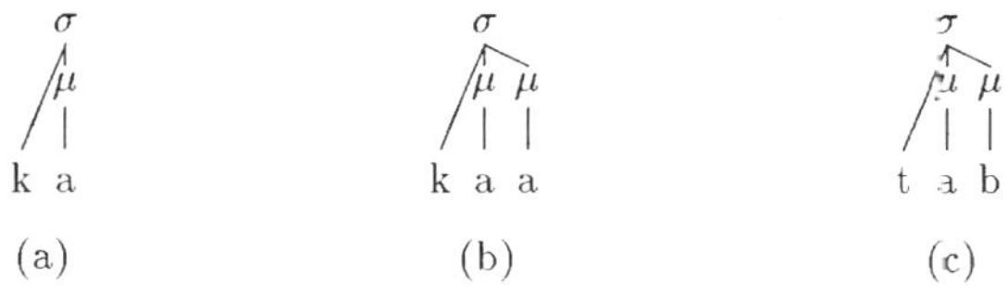

Fig. 2.8. Arabic syllabic structure: (a) open light, (b) open heavy, (c) closed heavy. A node σ is linked to a consonant. The first mora μ is linked to a vowel. The second μ may be associated with either a vowel as in (b) or a consonant as in (c).

The moraic analysis also builds on the notion of *extrametricality* (Liberman and Prince, 1977): At the right edge of stems, all Arabic stems – nominal and verbal – must end in a consonant that is considered to be an extrametrical syllable, denoted by σ_x. Based on this notion, the nominal stems in Table 2.2, (a)–(e), are analyzed moraically in Fig. 2.9. The subtitles indicate syllable-weight patterns, with L representing light syllables and H representing heavy syllables. This analysis shows that the Arabic nominal stem consists of at least two morae and at most two syllables, in addition to the obligatory final σ_x. This is known as the *Minimal and Maximal Stem Constraint.*

McCarthy (1993) claims that there are no HL noun patterns in Arabic. In other words, the forms in Table 2.2, (f) and (g), are atemplatic.[5] McCarthy found that CVVCVC triliteral forms such as /xaatam/ "signet ring" are rare. (Almost all other CVVCVC triliteral forms such as /kaatib/ are active participle forms of the verb, measure 1; their derivation is similar to the derivation of the verb /kaatab/, measure 3, in Section 2.3 below.) Quadriliteral forms like /ĵundub/ are formed by organizing the consonants and vowels in accordance to well formedness in Arabic syllable structure.

One aspect of the moraic analysis has not been mentioned yet: template satisfaction, that is, the association of melodic elements with patterns, especially since moraic theory does not distinguish between CVV and CVC syllables. The final syllable of a stem is predictable: a bimoraic final syllable is CVC in monosyllabic stems as in Fig. 2.9(a), and CVV in bisyllabic ones as in Fig. 2.9(c)–(e).

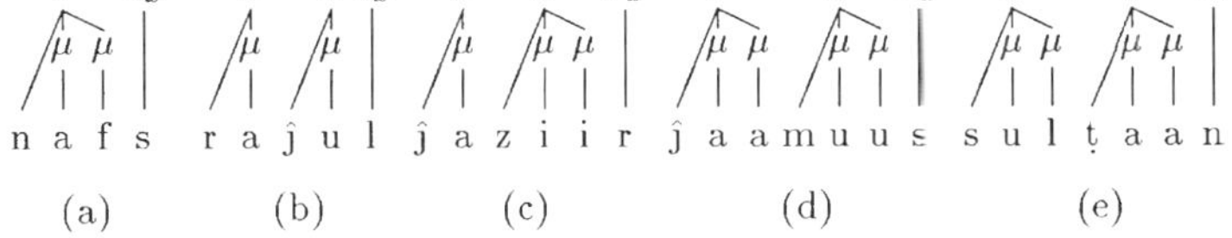

Fig. 2.9. Moraic analysis of the nominal classes in Table 2.2: (a) H, (b) LL, (c) LH, (d) HH, (e) HH. The subtitles indicate syllable-weight patterns, with L representing light syllables and H representing heavy syllables.

[5] This claim was affirmed by Kiraz (1996d) for Syriac.

The initial syllable, however, is not predictable, but it can be determined from the length of the root morpheme: a bimoraic initial syllable is CVV in triliteral roots as in Fig. 2.9(d), and CVC in quadriliteral roots as in Fig. 2.9(e).

2.3 The Affixational Approach

McCarthy (1993) departed radically from the notion of root-and-pattern morphology in the description of the Arabic verbal stem (see Table 2.1). In his new proposal, he argues that Arabic measure 1, /katab/, is templatic, having the moraic template in Fig. 2.10. The remaining measures are derived from the measure 1 template by affixation; they have no templates of their own. This kind of approach was also proposed by Bat-El (1989).

The simplest affixational operation is mere prefixation, for example, {n} + measure 1 $\rightarrow$ /nkatab/ (measure 7). Measures 4 and 10 are derived in a similar fashion, but they undergo a phonological rule of syncope,

$$V \rightarrow \epsilon \;/\; \#CVC\_\_\_\; CVC\#$$

where the pound symbol denotes the stem's left and right boundaries. The rule states that a vowel V becomes ϵ (i.e., is deleted) in the given context. Hence, for measure 4: {ʔa} + /katab/ produces underlying */ʔakatab/. Applying the syncope rule produces /ʔaktab/. Similarly for measure 10, {sta} + /katab/ produces underlying */stakatab/, which in turn produces /staktab/ after the application of the rule.

The remaining measures are derived by affixation under *prosodic circumscription* (PC), a notion introduced by McCarthy and Prince (1990a). Prosodic circumscription defines the domain of morphological operations. Normally, the domain of a typical morphological operation is a grammatical category (root, stem, or word), resulting in prefixation or suffixation. Under prosodic circumscription, however, the domain of a morphological operation is a prosodically delimited substring within a grammatical category, often resulting in some sort of infixation. Prosodic circumscription makes use of a parsing function with two arguments, $\Phi_{(C,E)}$: The function Φ returns the constituent C, which sits on the edge E (where E is in {`right`, `left`}) of the input. The result is a factoring of the input into *kernel*, which is the string returned by the parsing function, and *residue*, which is the remainder of the input. For example, the function $\Phi_{(\sigma_\mu,\texttt{left})}$ returns the monomoraic syllable σ_μ at the left edge of the input. Say the input is /katab/; applying the

Fig. 2.10. Arabic verbal template for measure 1 from which other measures are derived.

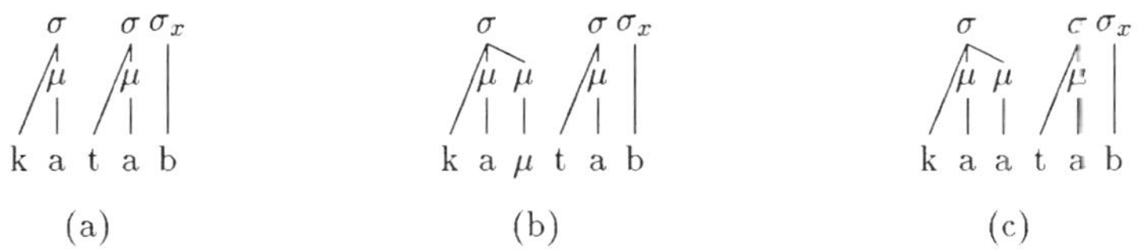

Fig. 2.11. Derivation of /kaatab/. The base template in (a) is prefixed with μ (b), causing the first syllable to become bimoraic. Then, the vowel [a] spreads (c).

parsing function $\Phi_{(\sigma_\mu,\mathtt{left})}$ factors it into (i) kernel /ka/ (the monomoraic syllable at the left), and (ii) residue, or the remainder of the input, /tab/.

There are two types of prosodic circumscription: *positive* and *negative*. In positive prosodic circumscription, the domain of the operation in question is the kernel. In negative prosodic circumscription, the domain is the residue. As a way of illustration, consider the passive of measure 8, /ktutib/. It is derived by the affixation of a {t} to the passive base template /kutib/ under negative prosodic circumscription. The operation is 'prefix {t}' and the parsing function is $\Phi_{(\mathtt{C},\mathtt{left})}$, where C stands for consonant. Applying the parsing function on /kutib/ parses it into the kernel /k/ (the consonant at the left edge) and the residue /utib/ (the remainder of the original string). Recall that in negative prosodic circumscription, the operation applies to the residue. Applying 'prefix {t}' to /utib/ produces /tutib/. Putting the kernel back in its original place results in /ktutib/.

Likewise, the passive of measure 2, /kuttib/, is derived by the doubling of the [t] in the passive base template /kutib/. This is achieved by prefixing a mora to the base template under negative prosodic circumscription. The operation is 'prefix μ' and the parsing function is $\Phi_{(\sigma_\mu,\mathtt{left})}$. Applying the parsing function on /kutib/ parses it into the kernel /ku/ (the monomoraic syllable at the left edge) and the residue /tib/. Hence, applying 'prefix μ' to /tib/ produces /μtib/. The new mora is filled by the spreading of the adjacent consonant [t], resulting in /ttib/. Putting the kernel back in its original place results in /kuttib/.

Measure 3 is derived by prefixing the base template with μ. The process is illustrated in Fig. 2.11. After prefixation, the first syllable becomes bimoraic, which causes the vowel [a] to spread.

The remaining (rare) measures[6] can be analyzed along similar lines by preassociating the second radical with the first σ node of the base template.

2.4 The Broken Plural

Another challenging phenomenon in South Semitic (Arabic and Ethiopic) is the *broken plural*, also called the *internal plural*, which involves considerable internal changes in the stem. Consider the Arabic nominal classes in Table 2.3.

[6] In Wehr's dictionary of Modern Standard Arabic, measures 9, 11, 12, and 14 occur 17, 1, 7, and 1 times, respectively. Measures 13 and 15 do not occur at all (Daniel Ponsford, personal communication).

Table 2.3. *Arabic broken plural forms classified by the CV pattern of their singulars*

	Pattern	Singular	Plural	Gloss
(a)	CVCC	nafs	nufuus	soul
(b)	CVCVC	raĵul	riĵaal	man
(c)	CVCVVC	ĵaziir	ĵazaaʔir	island
(d)	CVVCVVC	ĵaamuus	ĵawaamiis	buffalo
(e)	CVCCVVC	sulṭaan	salaaṭiin	sultan
(f)	CVVCVC	xaatam	xawaatim	signet-ring
(g)	CVCCVC	ĵundub	ĵanaadib	locust

Note: There are many plural types other than those listed in the table.

McCarthy and Prince (1990a) argue that the broken plural in Arabic is derived from the singular stem, not from the consonantal root; hence, /ĵundub/ "locust" produces /ĵanaadib/ "locusts." Further, they argue that broken plurals have the iambic (i.e., light–heavy) template depicted in Fig. 2.12. An informal account of the derivation of the plural from the singular is illustrated by deriving /ĵanaadib/ from /ĵundub/: The first two morae of the singular, that is, /ĵun/, are mapped onto the iambic template in Fig. 2.12. The consonants link to syllable nodes, while the vowel [u] spreads over the three morae, yielding the representation in Fig. 2.13(a). Then, the default plural vocalism {ai} overwrites the singular one by the spreading of [a], yielding the representation in Fig. 2.13(b); the final vowel [i] remains unlinked. Finally, the remaining part of the singular, that is, /dub/, is added and the unlinked [i] overwrites the original vowel [u] as shown in Fig. 2.13(c).

This process is accomplished by positive prosodic circumscription (see Section 2.3). The constituent C in the parsing function $\Phi_{(C,E)}$ is the minimal word, denoted by W_{min}, which consists of two morae. Since melody mapping in Arabic is left to right, the edge E is `left`. The parsing function is then $\Phi_{(W_{\text{min}},\text{left})}$. After the function parses a singular stem, it returns the kernel that maps onto the iambic template, with the default plural vocalism {ai} overwriting the singular one. The residue is then added.

The parsing results of the examples cited above are given in Table 2.4. Starting from the bottom of the list, the derivations of the form in Table 2.4(e) and (g) follow the example in Fig. 2.13. The kernel /ĵun/ maps onto the iambic template, the plural

Fig. 2.12. Broken plural iambic template.

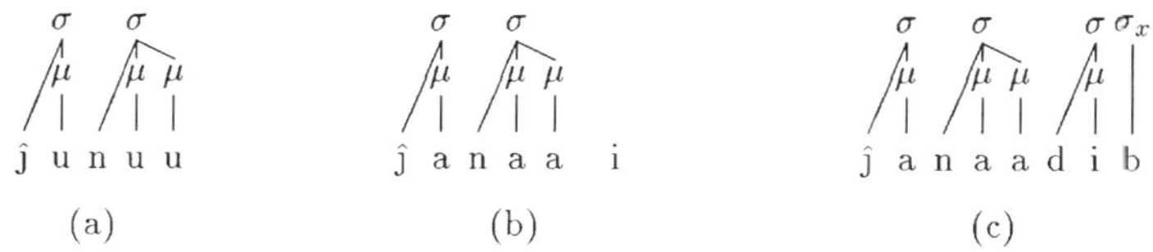

Fig. 2.13. Derivation of /ĵanaadib/ from the singular /ĵundub/. The first two morae of the singular, /ĵun/, are mapped onto the iambic template of Fig. 2.12. The consonants link to syllable nodes; [u] spreads over the three morae (a). Then, the plural vocalism {ai} overwrites the singular one by the spreading of [a] with the final [i] remaining unlinked (b). Finally, the remaining part of the singular, /dub/, is added and the unlinked [i] overwrites the original [u] (c).

vocalism {ai} overwrites the singular one, and the residue /dub/ is suffixed with [i] of the plural vocalism replacing [u].

The derivation of the forms in Table 2.4(d) and (f), for example, from /ĵaamuus/ to /ĵawaamiis/, is illustrated in Fig. 2.14. The kernel, that is, /ĵaa/, maps onto the iambic template as in Fig. 2.14(a), with the spreading of [a]. Since there is no consonant to fill the second σ node, a [w] is inserted as shown in Fig. 2.14(b). The insertion of [w] can be expressed by the default rule $\epsilon \rightarrow$ w when required by syllabic well formedness (recall that ϵ denotes the empty string). Finally, the residue, that is, /miis/, is added as shown earlier. The result appears in Fig. 2.14(c). It is worth noting that the length of [i] is carried over from the singular stem because the residue is not affected by template mapping operations.

The form in Table 2.4(c) adds some complications. Here, the parsing function splits the second syllable into two parts. For example, parsing /ĵaziir/ results in the kernel /ĵazi/ and the residue /ir/. The former maps onto the iambic template as in earlier examples; this is illustrated in Fig. 2.15(a). Next, the residue is added, the vocalism is overwritten by the plural one, and the $\epsilon \rightarrow$ w rule is invoked (see above) since the residue does not constitute a syllable, resulting in the σ node being linked to [w] as shown in Fig. 2.15(b). Finally, a phonological rule of glide realization, where [w] becomes [ʔ], is applied, resulting in Fig. 2.15(c).

Table 2.4. *Derivation of the broken plurals*

	Singular	Kernel	Residue	Plural	Gloss
(a)	nafs	naf	s	nufuu + s	souls
(b)	raĵul	raĵu	l	riĵaa + l	men
(c)	ĵaziir	ĵazi	ir	ĵazaa + ʔir	islands
(d)	ĵaamuus	ĵaa	muus	ĵawaa + miis	buffalos
(e)	sulṭaan	sul	ṭaan	salaa + ṭiin	sultans
(f)	xaatam	xaa	tam	xawaa + tim	signet rings
(g)	ĵundub	ĵun	dub	ĵanaa + dib	locust

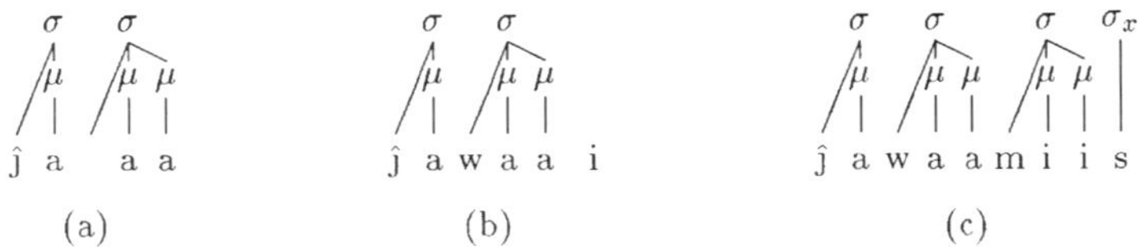

Fig. 2.14. Derivation of /ĵawaamiis/ from /ĵaamuus/. The kernel, /ĵaa/, maps onto the iambic template (a). A [w] is inserted to fill the second σ node (b). Finally, the residue, /miis/, is added (c).

The forms in Table 2.4(a) and (b) are bimoraic. Their derivation is straightforward. However, (i) the plural vocalism may be one of four – {u}, {ia}, {a}, or {au} – it is lexically marked; and (ii) since the residue is an extraprosodic syllable, the second vowel (if any) is deleted by stray erasure. The derivation precess of /riĵaal/ is illustrated in Fig. 2.16. The kernel, that is, /raĵ/, maps onto the iambic template with its plural melody {ia} as in Fig. 2.16(a). The residue, that is, /ul/, is added after deleting the vowel [u] by stray erasure as shown in Fig. 2.16(b).

2.5 Beyond the Stem

So far, this chapter has been concerned with stem morphology in Semitic languages since it is this particular problem that is computationally challenging. For completeness, this section briefly describes other aspects of Semitic morphology, especially those that pose computational morphotactic challenges such as circumfixation.

2.5.1 Morphotactics

Semitic makes extensive use of prefixation and suffixation. In the Hebrew Bible, for example, 51% of the words have at least one prefix and 19.8% have at least one suffix.

Morphosyntactic properties may be expressed differently across the family of Semitic languages. While conjunction is expressed by the prefix {wa} in Arabic

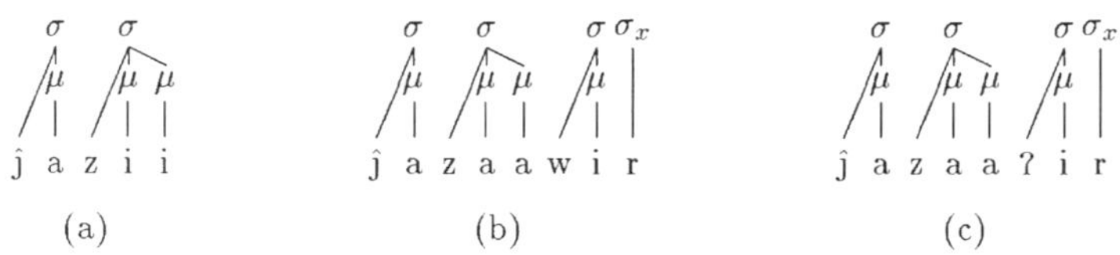

Fig. 2.15. Derivation of /ĵazaaʔir/ from /ĵaziir/. The kernel /ĵazi/ maps onto the iambic template (a). Then, the residue /ir/ is added, the vocalism is overwritten by the plural one, and the $\epsilon \rightarrow$ w rule is invoked (b). Finally, a phonological rule of glide realization is applied, resulting in (c).

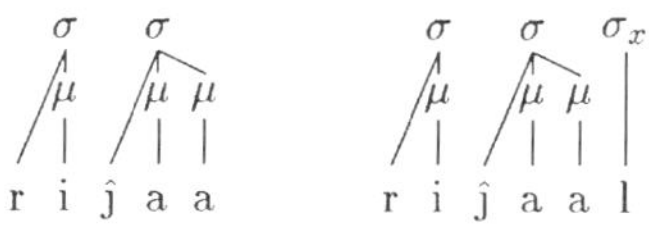

Fig. 2.16. Derivation of /riĵaal/ from /raĵul/. The kernel, /raĵ/, maps onto the iambic template and the stem's plural melody {ia} is applied (a). Then, the residue, /ul/, is added after deleting [u] by stray erasure (b).

(e.g., /wakatab/ "and he wrote"), Hebrew (e.g., /wəkātab/), and Syriac (e.g. /waktab/), the definite article is expressed by the prefix {ʔal} in Arabic (e.g., /ʔl-kitaab/ "the book"), the prefix {ha} in Hebrew (e.g., /hasēfer/ "the book"), and the suffix {å} in early Syriac (e.g., /ktåbå/).[7]

Having said that, the semantics of a particular prefix in a particular Semitic language may be highly ambiguous. When prefixed to nominals, the Syriac prefix {la} may stand for "to" or may be an object marker, for example, /hab ʔegartå lamhaymnå/ "give the letter *to* the believer" (literally, "give letter to-believer"), and /mħå lamhaymnå/ "[he] hit [the] believer." David (1896) enumerates 16 syntactic and semantic usages of the Syriac prefix {da}.

Suffixes are used for various morphological markings. In nominals, Arabic employs suffixes for case endings, while Syriac employs suffixes to mark what Western grammarians call "nominal state." In verbs, most, if not all, Semitic languages employ suffixes for object and possessive markers.

In addition to prefixation and suffixation, Semitic also employs circumfixation in verbal morphology. Imperfect (i.e., future) verbs are usually marked with circumfixes with inflectional markers for number, person, and gender (e.g., Syriac /nektbūn/ "they shall write" with the circumfix {ne-ūn}). While prefixation and suffixation can be easily handled within current frameworks of computational morphology (to be introduced shortly in the next chapter), circumfixation poses some difficulties since the prefix and suffix portion of the circumfix must always agree in number, person, and gender, something that is computationally more costly than simple prefixation and suffixation.

2.5.2 *Phonological Effects*

The morphological word that is derived from lexical elements (such as pattern, root, and vocalism) may undergo a number of phonological processes before a surface form is produced. The Syriac pattern {CVCVC}, root {ktb}, and vocalism {a}, for example, produce the morphological word */katab/ "to write." However, short vowels in open syllables are deleted in Syriac. The actual surface form is then /ktab/ with the deletion of the first [a].

[7] The suffix {å} has lost this function in later Syriac.

While such phonological processes are not uncommon in most languages, Semitic tends to be more rich in its phonological transformations because of the presence of three letters of the alphabet known in native grammars as *weak letters*, that is, [ʔ], [w], and [y]. Words that are derived from roots that contain at least one of these letters are bound to undergo phonological processes. (See Arabic /qaama/ "stood up" from the root {qwm} in the quotation at the beginning of the next chapter.) Out of the unique triliteral roots that appear in the Syriac New Testament, 40.5% contain at least one weak letter; 31.5% of the Arabic roots in the dictionary of Wehr (1971) are weak.

The large number of phonological processes of course adds to the complexity of a computational system. The nature of these processes, however, can be handled within the framework of current computational morphology systems, which are introduced next.

3 Survey of Finite-State Morphology

> The underlying form of *qaama* 'stood up' is *qawama*. . . . This had led some people to believe that such forms, in which the underlying level is not identical with the surface form, at one time were current, in the sense that people once used to say instead of *qaama zaydun: qawama zaydun* 'Zaid stood up'. . . . This is not the case, on the contrary: these words have always had the form that you can see and hear now.
>
> Ibn Jinnî (*c.* 932–1002)
> *al-Khaṣâ'iṣ*

During the past decade and a half, two-level morphology, introduced by Koskenniemi (1983), has become ubiquitous as a computational model. It has been applied to a variety of natural languages, including Akkadian, Arabic, and Hebrew. This chapter describes two-level morphology and reviews earlier proposals for handling nonlinear Semitic operations.

Section 3.1 discusses finite-state morphology, in particular Koskenniemi's two-level model and the original work of Ronald Kaplan and Martin Kay on which the two-level model was based. Section 3.2 gives an outline of the developments in two-level formalisms that are of relevance to the current work.

3.1 The Finite-State Approach

Finite-state morphology aims at analyzing morphology within the computational power of finite-state automata (see Section 1.2.2). It is by far the most popular approach in the field. This section briefly reviews the development of finite-state morphology.

3.1.1 Kay and Kaplan's Cascade Model (1983)

The notion of using FSTs to model phonological rules dates back to the early work of Johnson (1972). Independently, Kay and Kaplan (1983), in an unpublished work,[1] arrived at a similar conclusion and presented the mathematical

[1] Later published as Kaplan and Kay (1994), on which the current discussion is based.

tools required for the compilation into FSTs of regular rewrite rules of the form

$$\phi \rightarrow \psi / \lambda \_\_\_ \rho$$

where ϕ, ψ, λ, and ρ are regular expressions, with ϕ designating the input, ψ designating the output, and λ and ρ designating the left and right contexts, respectively. Rules are marked with precedence (i.e., which rule applies first) and direction (i.e., whether a rule applies to the string in question left to right, right to left, or simultaneously).

Each rule is compiled into a finite-state transducer. The relation between lexical and surface strings, for example, is taken as the composition of the FSTs that sanction their mapping as depicted Fig. 3.1. As a way of illustration, consider the Syriac derivation of /kθav/ "to write" from the underlying stem */katab/. The derivation makes use of two rules. These are the spirantization rule (ignoring changes in place of articulation),

$$[-\text{ CONTINUANT}] \rightarrow [+\text{ CONTINUANT}] \; / \; \text{V} \_\_\_$$

which maps [t] to [θ] and [b] to [v] postvocalically, and the vowel-deletion rule,

$$\text{V} \rightarrow \epsilon \; / \; \text{C} \_\_\_ \text{CV}$$

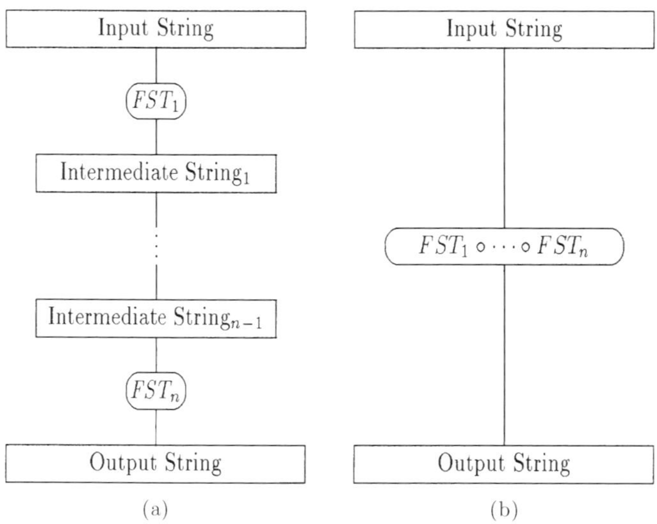

Fig. 3.1. (a) Cascade model of regular rewrite rule systems. (b) The relation between lexical and surface strings is taken as the composition of the FSTs that sanction their mapping.

which deletes (short) vowels in open syllables. The spirantization rule maps */katab/ into */kaθav/, and the vowel deletion rule maps */kaθav/ into /kθav/. Note that the two rules must apply in this order; otherwise, the spirantization rule will fail to apply on [t] resulting in the undesired */ktav/.

More formally, let L represent the FST that accepts only the identity of the string */katab/, and let M_1 and M_2 represent the FSTs for the above two rules, respectively. The direct mapping from */katab/ into /kθav/ is simulated by the composition $L \circ M_1 \circ M_2$.

In this model, an analysis that involves n ordered rules requires n FSTs running on $n + 1$ tapes, with $n - 1$ tapes being intermediate ones. As n increases, the number of intermediate tapes increases as well. Though merging all FSTs into one FST is possible by composing and minimizing all transducers, doing so results in huge intermediate machines that make the process, at least for the computer devices of that time, computationally infeasible. Modern machinary, however, can cope with this model. For example, the Bell Labs text-to-speech system (Sproat, 1997) implements the Kaplan and Kay model, albeit by employing another algorithm for compiling rules into FSTs (see Mohri and Sproat, 1996).

3.1.2 Koskenniemi's Two-Level Model (1983)

Koskenniemi (1983), working in the domain of morphology, proposed that the FSTs that represent rules should run in parallel, rather than serial, composition. In other words, the machinary has only two tapes, which Koskenniemi called *lexical tape* and *surface tape*. Since only two tapes are visible to all transducers, the model was named *two-level morphology*. Figure 3.2 depicts this parallel model. Here, the direct relation between the lexical and surface strings is taken as the intersection of all transducers.

Koskenniemi devised a formalism for expressing two-level rules that sanction lexical-surface pairs of symbols of the form

$$\tau \; \{\Rightarrow, \Leftarrow, \Leftrightarrow\} \; \lambda \_\_\_ \; \rho$$

where τ is a pair of symbols of the form LexicalSymbol:SurfaceSymbol, λ is the left context and ρ is the right context, both contexts being sequences of pairs of symbols. The operators are as follows: $\Rightarrow$ for context restriction (meaning "only but not always") rules, $\Leftarrow$ for surface coercion (meaning "always but not only") rules, and $\Leftrightarrow$ for composite rules.[2] For example, the abstract rule

$$\text{a:b} \Rightarrow \text{c:d} \_\_\_ \; \text{e:f}$$

[2] Some implementations (Karttunen and Beesley, 1992, and earlier works) make use of a fourth exclusion operation, $/\!\!\Rightarrow$.

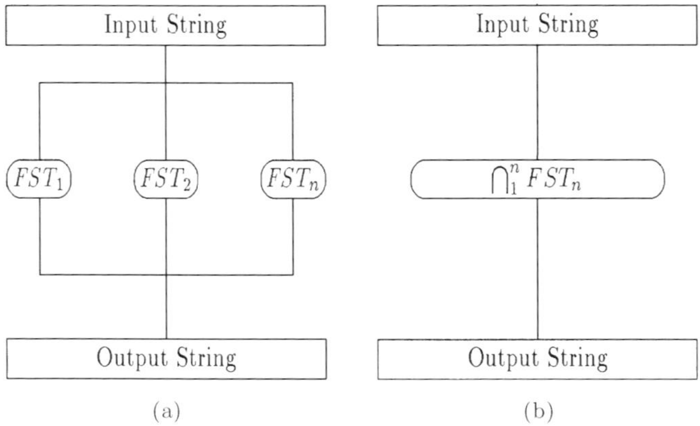

Fig. 3.2. (a) Parallel model of two-level morphology. FSTs that represent rules run in parallel. The machinary sees only two tapes: lexical and surface. (b) The direct relation between the lexical and surface strings is equivalent to the intersection of all transducers.

states that [a] maps to [b] only when preceded by [c] corresponding to [d] and followed by [e] corresponding to [f]. However, [a] may map to any other symbol in the same context if sanctioned by another rule. This rule maps the lexical string "cae" to the surface string "dbf". The abstract rule

$$\text{a:b} \Leftarrow \text{c:d} \;\_\_\_\; \text{e:f}$$

states that [a] must map to [b] in the given context, but not necessarily only in the stated context. The composite rule

$$\text{a:b} \Leftrightarrow \text{c:d} \;\_\_\_\; \text{e:f}$$

is basically a shorthand for combining the two rules (meaning "always and only").

The following [e]-deletion rule demonstrates the deletion of [e] in English /moved/, from the lexical morphemes {move} and {ed} (cf. p. 22):

$$\text{e:0} \;\Leftrightarrow\; \text{v:v} \;\_\_\_\; \beta\text{:0 (i:i} \cup \text{e:e)}$$

The rule states the deletion of lexical [e] in {move} in the context shown. The null symbol [0] is a genuine symbol that represents the empty string ε. The reason [0] must be used instead of ϵ is that ϵ-containing transducers are not necessarily closed under intersection, a crucial operation in the two-level model (see p. 20).

Another aspect of Koskenniemi's work is morphotactics. In the two-level model, morphotactics was implemented in a finite-state manner by using "continuation patterns/classes," in which each lexical entry was marked with a set of classes of morphemes that may follow.

Koskenniemi's proposal proved to be successful and was implemented in various systems (Karttunen, 1983; Antworth, 1990; Karttunen, 1993). However, it fell short of analyzing complex nonlinear phenomena.

3.2 Developments in Two-Level Formalisms

This section examines the developments and augmentations of two-level formalisms that are of relevance to the current work. Subsection 3.2.1 gives the background of rule features. The remaining subsections outline the development of the formalism used in subsequent chapters.

3.2.1 Bear's Proposals (1986, 1988)

Two important proposals were put forward by Bear, the first concerning morphotactics and the second concerning negative rule features.

(Bear, 1986) noted that the implementation of morphotactics in the form of "continuation patterns/classes" is inadequate for encoding long-distance dependencies, such as {en} and {able} in /*en*joy*able*/, and requires the use of ad hoc special symbols in the lexicon and rules. He proposed replacing continuation classes by a unification-based grammar for morphotactic parsing. This approach was later adopted in various implementations (Beesley, Buckwalter, and Newton, 1989; Trost, 1990; Ritchie et al., 1992; Antworth, 1994, inter alia).

Additionally, Bear (1988) pointed out that earlier two-level systems did not provide for an easy way to let the two-level rules know about individual idiosyncrasies in lexical entries; instead, special diacritics were coded in lexical entries in order to allow rules to apply to a subset of the lexicon. An example of this approach is the insertion of [e] in English plurals: /potato/, for example, takes an epenthetic [e] in the plural, forming /potatoes/, while /piano/ does not take an [e]. Bear proposed that lexical entries may be associated with negative rule features indicating that certain rules do not apply to marked entries. For example, the lexical entry for /piano/ would be marked with the feature [epenthesis -], preventing the epenthetic rule from applying to it.

3.2.2 Black et al.'s Formalism (1987)

It was pointed out by Black et al. (1987) that previous two-level rules affect one character at a time, resulting in the need for more than one rule to describe a single change. They proposed a formalism that maps between (equal numbered) sequences of surface and lexical characters as follows:

$$\text{SURF}\{\Rightarrow, \Leftarrow\}\text{LEX}$$

where $\Rightarrow$ and $\Leftarrow$ are the operators for optional and obligatory rules, respectively.

s	t	a	b	leβi	t	y	*lexical*
1	1	1	1	2	1	1	
s	t	a	b	il0i	t	y	*surface*

Fig. 3.3. Partitioning of /stability/ into lexical-surface subsequences is indicated by dotted lines; numbers indicate the rules that sanction the respective subsequences.

The interpretation of this formalism differs from that of Koskenniemi. Here, a lexical string maps to a surface string if and only if there is a partitioning of the surface string into surface subsequences such that each subsequence is a SURF of a $\Rightarrow$ rule and the lexical string is equal to the concatenation of the corresponding LEX strings. Further, any subsequence of the lexical string that is a LEX of a $\Leftarrow$ rule must correspond to the surface string given in the corresponding SURF of the same rule. Black et al. (1987) noticed that, in practice, for each $\Leftarrow$ rule there is a corresponding $\Rightarrow$ rule; they suggested collapsing such pairs of rules into a single composite rule with the operator $\Leftrightarrow$.

As a way of illustration, the mapping of English /stability/ to the lexical morphemes {stable} and {ity} is described by the following rules:

$$\text{R1} : \text{X} \Rightarrow \text{X}, \text{ where X is any symbol}$$

$$\text{R2} : \text{il0i} \Leftrightarrow \text{le}\beta\text{i}$$

R1 is the identity rule that maps any symbol to itself. R2 maps lexical /leβi/ into surface /il0i/. The sequence of the rules sanctioning the mapping is shown in Fig. 3.3. The partitioning into lexical-surface subsequences is indicated by dotted lines. The numbers between the lexical and surface strings indicate the rules that sanction the subsequences.

Notice that this formalism does not allow the output of one application of a rule to serve as context for subsequent applications of the same rule. For this to be remedied, contexts must be stated explicitly in rules.

3.2.3 Ruessink's Formalism (1989)

Developing the above formalism, Ruessink (1989) added explicit contexts and allowed unequal sequences even in the center of the rule (SURF and LEX), thus dispensing with the '0' symbol in Koskenniemi's original formalism.[3] Dispensing with '0' meant that the interpretation of $\Leftarrow$ rules had to be modified: $\Leftarrow$ rules in

[3] Although this is more elegant than earlier formalisms, it will be shown that in order to remain within finite-state power, a rule compiler must ensure that the centers of a rule are of equal length by automatically padding an auxiliary symbol, say '0' (see Sect. 7.3.1).

Ruessink's version can only apply to subsequences sanctioned by $\Rightarrow$ rules. The new formalism follows:[4]

$$\text{LLC} - \text{Lex} - \text{RLC}\{\Rightarrow, \Leftrightarrow\}$$
$$\text{LSC} - \text{Surf} - \text{RSC}$$

where LLC denotes the left lexical context, Lex denotes the lexical form, and RLC denotes the right lexical context. LSC, Surf, and RSC are the surface counterparts. The context denoted by an asterisk is always satisfied. The operator $\Rightarrow$ states that Lex *may* surface as Surf in the given context, while the operator $\Leftrightarrow$ adds the condition that when Lex appears in the given context, then the surface description *must* satisfy Surf. The latter caters for obligatory rules. A lexical string maps to a surface string if and only if they can be partitioned into pairs of lexical-surface subsequences, where (i) each pair is licensed by a $\Rightarrow$ rule and (ii) no pair violates a $\Leftrightarrow$ rule.

For ease of presentation, rules may contain variables described with a "where" clause, as shown in R1 in Fig. 3.4(a).

Consider again the analysis of English /stability/. It can be achieved with the use of the rules in Fig. 3.4(a). R1 is the identity rule that maps any symbol to itself. R2 maps lexical /le/ to surface /il/ in the given context. R3 is the boundary symbol deletion rule. The partitioning into lexical-surface subsequences is depicted in Fig. 3.4(b). The numbers indicate the rules that sanction the subsequences. The rules, however, do not prevent */stableity/ from surfacing, as depicted in Fig. 3.4(c), since none of the subsequences violate R2. This is so because there is no subsequence in the analysis that matches the center of R2 (note that [l] and [e] on the lexical tape belong to different subsequences). This problem is due to the semantics of obligatoriness, as will be described shortly (cf. Sections 3.2.5 and 3.2.6).

3.2.4 Pulman and Hepple's Feature Representation (1993)

Pulman and Hepple (1993) extended the above formalism by adding rule features following Bear (1988; see Section 3.2.1). Here, each rule may be associated with a feature structure (unordered set of *attribute* = *value pairs*, where *attribute* is a feature label and *value* is an atom, a variable, or another feature structure). Each

[4] In Ruessink's formalism, lexical expressions appear to the left of the operator, while surface expressions appear to the right:

$$\text{LLC} - \text{Lex} - \text{RLC}\{\Rightarrow, \Leftrightarrow\}\,\text{LSC} - \text{Surf} - \text{RSC}$$

However, because of the limited width of the page and to ease comparison between rules and multitape illustrations in subsequent chapters (which depict lexical tapes on top of surface tapes, e.g. Fig. 5.4), lexical expressions are aligned on top of their surface counterparts.

```
       *  -  X  -  *   ⇒
R1:
       *  -  X  -  *

       where X is any symbol

       b  -  le -  βi  ⇔
R2:
       b  -  il -  i

       *  -  β  -  *   ⇔
R3:
       *  -  ε  -  *
```

(a)

s	t	a	b	le	β	i	t	y	*lexical*
1	1	1	1	2	3	1	1	1	
s	t	a	b	il		i	t	y	*surface*

(b) /stability/

s	t	a	b	l	e	β	i	t	y	*lexical*
1	1	1	1	1	1	3	1	1	1	
s	t	a	b	l	e		i	t	y	*surface*

(c) */stableity/

Fig. 3.4. Two-level analysis of /stability/, using Ruessink's formalism. (a) R1 is the identity rule; R2 maps lexical /le/ to surface /il/; R3 is the boundary-deletion rule. Partitioning into lexical-surface subsequences is depicted in (b); the numbers indicate the rules that sanction the subsequences. The rules, however, do not prevent */stableity/ from surfacing (c).

lexical entry in the lexicon (e.g., morpheme) may be associated with a feature structure as well.

The following constraints were added to the interpretation of Ruessink's formalism: the feature structure associated with the lexical entry containing a licensed pair of lexical-surface subsequence must unify with the feature structure of the rule that sanctions that particular pair. For example, assume that the lexicon contains the three abstract morphemes {abcd}, {ef}, and {ghi}, which are associated in the lexicon with the feature structures l_1, l_2, and l_3, respectively, as in Fig. 3.5(a). Now assume that there is a partitioning of lexical-surface subsequences as in Fig. 3.5(b), where r_i, $1 \leq i \leq 9$ is the feature structure associated with the rule that sanctions pair i. For the partitioning to be valid, r_1, r_2, r_3, and r_4 must unify with l_1, the feature structure associated with {abcd} in the lexicon; r_5 and r_6 must unify with l_2, the feature structure associated with {ef} in the lexicon;

Entry	Feature structure
abcd	l_1
ef	l_2
ghi	l_3

(a) Lexicon

a	b	c	d	e	f	g	h	i	*lexical*
r_1	r_2	r_3	r_4	r_5	r_6	r_7	r_8	r_9	
a	b	c	d	e	f	g	h	i	*surface*

(b) Lexical-Surface Analysis

Fig. 3.5. Feature example demonstrating how rule and lexical features unify. The abstract morphemes in (a) are associated with feature structures. Each rule sanctioning a lexical-surface subsequence in the analysis in (b) is associated with a feature structure r_i. For the partitioning to be valid; r_1–r_4 must unify with l_1, r_5 and r_6 with l_2, and r_7–r_9 with l_3.

and r_7, r_8, and r_9 must unify with l_3, the feature structure associated with {ghi} in the lexicon.

The Pulman–Hepple version of the formalism has some advantages over previous two-level formalisms.

(i) It allows mappings between lexical and surface strings of unequal lengths, making it easier to write prosodic morphological rules (cf. Section 5.2).[5]

(ii) The ability to use unification for representing sequences allows a lexical entry to include variables; for example; the vowel V in the Arabic verbal prefix morpheme {tV} can be determined from the vowel of the following stem: [a] in /takaatab/ and [u] in /tukuutib/ (cf. Sect. 6.3). As long as such variables are predefined over a finite set of possible values, one remains within finite-state power.

(iii) It covers within its definition rule features that are very helpful in writing complex Semitic morphophonology systems.

Two subsequent implementations of the formalism discovered a problem in the interpretation of obligatory rules. These are discussed below.

[5] When the rules are compiled into automata, a preprocessing stage makes all expressions equal in length (see Sect. 7.3.1).

3.2.5 Carter's Note on Obligatory Rules (1995)

It was pointed out by Carter (1995) that although the Pulman–Hepple formalism allows the mapping of sequences of unequal lengths, the grammar writer cannot practically take advantage of this feature in obligatory rules.

Recall from Section 3.2.3 that the rules in Fig. 3.4(a) do not prohibit the analysis of */stableity/ in Fig. 3.4(c). This is so because the semantics of obligatoriness is not bidirectional: the *lexical* element of a subsequence and the contexts correspond to the *surface* element of the same subsequence; the opposite does not hold (Carter, 1995, Section 4.1).

To resolve the problem within the current definition of the formalism, two separate rules are required for the mapping of lexical /le/ to surface /il/: R2 and R3 in Fig. 3.6(a). The proper analysis is given in Fig. 3.6(b). In order to avoid such complications, the definition of obligatoriness had to be reexamined.

$$\text{R1:}\quad \begin{array}{ccccc} * & - & \text{X} & - & * \\ * & - & \text{X} & - & * \end{array} \Rightarrow$$

where X is any symbol

$$\text{R2:}\quad \begin{array}{ccccc} \text{b} & - & \text{l} & - & \text{e}\beta\text{i} \\ \text{b} & - & \text{i} & - & \text{li} \end{array} \Leftrightarrow$$

$$\text{R3:}\quad \begin{array}{ccccc} \text{l} & - & \text{e} & - & \beta\text{i} \\ \text{i} & - & \text{l} & - & \text{i} \end{array} \Leftrightarrow$$

$$\text{R4:}\quad \begin{array}{ccccc} * & - & \beta & - & * \\ * & - & \epsilon & - & * \end{array} \Leftrightarrow$$

(a)

s	t	a	b	l	e	β	i	t	y	*lexical*
1	1	1	1	2	3	4	1	1	1	
s	t	a	b	i	l		i	t	y	*surface*

(b)

Fig. 3.6. Derivation of /stability/ that prevents */stableity/; two separate rules (R2 and R3) are required for the mapping of lexical /le/ to surface /il/.

3.2.6 Redefining Obligatoriness: Grimley-Evans, Kiraz, and Pulman (1996)

Recall from Section 3.2.3 that in the above formalism, a lexical string maps to a surface string if and only if both strings can be partitioned into pairs of lexical-surface subsequences, where (i) each pair is licensed by a $\Rightarrow$ rule and (ii) no pair violates a $\Leftrightarrow$ rule.

There are two problems with the second condition: first, the grammar writer cannot practically take advantage of mapping lexical-surface subsequences of unequal lengths as described above (Section 3.2.5); second, the condition does not cater for epenthetic rules (discussed below). Grimley-Evans, Kiraz, and Pulman (1996) reexamined and redefined obligatoriness to resolve the two problems.

As a way to allow the grammar writer to express mappings of unequal lengths, condition (ii) was modified to read "*no sequence of adjacent pairs* violates a $\Leftrightarrow$ rule" (modifications to the earlier definition are shown in italic). Hence, the undesired analysis in Fig. 3.4(c) will fail since the two adjacent subsequences, [l] and [e], violate R2 of the grammar. This is so because lexical /le/ matches LEX in R2 and all contexts are satisfied, but surface /le/ does *not* match SURF in R2.

As for the case of epenthetic rules, consider the rules in Fig. 3.7. The epenthetic rule R2 states that [b] *must* be inserted in the surface if preceded by lexical [c] mapping to surface [c] and followed by lexical [d] mapping to surface [d]. In other words, the lexical sequence /cd/ is *not* allowed to surface as /cd/. The formalism fails to capture this case, as the undesired partitioning in Fig. 3.7(b) illustrates. Both

$$\text{R1:}\quad \begin{matrix} * & - & X & - & * & \Rightarrow \\ * & - & X & - & * & \end{matrix}$$

where $X \in \{c,d\}$

$$\text{R2:}\quad \begin{matrix} c & - & \epsilon & - & d & \Leftrightarrow \\ c & - & b & - & d & \end{matrix}$$

(a)

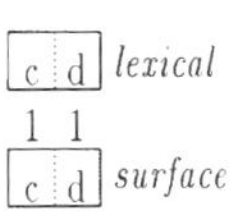

(b)

Fig. 3.7. Example of epenthetic rules (a). R1 is the identity rule; R2 inserts [b] between [c] and [d]. Hence, the lexical sequence /cd/ in (b) is invalid.

subsequences in Fig. 3.7(b) are licensed by R1 and neither of them violates R2. Condition (ii) was further modified to read "no sequence of *zero or more* adjacent pairs violates a ⇔ rule". With this definition of obligatoriness, the undesired derivation in Fig. 3.7(b) fails since there is a zero subsequence (in fact an infinite number of such a subsequence) between the two shown subsequences, which violates R2.

The final interpretation of the formalism follows. A lexical string maps to a surface string if and only if they can be partitioned into pairs of lexical-surface subsequences, where (i) each pair is licensed by a ⇒ rule and (ii) no sequence of zero or more adjacent pairs violates a ⇔ rule. This final definition of the formalism is used in subsequent chapters.

4 Survey of Semitic Computational Morphology

> The words are noun, verb and particle which brings a meaning that is neither noun nor verb. Noun is *rajul* 'man', *faras* 'horse'. Verbs are patterns derived from the expression of the events of the nouns; they have forms to indicate what is past; and what will be but has not yet happened; and what is being and has not yet been interrupted.... These patterns are derived from the expression of the events of the nouns; they have many different forms which will be explained, God willing.... As for those words that bring a meaning that is neither noun nor verb, they are like *thumma* 'then', *sawfa* [particle of the future], the *w* used in oaths, the *l* used in annexion, etc.
>
> Sîbawayhi (d. 793)
> *al-Kitaab*

> [Sibawaih's] phonetic description of the Arabic script ... was ahead of preceding and contemporary western phonetic science. He and other Arab grammarians were able to set out systematically the organs of speech and the mechanism of utterance.
>
> R. H. Robins
> *A Short History of Linguistics*

A major obstacle in mainstream two-level morphology is that the lexical level consists of the *concatenation* of the lexical forms in question. This makes it extremely difficult, if not impossible, to apply mainstream two-level notation to the autonomous morphemes of Semitic. Other cases of nonlinear morphology, for example, infixation and reduplication, can be handled within standard two-level models, though this requires the use of diacritics and clumsy notation in lexical entries and rules (for examples, see Antworth 1990, Section 6.4.4). A number of proposals for handling nonlinear morphology in a more interesting way have appeared in the past decade. This chapter gives a brief description of them in chronological order.

4.1 Kay's Approach to Arabic (1987)

Kay (1987) proposed a finite-state approach for handling Arabic nonconcatenative morphology. The approach follows the CV analysis of Arabic (see Section 2.1). Kay's proposal uses four-tape automata and adds some extensions to traditional FSTs. Transitions are marked with quadruples of elements (for vocalism, root,

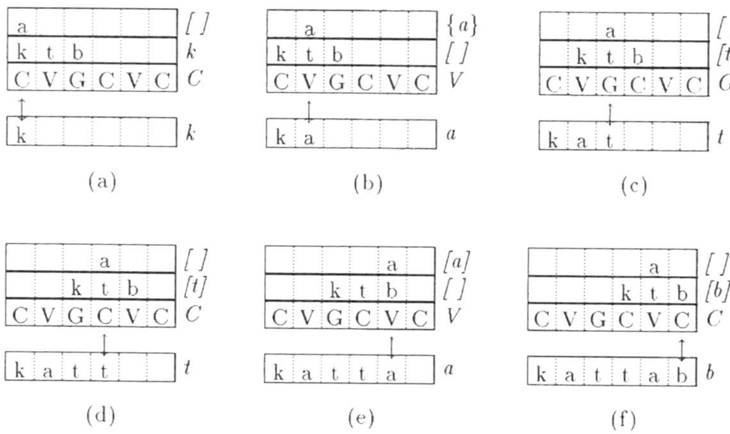

Fig. 4.1. Kay's analysis of Arabic /kattab/. The four tapes are (from top to bottom) the vocalism, root, pattern, and surface tapes. Transition quadruples are shown at the right side of the tapes. The ↕ between the lower surface tape and the lexical tapes indicates the current symbols under the read–write heads.

pattern, and surface form, respectively), where each element is a pair: a symbol and an instruction concerning the movement of the tape's head. Kay uses the following notation: An unadorned symbol is read and the tape's head moves to the next position. A symbol in brackets, [ ], is read and the tape's head remains stationary. A symbol in braces, { }, is read and the tape's head moves only if the symbol is the last one on the tape. Kay used this notation to have CV elements in the pattern tape select which of the other (root and vocalism) tapes to read from.

The transitions for the analysis of Arabic /kattab/ (measure 2) is shown in Fig. 4.1. The four tapes are, from top to bottom, the vocalism tape, root tape, pattern tape, and surface tape. Transition quadruples are shown at the right side of the tapes. The up-and-down arrow between the lower surface tape and the lexical tapes indicates the current symbols under the read–write heads. After the first transition on the quadruple ⟨[ ], k, C, k⟩ in Fig. 4.1(a):

(i) no symbol is read from the vocalism tape;
(ii) [k] is read from the root tape and the tape's head is moved;
(iii) [C] is read from the pattern tape and the tape's head is moved; and
(iv) [k] is written on the surface tape and the tape's head is moved.

In a similar manner, after the second transition on the quadruple ⟨{a}, [ ], V, a⟩ in Fig. 4.1(b):

(i) [a] is read from the vocalism tape, but the tape's head remains stationary;
(ii) no symbol is read from the root tape;

(iii) [V] is read from the pattern tape and the tape's head is moved; and
(iv) [a] is written on the surface tape and the tape's head is moved.

At the final configuration, all the tapes have been exhausted and the desired form appears on the surface tape.

Kay makes use of a special symbol, G, to handle gemination. When reading G on the pattern tape, the machine scans a symbol from the root tape without advancing the read head of that tape.

Kay's model has a number of shortcomings. Some of these have already been pointed out by Bird and Ellison (1992, Section 5.1). For instance, the introduction of ad hoc symbols to templates (e.g., G for gemination) moves away from the spirit of association in autosegmental phonology, which Kay wanted to model; other special symbols must also be added to completely implement the rest of the paradigm under question (e.g., vowel spreading). Additionally, this approach also requires the grammar writer to annotate the lexical segments in order for the control notation to work.

However, Kay's usage of four-tape machines is very attractive, as it allows for specifying the various tiers of an autosegmental representation. We shall expand on Kay's multitape notion in subsequent chapters.

4.2 Kataja and Koskenniemi's Approach to Akkadian (1988)

Working within standard two-level morphology, Kataja and Koskenniemi (1988) describe a system that handles Akkadian stems. (Arabic examples are used instead here.) The general architecture of the system appears in Fig. 4.2. Lexical entries take the following form: a verb such as /nkutib/ (measure 7, passive) is described by the regular expressions:

$$\Sigma_1^* \text{ k } \Sigma_1^* \text{ t } \Sigma_1^* \text{ b } \Sigma_1^*$$

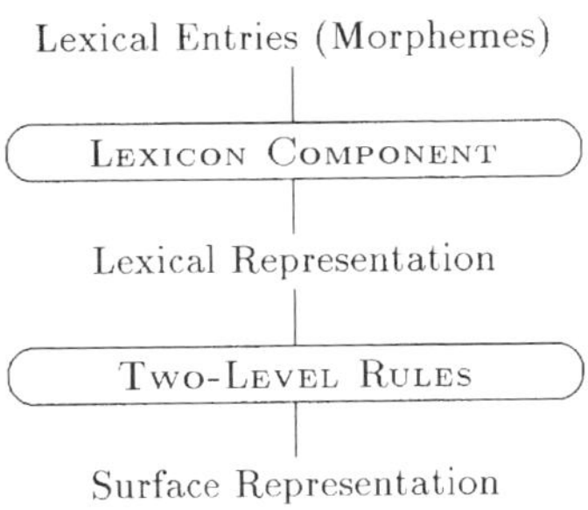

Fig. 4.2. Architecture of Kataja and Koskenniemi's Akkadian System. The lexicon component takes the intersection of roots and pattern expressions, and produces verbal stems. The stems are fed onto the lexical tape of a standard two-level system.

and

$$n\ \Sigma_2\ u\ \Sigma_2\ i\ \Sigma_2$$

where Σ_1 is the alphabet of the vocalism and affixes and Σ_2 is the alphabet of the root. The former describes the root {ktb} with symbols from the pattern alphabet appearing freely throughout the root. The latter describes measure 7.

The lexicon component of the system takes the intersection of the two expressions and produces the verbal stem /nkutib/, which is fed onto the lexical tape of a standard two-level system. Note that this will work properly only if Σ_1 and Σ_2 are mutually exclusive. The two-level rules take care of conditional phonetic changes (assimilation, deletion, etc.) and produce /ʔinkutib/ since Arabic initial consonant clusters, CC, require a prosthetic /ʔi/.

The difference between this system and a standard two-level model is the way in which the system searches the lexicon by means of the lexical component. Instead of taking the intersection of lexical entries in advance, the system can do simultaneous searches in the lexica to simulate intersection.

This intersection approach has two shortcomings. The intersection of the two lexica works only if Σ_1 and Σ_2 above are disjoint. As this is not the case in Semitic, one has to introduce ad hoc symbols in the alphabet to make the two alphabets disjoint. (For an alternative intersection approach, see Section 4.9.)

More serious is the fact that bidirectionality of two-level morphology (i.e., morphemes mapping to surface forms and vice versa) is lost. Once intersection is performed, the result is an accepting automaton that represents stems rather than independent morphemes. Hence, intersection is a destructive operator in the sense that its arguments cannot be attained back from the result.

4.3 Beesley's Approach to Arabic (1989, 1990, 1991)

In a number of papers, Beesley and colleagues report a working system for Arabic (Beesley, Buckwalter, and Newton, 1989; Beesley, 1990; Beesley, 1991). This is probably the largest reported system for Arabic morphology.[1] The lexicon contains approximately 5000 roots, which would cover all roots in Modern Standard Arabic (Wehr, 1971). Each entry is marked to show which verbal and nominal patterns a root can combine with. Another lexicon holds verbal and nominal patterns. The lexical access was named "detouring," which simulates the intersection of two lexica. (Sproat, 1992, pp. 163–165 gives a possible algorithm for "detouring.")

The system was tested on newspaper texts. For each word, the system returned (i) the appropriate lexical strings with the root and pattern intersected together as

[1] There are activities, some of which are commercial, in the Middle East on computational morphology. Reports on some can be found in the various proceedings of the International Conferences and Exhibitions on Multi-Lingual Computing (published by Center of Middle Eastern Studies, University of Cambridge).

a stem, (ii) the root and pattern separated, (iii) lists of features, and (iv) a rough English meaning (Beesley, personal communication).

A more recent version of this system is described by Beesley (1996, et seq.), with an excellent demo available on the Internet.[2]

Unlike the above intersection approach, Beesley's new method maintains bidirectionality by a direct mapping of each root and pattern pair to their respective surface realization. The lexical description (Beesley, 1996, personal communication) gives the root and pattern superficially concatenated in the form

$$\text{[ktb\&CaCaC]} \tag{4.1}$$

The brackets are special symbols that delimit the stem, and the ampersand is another special symbol that separates the root from the pattern; it is not the intersection operator. For each root and pattern pair, a rule of the following form is generated automatically:

$$\text{[ktb\&CaCaC]} \rightarrow \text{katab} \tag{4.2}$$

Each rule of the form in Eq. (4.2) is compiled into a transducer, which is then applied by composition to the identity transducer of the corresponding lexical description in Eq. (4.1). The result is a transducer that maps the string "[ktb&CaCaC]" into "katab." It is worth noting that rules of the form in Eq. (4.2) are reminiscent of Chomsky's early transformational rules for Hebrew stems (Chomsky, 1951).

(As the ampersand in the two equations above is a concrete symbol, no real intersection, in the set-theoretic sense, takes place.)

One disadvantage of this method is that it requires a huge number of rules (no. of roots × no. of vocalisms × no. of patters in the worst case) of the form in Eq. (4.2) to be compiled into their respective transducers, literally thousands of rules. Additionally, the entire set of m transducers (or subsets, one subset at a time) need to be put together into one (or more) transducer(s) by means of intersection (if the transducers are ϵ free) or composition. Although this takes place during the development of the grammar, rather than at run time, the inefficiency that results in the compilation process is apparent from the fact that a linguistic phenomenon (here, the linearization of stems) is conveyed by applying a rule to every single stem of the language. As one does not provide a rule to delete [e] in English /move + ing/ and another to delete the same in /charge + ing/, and so on, but a single [e] deletion rule that applies throughout the entire language, stems in Semitic ought to be realized by rules that represent the phenomenon itself, not every single instance of the phenomenon.

4.4 Kornai's Linear Coding (1991)

Kornai (1991) proposed modeling autosegmental phonology (see p. 3) by using FSTs, in which autosegmental representations are coded as linear strings. Various

[2] URL: `http://www.rxrc.xerox.com/research/mltt/arabic`.

Fig. 4.3. Autosegmental representation of /kpòlò/.

encodings were evaluated with respect to four desiderata: computability, compositionality, invertibility, and iconicity. To illustrate one encoding, consider the autosegmental representation of the Ngbaka verb /kpòlò/ "return" in Fig. 1.1 (repeated in Fig. 4.3). The corresponding linear coding in Kornai's system is given in the following example:

`L0k b L0p b L1o b L1o`

The coding `L0k` indicates the absence of an association line between [L] on the upper tone tier and [k] on the lower stem tier. The keyword `b` advances the bottom tape only. The next two keywords are similar to the two preceding ones, respectively. The keyword `L1o` indicates the existence of an association line between [L] and [o]. Kornai also uses the keyword `t` (which does not feature in this example) to advance the top tape only. Such linear encodings are converted into traditional finite-state transducers. (See comments on the coding approach at the end of Section 4.5.)

4.5 Bird and Ellison's One-Level Approach (1992, 1994)

Bird and Ellison (1994)[3] proposed a model based on one-level phonology, a finite-state version of declarative phonology, using FSAs to model representations and rules. Their model employs an encoding scheme for the representation of autosegmental diagrams. Recall that every pair of autosegmental tiers constitutes a *chart* (or plane). This is illustrated for the case of Arabic /kattab/ in the form of a triangular prism as in Fig. 4.4. Each morpheme sits on one of the prism's three longitudinal edges: the pattern on edge 1–2, the vocalism on edge 3–4, and the root on edge 5–6. Moreover, the prism has three longitudinal charts (or plane): the pattern–vocalism chart (1-2-3-4), the pattern–root chart (1-2-6-5), and the root–vocalism chart (3-4-5-6). The corresponding encoding of the diagram is

Tier 1	a:2:0:0
Tier 2	C:0:1:0 V:1:0:0 C:0:1:0 C:0:1:0 V:1:0:0 C:0:1:0
Tier 3	k:0:1:0 t:0:2:0 b:0:1:0

Each expression is an $(n + 1)$ tuple, where n is the number of charts. The first element in the tuple represents the autosegment. The positions of the remaining elements in the tuple indicate the chart in which an association line occurs, and the numerals indicate the number of association lines on that chart. For example, the expression a:2:0:0 states that the autosegment 'a' has two association lines on

[3] The original work appeared as Bird and Ellison (1992).

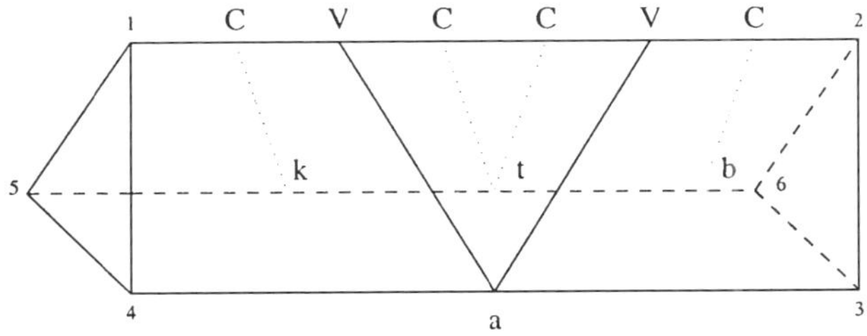

Fig. 4.4. Triangular prism (Pulleyblank, 1986), demonstrating the autosegmental representation of Arabic /kattab/.

the first (i.e., pattern–vocalism) chart, zero lines on the second (i.e., pattern–root) chart, and zero lines on the third (i.e., root–vocalism) chart.

Bird and Ellison (1994) provide tools for converting such encodings into finite-state devices, which they call state-labeled finite automata (SFA). Their machines are no more expressive than traditional FSAs.[4]

Their one-level analysis of Arabic takes the following form: three SFAs represent a pattern morpheme, a root morpheme, and a vocalism morpheme, respectively. The surface form is obtained by taking the intersection of the three automata.

Bird and Ellison question if their approach will "cover all possible generalizations about Arabic verbal structure" (p. 87). It would definitely be worth investigating how a higher-level autosegmental description of Semitic can be compiled algorithmically into their machines directly.

It was mentioned above that the intersection approach lacks bidirectionality. It is possible, though this has not been tested, that the indices in Bird and Ellison's method can play a role in claiming the various morphemes of a particular surface form.

4.6 Wiebe's Multilinear Coding (1992)

Wiebe (1992) proposed another encoding for representing autosegmental phonology following Kornai's four desiderata (see Section 4.4). This is illustrated by showing the encoding of the autosegmental representation of Arabic /kattab/ (measure 1). The autosegmental representation is given in Fig. 2.4, repeated in Fig. 4.5. The corresponding multilinear coding is

a11
C2V1C2C2V1C2
k2t22b2

A numeral *n* following an autosegment indicates that it has an association on chart *n*. An autosegment that is linked *m* times is followed by *m* repetitions of *n*, for example, a11 and t22.

[4] These machines are identical to Moore machines (Moore, 1956).

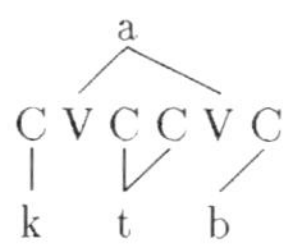

Fig. 4.5. Autosegmental representation of Arabic /kattab/.

The multilinear encoding is processed by devices that Wiebe calls multitape state-labeled finite automata.[5] Labels here are associated with states rather than transitions.

The computational power of Wiebe's version of these machines exceeds the power of conventional transducers. Wiebe's machines can accept context free, and even some context sensitive, languages.

4.7 Pulman and Hepple's Approach to Arabic (1993)

Pulman and Hepple (1993) proposed a formalism for bidirectional segmental phonological processing (cf. Section 3.2.4) and proposed using it for Arabic in the following manner: A stem like /takattab/ (measure 5) is simply expressed with the rule

$$\begin{array}{ccccccc} * & - & C_1\,C_2\,C_3 & - & * & \Rightarrow \\ * & - & t\,a\,C_1\,a\,C_2\,C_2\,a\,C_3 & - & * & \end{array}$$

where C_i represents the ith radical of the root {ktb}. Note that the pattern and vocalism morphemes are embedded in the surface expression of the rule.

The above formalism is appealing and will be expanded upon in the rest of this work. The form of the Arabic rules above, however, would require that morphemes (e.g., the prefix {ta} and the vocalism) be coded in rules rather than the lexicon.

4.8 Narayanan and Hashem's Three-Level Approach (1993)

Narayanan and Hashem (1993) proposed an extension to the traditional two-level model by adding a third abstract level of automaton representation "at which classes of inflectional phenomena are given an abstract representation." Under this framework, patterns of inflection constitute an abstract automaton component that sits on top of a standard two-level system.

Their Arabic implementation assumes that nominal forms are entered in the lexicon as stems. The automata represent various nominal inflections (prefixation and suffixation), which are in fact concatenative. The treatment of the verbal system employs two-way transducers (transducers with a reading head that can move to

[5] The machines in Bird and Ellison (1994) differ in definition and computational power from those of Wiebe (1992), though both have a somewhat similar name. Wiebe (1992), borrowed the name from Bird and Ellison (1992).

Table 4.1. *Transitions for Arabic /katab/ and /kutib/*

From State	Move to State	On Lexical	And Surface
1	2	[C,r,1]	[C_,r,0]
2	3	[C,r,1]	[C_,r,1]
3	4	[C,r,1]	[C,r,1]
4	5	[β,r,1]	[ε,r,1]
5	6	[V,r,1]	[[V,l,3],[ε,r,3]]
6	7	[V,r,1]	[[V,l,1],[ε,r,2]]

Note: An arc is marked with a pair Lex:Surf, where each element of the pair is a triple $[x, d, n]$, which indicates that after moving n positions in direction $d \in \{\texttt{left},\texttt{right}\}$, read–write the string x on the tape in question.

the left and right) with ε moves, mapping unequal sequences of symbols. The transitions for deriving Arabic /katab/ (measure 1) are listed in Table 4.1 (a simplified version is given here). Each arc is marked with a pair Lex:Surf as in traditional transducers. Each of the elements of the pair is a triple $[x, d, n]$, which indicates that after moving n positions in direction $d \in \{\texttt{left},\texttt{right}\}$, read–write the string x on the tape in question.

The above machine transduces the lexical strings ⟨ktb β aa⟩ and ⟨ktb β ui⟩ into ⟨katab⟩ and ⟨kutib⟩, respectively. For example, in the first case, after reaching state 5, the output would be ⟨k_t_b⟩ with the read–write head on [b]. The transition to state 6 moves the head three positions to the left and writes the desired vowel; then the head moves back to its original position with ⟨kat_b⟩ on the output tape. The transition to state 7 is similar, resulting in ⟨katab⟩ on the surface tape.

In their handling of nominal stems, Narayanan and Hashem consider stems, rather than patterns, roots, and vocalisms; hence, the question of nonlinearity is avoided. One would assume that a nonlinear approach to nominals would follow their verbal treatment. It is not clear, however, how the third level of abstract two-way transducers interacts with the traditional two-level system.

4.9 Beesley's Intersection Approach

It was mentioned (Section 4.2) that the intersection of lexica approach works only if the root and pattern–affixes alphabets are disjoint. As this is not the case in Semitic, one has to introduce ad hoc symbols in the alphabet to make the two alphabets disjoint. Alternatively, Beesley (forthcoming) introduces an ingenious, but cumbersome, bracketing mechanism. Kataja and Koskenniemi's expression Σ_1^* k Σ_1^* t Σ_1^* b Σ_1^* and n Σ_2 u Σ_2 i Σ_2 become

$$A^* \langle \mathrm{k} \rangle A^* \langle \mathrm{t} \rangle A^* \langle \mathrm{b} \rangle A^* \quad (4.3)$$

where $A = \Sigma - \{ \langle, \rangle \}$ (I have changed Beesley's braces into angle brackets in order to not confuse set notation), and

$$B^* \text{ u } B^* \text{ i } B^* \tag{4.4}$$

where $B = \Sigma - V$, and V is the disjunction of all vowels, respectively. Finally, each measure is given by an expression; for instance, Arabic Form V (e.g., /takattab/, where the first [t] is an affix not related to the [t] of the root) is

$$\text{t}VCVC\text{X}VC \tag{4.5}$$

where C is

$$\langle\{ \text{k,t,b} \}\rangle \tag{4.6}$$

(i.e., the disjunction of the root symbols surrounded by angle brackets). The symbol "X" in Expression (4.5) indicates gemination in a way reminiscent of Kay's "G" symbol. The intersection of Expressions (4.3), (4.4), and (4.5) result in /takatXab/ (X is dealt with by later rules). The disjunction of all such intersections results in what one may call a "quasi-lexicon," that is, the lexical side of subsequent two-level transducers that deal with linear phenomena (setting aside long-distance dependencies). Given r roots (*ca.* 4000 in Modern Standard Arabic), v vocalisms, and p patterns (a few hundred for $v \times p$, depending on the linguistic framework used), Beesley's bracketing algorithm has to perform m intersections, where $r \ll m < r \times v \times p$ (since each root only intersects with lexically defined subsets of the patterns), which proves to be quite costly (See Kiraz (2000) for a comparison between the above algorithm and the one we are about to describe in this book.)

4.10 Where to Next?

The next chapter presents a new general model building on the proposal of Kay (1987), see Section 4.1, and the formalism presented by Pulman and Hepple (1993), see Section 3.2.4.

5 A Multitier Nonlinear Model

> Let whoever is strong in the subject add more, of his own knowledge; as for us, we have done as much as we can. The person who is not up to the subject should keep his mouth shut, and not laugh at our efforts. Let this suffice for the discerning.
>
> Ḥunayn bar Isḥâq († 876)

> [Phonological] ambiguity is due to either vowel letters or consonantal letters. The Syriac alphabet is ambigious in both – [e.g.] in vowel letters since the single sign of *Alaph* may be vocalized with any one of the different vowels . . . and in consonantal letters since the letter *Kaph* may be pronounced sometimes with hardening [k], and sometimes with softening [x]. . But this is not the case with those of perfect alphabets, whose tongue is Greek, Latin, Coptic or Armenian. . . . Simply by looking at their letters, they can fly unburdened over passages they have never known before, that are not marked by diacritic symbols, and that they have never previously heard.
>
> Bar Ebroyo (1226–1286)
> *Ṣemḥe*, iv. i §1.

This chapter outlines a new model for computational morphology that is capable of analyzing the nonlinear problems described in Chapter 2. This model consists of three components: lexicon, rewrite rules, and morphotactics.

Section 5.1 gives a brief overall description of the model. Section 5.2 outlines the lexical component. Section 5.3 presents the rewrite rules component. Section 5.4 presents the morphotactic component. Finally, Section 5.5 discusses further extensions to the model.

(Readers who are not interested in the formal aspects of this model may skip the subsections named "Formal Description." These sections, however, are essential for the reader who is interested in the compilation algorithms of Chapter 7.)

5.1 Overall Description

Recall from Chapter 2 that a Semitic stem is derived in a nonlinear manner from at least three morphemes. Arabic /katab/ "to write – PERF ACT," for example, is derived from the pattern morpheme {CVCVC}, the root morpheme {ktb}, and the vocalism morpheme {a}. The autosegmental representation of the stem is repeated in Fig. 5.1. Further, recall from Chapter 3 that the established practice in

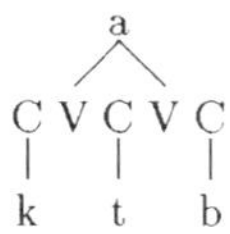

Fig. 5.1. Autosegmental representation of Arabic /katab/.

computational morphology is two-level morphology, which makes use of finite-state transducers to describe the mapping between the lexical level and the surface level.

In the case of Semitic, the lexical level of a lexical-surface analysis consists of three lexical morphemes: pattern, root, and vocalism. The model presented here assumes two levels of linguistic description in recognition and synthesis. The lexical level employs *multiple* representations (e.g., for patterns, roots, and vocalisms), while the surface level employs only *one* representation. The upper bound on the number of lexical representations is not only language specific, but also grammar specific.

There is a linguistic motivation behind this approach. When a word is uttered, it is pronounced in a linear string of segments; that is, the multitier lexical representation is linearized at the surface level. McCarthy (1986) calls this process *tier conflation*. Consider for example the autosegmental structure in Fig. 5.2(a) of Arabic /yaktubna/ "they (FEM) are writing," which consists of the following morphemes (from top to bottom): the circumfix morpheme {y-na} "IMPF PL 3RD FEM," the vocalism morpheme {au} "IMPF ACT," the corresponding CV pattern morpheme and the root morpheme {ktb} "notion of writing." Tier conflation is performed as follows: after associating the root consonants with the Cs and the vocalism vowels with the Vs, one folds together the consonants and vowels of the stem onto a single tier as shown in Fig. 5.2(b). The same operation is performed on the remaining morphologically determined tiers, resulting in the linearized configuration in Fig. 5.2(c). In other words, the various lexical tiers in the underlying representation end up in a single tier in the surface level.

In this vein, the lexicon component of the model presented here consists of multiple sublexica, each representing entries for a particular lexical representation

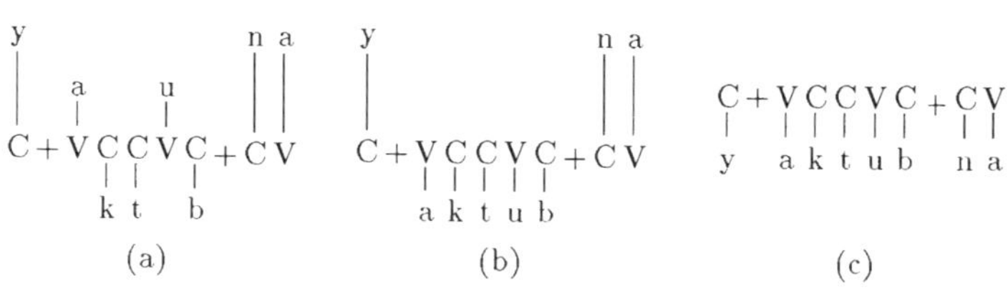

Fig. 5.2. (a) Tier conflation in Arabic /yaktubna/. After associating the root consonants with Cs and the vocalism vowels with Vs, both consonants and vowels are folded together onto a single tier (b). The same applies to the remaining tiers, resulting in a linearized configuration (c).

or tier. The rewrite rules component maps the multiple lexical representations to a surface representation. Finally, the morphotactic component enforces morphotactic constraints.

The rest of this chapter gives a detailed description of the three components. Each component is described by using two accounts: intuitive followed by formal. The latter can be skipped without any loss of continuity (though formal definitions are necessary for understanding the discussion in Chapter 7).

Throughout the following discussion, a tuple of strings represents a surface-lexical mapping, where the first element of the tuple represents the surface form and the remaining elements represent lexical forms. For instance, the tuple of strings that represents the mapping of Arabic /katab/ to its lexical forms is ⟨katab,cvcvc, ktb,a⟩.[1] (The elements are surface, pattern, root, and vocalism.)

5.2 The Lexicon Component

The lexicon component provides the set of morphemes and/or lexemes of a particular language.

5.2.1 *Intuitive Description*

The lexicon in the current model consists of multiple *sublexica*, each sublexicon containing entries for one particular lexical representation (or tier in the autosegmental analysis). Since an n tuple contains $n-1$ lexical elements (the first of which is the surface representation), the lexicon component consists of $n-1$ sublexica. An Arabic lexicon for the example in Fig. 5.1 will have a pattern sublexicon, a root sublexicon, and a vocalism sublexicon. Other affixes that do not conform to the root-and-pattern nature of Semitic morphology (e.g., prefixes, suffixes, particles, etc.) have to be represented as well. One can either give them their own sublexicon or have them represented in one of the three sublexica. Since pattern segments are the closest – in terms of number – to surface segments, such morphemes are represented in the pattern sublexicon by convention.

For morphotactic purposes, each entry in a sublexicon is associated with a *category* of the form

$$\begin{bmatrix} \mathsf{cat} \\ \text{ATTRIBUTE}_1 = \text{value}_1 \\ \text{ATTRIBUTE}_2 = \text{value}_2 \\ \vdots \end{bmatrix}$$

where *cat* is an atom representing a (grammatical) category followed by an unordered list of *attribute* = *value* pairs. An *attribute* is an atomic label. A *value*

[1] Capital-initial strings will be used shortly to denote variables. For this reason, we represent the pattern {CVCVC} by using small letters.

can be an atom or a variable drawn from a predefined finite set of possible values.[2]

As a way of illustration, consider the Arabic verb /katab/ (depicted in Fig. 5.1) with the conjunction prefix {wa} "and" and the suffix {at} "SING 3RD FEM." The entries of the first sublexicon are

$$\text{wa}\begin{bmatrix}\textsf{conj}\end{bmatrix}$$

$$\text{cvcvc}\begin{bmatrix}\textsf{pattern}\\ \text{MEASURE} = 1\\ \text{VOICE} = \text{act}\end{bmatrix}$$

$$\text{at}\begin{bmatrix}\textsf{VIM}\\ \text{NUMBER} = \text{sing}\\ \text{PERSON} = \text{3rd}\\ \text{GENDER} = \text{fem}\end{bmatrix}$$

The first entry gives the prefix; here, the category does not have any *attribute* = *value* pairs. The second entry represents the pattern with its measure and voice specified in the associated category. The third entry gives the verbal inflexional marker (VIM) suffix with the related values for number, person, and gender.

The second sublexicon maintains the root entry (and any other root entries in a larger system):

$$\text{ktb}\begin{bmatrix}\textsf{pattern}\\ \text{MEASURE} = \{1,2,3,4,5,6,7,8,10\}\end{bmatrix}$$

Recall (see p. 28) that roots do not take all verbal measures; rather, each root occurs in the literature in a subset of the measures. This subset is indicated in value of the measure attribute (one gets such information from dictionaries and corpora).

The third lexicon maintains the vocalism (and any other vocalisms in a larger system):

$$\text{a}\begin{bmatrix}\textsf{vocalism}\end{bmatrix}$$

The category associated with the vocalism may of course incorporate *attribute* = *value* pairs if the need arises.

5.2.2 *Formal Description*

The following definitions assume a system that makes use of n tuples of expressions, out of which $n - 1$ are lexical.

> **Definition 5.2.1** A *category* is a pair (Cat, AV) with Cat as an atom denoting a (grammatical) category and AV as an unordered list of *attribute* = *value* pairs, where *attribute* is an atomic label and *value* is either an atom or a variable drawn from a predefined finite set of possible values. □

[2] It is also possible to extend the above formalism in order to allow *value* to be a category, though this takes us beyond finite-state power.

Example 5.2.1 The category of the above Arabic suffix {at} is (VIM, [number = sing, person = 3rd, gender = fem]). □

Definition 5.2.2 A *lexical entry* over some alphabet Σ is a pair (W,C) where W ∈ Σ^* is a string denoting a lexical word and C is a category. □

Remark 5.2.1 In the domain of morphology, W above is usually a morpheme or a stem. □

Example 5.2.2 Let Σ = { a,c,t,v,w } be the alphabet of the first sublexicon in the example of the preceding subsection. The lexical entry of the pattern is (cvcvc, (pattern, [measure = 1, voice = act])). □

Definition 5.2.3 A *sublexicon* over the alphabet Σ is a set of lexical entries over Σ. □

Definition 5.2.4 A *lexicon* over the alphabets $(\Sigma_1, \ldots, \Sigma_{n-1})$ is an $(n-1)$ tuple $(L_1, \ldots, L_{n-1})$ such that each L_i is a sublexicon over Σ_i, $1 \leq i \leq n-1$. □

5.3 The Rewrite Rules Component

The rewrite rules component maps the multiple lexical representations to a surface representation. It also provides for phonological, orthographic, and other rules.

5.3.1 Intuitive Description

The current model makes use of the formalism presented in Section 3.2.2, shown again below, with additional extensions to cater for multiple lexical forms.

$$\begin{array}{ccccc} \text{LLC} & - & \textsc{Lex} & - & \text{RLC} \quad \{\Rightarrow, \Leftrightarrow\} \\ \text{LSC} & - & \textsc{Surf} & - & \text{RSC} \end{array}$$

LLC denotes the left lexical context, LEX denotes the lexical form, and RLC denotes the right lexical context. LSC, SURF, and RSC are the surface counterparts. Recall that the context denoted by an asterisk is always satisfied; that is, it represents a Kleene star (i.e., Σ^* where Σ is the alphabet). Capital-initial expressions are variables over predefined finite sets of symbols and are expressed with a "where" clause.

The operator ⇒ is the context restriction operator. It states that LEX *may* surface as SURF in the given context. The operator ⇔ adds surface coercion constraints: when LEX appears in the given context, then the surface description *must* satisfy SURF. A lexical string maps to a surface string if and only if they can be partitioned into pairs of lexical-surface subsequences, where (i) each pair is licensed by a ⇒ rule, and (ii) no sequence of zero or more adjacent pairs violates a ⇔ rule.

The following extensions are adopted: All expressions on the upper lexical side of the rules (LLC, LEX, and RLC) are tuples of strings of the form $\langle x_1, x_2, \ldots, x_{n-1}\rangle$. The ith element in the tuple refers to symbols in the ith sublexicon of the

$$\text{R1:}\quad \frac{* \;-\; \langle \mathrm{c},\mathrm{X},\varepsilon\rangle \;-\; *}{* \;-\; \mathrm{X} \;-\; *} \Rightarrow$$

where X is a consonant.

$$\text{R2:}\quad \frac{* \;-\; \langle \mathrm{v},\varepsilon,\mathrm{X}\rangle \;-\; *}{* \;-\; \mathrm{X} \;-\; *} \Rightarrow$$

where X is a vowel.

$$\text{R3:}\quad \frac{\langle \mathrm{v},\varepsilon,\mathrm{X}\rangle\, * \;-\; \mathrm{v} \;-\; *}{* \;-\; \mathrm{X} \;-\; *} \Rightarrow$$

where X is a vowel.

Fig. 5.3. Rules for the derivation of Arabic /katab/. R1 and R2 sanction root consonants and vowels, respectively; R3 handles vowel spreading.

lexical component. When a lexical expression makes use of only the first sublexicon, the angle brackets can be ignored. Hence, the LEX expression $\langle x, \epsilon, \ldots, \epsilon\rangle$ and x are equivalent; in lexical contexts, $\langle x, *, \ldots, *\rangle$ and x are equivalent.

The formalism is illustrated in Fig. 5.3.[3] The rules derive Arabic /katab/ from the pattern morpheme {cvcvc} "verbal measure 1," the root morpheme {ktb} "notion of writing," and the vocalism morpheme {a} "PERF ACT" (cf. Fig. 5.1). R1 sanctions root consonants by mapping a [c] from the first (pattern) sublexicon, a consonant [X] from the second (root) sublexicon, and no symbol from the third (vocalism) sublexicon to surface [X]. R2 sanctions vowels in a similar manner. R3 allows the spreading of the vowel: if a vowel [X] has previously occurred, that is, LLC is "$\langle$v,ε,X$\rangle$ *," then a [v] from the pattern sublexicon may map to that same vowel on the surface. The quality of the vowel on the surface is determined from LLC.

The mapping is illustrated in Fig. 5.4(a). The numbers between the surface and lexical expressions indicate the rules in Fig. 5.3 that sanction the shown

	a				*vocalism*
k		t		b	*root*
c	v	c	v	c	*pattern*
1	2	1	3	1	
k	a	t	a	b	*surface*

(a)

			a						*vocalism*
		k		t		b			*root*
w	a	c	v	c	v	c	a	t	*pattern & affixes*
0	0	1	2	1	3	1	0	0	
w	a	k	a	t	a	b	a	t	*surface*

(b)

Fig. 5.4. Lexical-surface analysis of Arabic /katab/ and /wakatabat/. Numbers indicate the rules in Fig. 5.3 that sanction the lexical-surface subsequences; empty slots represent the empty string ϵ; expressions are depicted from bottom to top: first the surface expression, and then the various lexical expressions.

[3] The rules will be modified in Section 6.1 to cater for other stems.

subsequences. Empty slots represent the empty string ϵ. Note that expressions are depicted from bottom to top: first the surface expression, and then the lexical expressions.

As stated above, morphemes that do not conform to the root-and-pattern nature of Semitic (i.e., prefixes, suffixes, particles, etc.) are given in the first sublexicon. The identity rule

$$\begin{array}{llllll} & * & - & \mathrm{X} & - & * \Rightarrow \\ \mathrm{R0:} & * & - & \mathrm{X} & - & * \\ & \multicolumn{5}{l}{\text{where } \mathrm{X} \notin \{\mathrm{c,v}\}} \end{array}$$

maps such morphemes to the surface. The rule basically states that any symbol not in { c,v } from the first sublexicon may surface. Figure 5.4(b) illustrates the analysis of /wakatabat/ from the morphemes given earlier on p. 71.

The rewrite rule component interacts with the lexical component in the following manner. The lexical forms produced by a rewrite rule must each represent a concatenation of lexical entries from the corresponding sublexicon. For example, for the analysis described by the tuple ⟨wakatabat, wa cvcvc at, ktb, a⟩ to be lexically valid, the first sublexicon must contain the entries {wa}, {cvcvc}, and {at}. Similarly, the second and third sublexica must contain the entries {ktb} and {a}, respectively.

5.3.2 *Formal Description*

As before, n tuples are used for lexical-surface mapping, with the first element representing surface forms and the remaining $n - 1$ elements representing lexical forms.[4]

5.3.2.1 *String Tuples*

String tuples, as opposed to symbol pairs in traditional two-level morphology, form the basic alphabet of the rewrite rules component.

Definition 5.3.1 Let $X = \langle x_1, x_2, \ldots, x_n \rangle$ and $Y = \langle y_1, y_2, \ldots, y_n \rangle$ be n tuples of strings. Their *n-way concatenation*, denoted by XY, is $\langle x_1 y_1, x_2 y_2, \ldots, x_n y_n \rangle$, that is, the tuple of strings formed by the concatenation of the corresponding elements in X and Y. □

Example 5.3.1 Let $S_1 = \langle \text{ab, cb, accb} \rangle$, $S_2 = \langle \text{bb}, \epsilon, \text{aca} \rangle$, and $S_3 = \langle \text{ca, bb, ac} \rangle$ be three 3-tuples of strings. The following concatenations are valid:

$$\begin{aligned} S_1 S_2 &= \langle \text{abbb, cb, accbaca} \rangle \\ S_2 S_1 &= \langle \text{bbab, cb, acaaccb} \rangle \\ (S_3)^2 &= \langle \text{caca, bbbb, acac} \rangle \end{aligned}$$

□

[4] Definitions in Section 5.3.2.1 are modeled after the ones in Kaplan and Kay (1994). Definitions 5.3.4, 5.3.13, and 5.3.15 ff. benefited from Ritchie (1992).

Remark 5.3.1 The tuple $X = \langle \epsilon, \ldots, \epsilon \rangle$ (all of whose elements are the empty string ϵ) is the identity for n-way concatenation. □

Definition 5.3.2 Let $S = \langle x_1, x_2, \ldots, x_n \rangle$ be an n tuple of strings. The **length** of S, denoted by $|S|$, is defined in terms of the lengths of the elements in S,

$$|S| = \sum_{i=1}^{n} |x_i|$$ □

Example 5.3.2 In Example 5.3.1, $|S_1| = 8$, $|S_2| = 5$, and $|S_3| = 6$. □

Definition 5.3.3 An n tuple of strings $\langle x_1, \ldots, x_n \rangle$ is said to be a *same-length n tuple of strings* if and only if $|x_i| = |x_j|$ for all $1 \leq i, j \leq n$. □

Example 5.3.3 In Example 5.3.1, S_3 is a same-length 3-tuple of strings whose elements are all of length two, while S_1 and S_2 contain elements of different lengths. □

5.3.2.2 *Partitions*

Recall (p. 73) that in the interpretation of the formalism, the mapping between lexical and surface forms requires the lexical-surface analysis to be partitioned into pairs of lexical-surface subsequences. The following definitions specify the notion of partitioning over tuples of strings.

Definition 5.3.4 Let S be a tuple of strings. A sequence $(P^1, \ldots, P^n)$ of tuples of strings is said to be an *n-way partition* of S if and only if $S = P^1 \cdots P^n$ (i.e., S is the n-way concatenation of P^i, $1 \leq i \leq n$). □

Definition 5.3.5 Each P^i, $1 \leq i \leq n$, in the above definition is called a *subsequence* of S. (Note that the superscript i does not denote exponentiation in this context.) □

Example 5.3.4 Let $S = \langle \text{ab, cdef, ghi} \rangle$ be a 3-tuple of strings; the following tuples of strings are partitions of S:

$$S_1 = (\langle \text{a, cd, gh} \rangle, \langle \text{b, ef, i} \rangle)$$
$$S_2 = (\langle \text{ab, c, g} \rangle, \langle \epsilon, \text{de, hi} \rangle, \langle \epsilon, \text{f}, \epsilon \rangle)$$
$$S_3 = (\langle \text{a, c, g} \rangle, \langle \epsilon, \epsilon, \epsilon \rangle, \langle \text{b, d, hi} \rangle, \langle \epsilon, \text{ef}, \epsilon \rangle)$$

See Fig. 5.5 for illustrations. □

Definition 5.3.6 Let S be a same-length tuple of strings. A sequence $(P^1, \ldots, P^k)$ of same-length tuples of strings is said to be a *same-length n-way partition* of S if and only if $S = P^1 \cdots P^k$. □

Example 5.3.5 Let $S = \langle \text{abcd, efgh} \rangle$ be a same-length 2-tuple of strings; the following tuples of strings are same-length two-way partitions of S:

$$S_1 = (\langle \text{ab, ef} \rangle, \langle \text{cd, gh} \rangle)$$
$$S_2 = (\langle \text{a, e} \rangle, \langle \text{bc, fg} \rangle, \langle \text{d, h} \rangle)$$
$$S_3 = (\langle \text{abc, efg} \rangle, \langle \epsilon, \epsilon \rangle, \langle \text{d, h} \rangle)$$ □

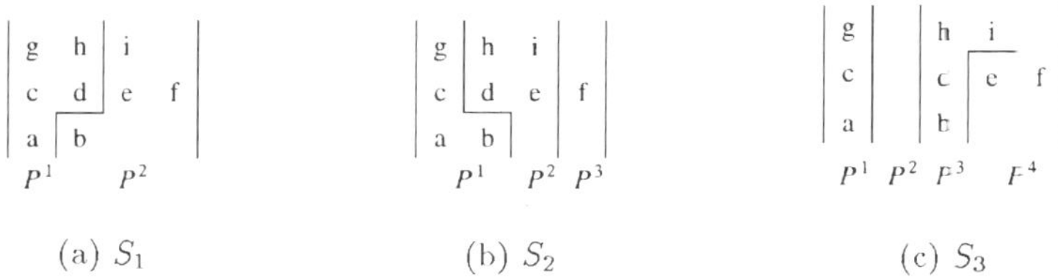

Fig. 5.5. Partitions of $S = \langle$ab, cdef, ghi$\rangle$: (a) S_1, (b) S_2, (c) S_3. P^n indicates the nth subsequence in a partition.

Definition 5.3.7 Let S be a tuple of strings; an *ϵ-free n-way partition* of S is an n-way partition of S that does not have any subsequence with length zero (i.e., a subsequence all of whose elements are ϵ). □

Example 5.3.6 In Fig. 5.5, S_1 and S_2 are ϵ-free three-way partitions of S, while S_3 has a subsequence of length zero, that is, the subsequence $P^2 = \langle \epsilon, \epsilon, \epsilon \rangle$. □

Definition 5.3.8 Let S be a same-length tuple of strings; an *ϵ-free same-length n-way partition* of S is a same-length n-way partition of S that does not have a subsequence with length zero. (See Definition 5.3.2 for the definition of "length.") □

Example 5.3.7 In Example 5.3.5, S_1 and S_2 are ϵ-free same-length two-way partitions of S, while S_3 has a subsequence of length zero, that is, the second subsequence. □

5.3.2.3 N-Way Prefixes and Suffixes

The following definitions specify n-way prefixes and n-way suffixes of tuples of strings. These definitions will be used in defining context restriction and surface coercion operations (see Section 5.3.2.6).

Definition 5.3.9 Let S_1 and S_2 be two tuples of strings. S_1 is said to be an *n-way prefix* of S_2 if and only if there is an n-way partition $(P^1, \ldots, P^k)$ of S_2 such that for some $j \in \{1, \ldots, k\}$, $S_1 = P^1 \cdots P^j$ (i.e., S_1 is the n-way concatenation of P^i, $1 \le i \le j$). □

Example 5.3.8 In Fig. 5.5(a), $P^1 = \langle$a, cd, gh$\rangle$ is a three-way prefix of S_1; so is the concatenation $P^1P^2 = \langle$ab, cdef, ghi$\rangle$. In a similar manner, in Fig. 5.5(c), the tuples of strings

$$
\begin{aligned}
P^1 &= \langle \text{a, c, g} \rangle \\
P^1P^2 &= \langle \text{a, c, g} \rangle \\
P^1P^2P^3 &= \langle \text{ab, cd, ghi} \rangle \\
P^1P^2P^3P^4 &= \langle \text{ab, cdef, ghi} \rangle
\end{aligned}
$$

are all three-way prefixes of S_3. □

Definition 5.3.10 Let S_1 and S_2 be two tuples of strings. S_1 is said to be an *n-way suffix* of S_2 if and only if there is an n-way partition $(P^1, \ldots, P^k)$ of S_2 such that for some $j \in \{1, \ldots, k\}$, $S_1 = P^j \cdots P^k$ (i.e., S_1 is the n-way concatenation of P^i, $1 \leq i \leq j$). □

Example 5.3.9 In Fig. 5.5(b), the tuples of strings

$$\begin{aligned} P^3 &= \langle \epsilon, \text{f}, \epsilon \rangle \\ P^2 P^3 &= \langle \epsilon, \text{def}, \text{hi} \rangle \\ P^1 P^2 P^3 &= \langle \text{ab}, \text{cdef}, \text{ghi} \rangle \end{aligned}$$

are all three-way suffixes of S_2. □

5.3.2.4 Two-Level Tuples

For purposes of describing rewrite rules, a special tuple of strings is defined that we shall call a "two-level tuple" since it will be used to map sequences between two linguistic descriptions (e.g., lexical and surface). Hence, the term "level" here does not refer to a "tape" in an automaton; rather, it refers to a linguistically motivated (multitiered) level of description.

Definition 5.3.11 A *two-level tuple* is an n-tuple of strings over some alphabets $(\Sigma_1, \ldots, \Sigma_n)$ of the form $\langle s, l_1, l_2, \ldots, l_{n-1} \rangle$, where $s \in \Sigma_1^*$ represents a surface string and $l_i \in \Sigma_{i+1}^*$, $1 \leq i \leq n-1$, represent lexical strings. □

Example 5.3.10 Consider the analysis in Fig. 5.4(a). The two-level tuple ⟨katab, cvcvc, ktb, a⟩ represents the surface string in its first element and the lexical strings (pattern, root, and vocalism, respectively) in its remaining elements. □

Definition 5.3.12 Let $S = \langle s, l_1, l_2, \ldots, l_{n-1} \rangle$ be a two-level tuple. We say that S is a *same-length two-level tuple* if and only if $|s| = |l_i| = |l_j|$ for all $1 \leq i, j \leq n-1$. □

Example 5.3.11 Consider the analysis in Fig. 5.4(a). By inserting the symbol '0' in the empty slots, we achieve the same-length two-level tuple ⟨katab, cvcvc, k0t0b, 0a000⟩. □

5.3.2.5 Rewrite Rules

Rewrite rules are defined over two-level tuples per the formalism on p. 73.

Definition 5.3.13 A *two-level rule* consists of a pair (C, LR), where C is a two-level tuple representing the center of the rule, and LR is a nonempty set of pairs (λ, ρ), with λ and ρ two-level tuples representing the left and right contexts, respectively. □

Example 5.3.12 Consider the analysis in Fig. 5.4(a). The rule sanctioning the first subsequence (i.e., representing R1 in Grammar 5.3, p. 74) is

(⟨k, c, k, ϵ⟩, { (*,*) }). The first element is the center of the rule. The set represents contexts. □

Definition 5.3.14 A *same-length two-level rule* is a two-level rule (C, LR), such that C is a same-length two-level tuple, and for all (λ, ρ) in LR, both λ and ρ are same-length two-level tuples. □

5.3.2.6 *Optional and Obligatory Rules*

Optional rules license a certain mapping in a given context, whereas obligatory ones enforce such mappings.

Definition 5.3.15 Let S be a two-level tuple and let

$$\mathcal{P} = (P^1, \ldots, P^{i-1}, P^i, P^{i+1}, \ldots, P^k), \quad 1 \leq i \leq k$$

be an n-way partition of S. We say that a two-level rule $(P^i$, LR) *contextually allows* P^i *in* $\mathcal{P}$ if and only if LR contains a pair (λ, ρ) such that λ is an n-way suffix of $P^1 \cdots P^{i-1}$ and ρ is an n-way prefix of $P^{i+1} \cdots P^k$. □

Definition 5.3.16 Let S be a two-level tuple and let

$$\mathcal{P} = (P^1, \ldots, P^{i-1}, P^i, \ldots, P^{j-1}, P^j, \ldots, P^k), \quad 1 \leq i \leq j \leq k$$

be an n-way partition of S with $P^i \cdots P^{j-1} = \langle s, l_1, \ldots, l_{n-1} \rangle$. We say that a two-level rule $(\langle s', l_1, \ldots, l_{n-1} \rangle$, LR) *coercively disallows* $P^i \cdots P^{j-1}$ *in* $\mathcal{P}$ if and only if LR contains a pair (λ, ρ) such that λ is an n-way suffix of $P^1 \cdots P^{i-1}$, ρ is an n-way prefix of $P^j \cdots P^k$, and $s \neq s'$. □

Remark 5.3.2 Notice that since i may be equal to j, the above definition states how a rule can coercively disallow a sequence of zero or more subsequences in $\mathcal{P}$ (see the discussion in Section 3.2.6). □

5.3.2.7 *Grammars*

A collection of rewrite rules constitutes a grammar. The following definitions give the formal description of such grammars.

Definition 5.3.17 A *two-level grammar* consists of a pair (CR, SC) in which CR (context restriction) and SC (surface coercion) are finite sets of two-level rules. □

Definition 5.3.18 Let G =(CR, SC) be a two-level grammar and S be a two-level tuple. We say that G accepts S if and only if there is an n-way partition $\mathcal{P} = (P^1, \ldots, P^k)$ of S such that (i) for each P^i, $1 \leq i \leq k$, there is at least one rule in CR which contextually allows P^i in $\mathcal{P}$, and (ii) there are no i, j with $1 \leq i \leq j \leq k$ such that there is a rule in SC which coercively disallows $P^i \cdots P^j$ in $\mathcal{P}$. □

5.3.2.8 Interaction with the Lexicon

Finally, the following definition states the interaction of the rewrite rules component with the lexical component.

Definition 5.3.19 Let G be a two-level grammar, $L = (L_1, \ldots, L_{n-1})$ be a lexicon, and $S = \langle s, l_1, \ldots, l_{n-1} \rangle$ be a two-level tuple. We say that S is *lexically accepted* if and only if (i) G accepts S, and (ii) for every l_i, $1 \leq i \leq n-1$, there is an ϵ-free one-way partition of l_i in the form $(W_i^1, \ldots, W_i^k)$ such that there is a pair $(W_i^j, C_i^j) \in L_i$ for all $1 \leq j \leq k$ (where C_i^j as before is some category). □

Remark 5.3.3 In the above definition, C^j plays a role when grammatical features are used (see Section 5.5.2). □

5.4 The Morphotactic Component

A lexicon and a two-level grammar fall short of defining the set of licit combinations of lexical forms. Consider the following identity rule:

$$\begin{array}{l} * \; - \; \mathrm{X} \; - \; * \;\; \Rightarrow \\ * \; - \; \mathrm{X} \; - \; * \\ \text{where X} \in \{\text{c, e, f, l, n, s, u}\} \end{array}$$

and some lexicon with entries for the morphemes {un}, {success}, and {ful}, which sanction English /unsuccessful/. The lexicon and the rule will not only sanction /unsuccessful/, but it will also allow any other combination of the morphemes in question: */successunful/, */fulsuccessun/, and so on, because nowhere in the lexical and rewrite rules components is the order of lexical forms defined.

In computational morphology, there are two schools of thought in this regard. The first uses "continuation patterns/classes" (Koskenniemi, 1983; Antworth, 1990; Karttunen, 1993), in which each class of morphemes is associated with a set of continuation classes defining the morphemes that can follow. The second adopts unification-based grammars with linear precedence relations (Bear, 1986; Beesley, Buckwalter, and Newton, 1989; Bird and Klein, 1994; Trost, 1990; Ritchie et al., 1992; Antworth, 1994, inter alia).

In what follows, two methods for handling Semitic morphotactics are presented: regular and context free.

5.4.1 Regular Morphotactics

A regular approach to morphotactics provides a mechanism under which Semitic morphemes can combine to form larger grammatical units within the expressiveness of regular languages.

Semitic morphotactics can be divided into two categories. *Templatic morphotactics* occurs when the pattern, root, vocalism, and possibly other morphemes join together in a nonlinear manner to form a stem. *Nontemplatic morphotactics* takes place when the stem is combined with other morphemes to form larger morphological or syntactic units. The latter can be divided in turn into two types: *linear nontemplatic morphotactics*, which makes use of simple prefixation and suffixation, and *nonlinear nontemplatic morphotactics*, which makes use of circumfixation.

Templatic morphotactics is handled implicitly by the rewrite rules component. For example, the rules in Fig. 5.3 that sanction stem consonants and vowels implicitly dictate the manner in which pattern, root, and vocalism morphemes combine. Hence, the morphotactic component need not worry about templatic morphotactics.

Linear nontemplatic morphotactics can be handled by means of regular operations, usually n-way concatenation in the multitiered case. Consider, for example, Arabic /wakatabat/ and its lexical-surface analysis in Fig. 5.4(b). The lexical-surface analyses of the prefix, stem, and suffix are $\langle$wa, wa, ε, $\varepsilon\rangle$ for the prefix, $\langle$katab, cvcvc, ktb, a$\rangle$ for the stem, and $\langle$at, at, ε, $\varepsilon\rangle$ for the suffix. Their n-way concatenation gives the tuple $\langle$wakatabat, wa cvcvc at, ktb, a$\rangle$. One may also use the "continuation patterns/classes" paradigm. Here, lexical elements will be marked with the set of morpheme classes that can follow on their own sublexicon. For example, the verbal pattern {cvcvc} will be marked with the suffix {at}. Note that both morphemes, {cvcvc} and {at}, belong to the same sublexicon.

The last case is that of nonlinear nontemplatic morphotactics. Normally this arises in circumfixation operations. The following morphotactic rule formalism is used to describe such operations:

$$\begin{aligned} A &\rightarrow \overbrace{P\,B\,S} \\ (P, S) &\rightarrow (p_1, s_1) \\ (P, S) &\rightarrow (p_2, s_2) \\ &\vdots \\ (P, S) &\rightarrow (p_n, s_n) \end{aligned}$$

A circumfix here is a pair (P, S) where P represents the prefix portion of the circumfix and S represents the suffix portion. The circumfixation operation $\overbrace{PBS}$ applies the circumfix (P, S) to B. As a way of illustration, consider the Syriac circumfixes of the imperfect verb in Table 5.1. The circumfixation of the unique circumfixes to the stem /ktob/ "to write – IMPF" is

$$\begin{aligned} \text{Verb} &\rightarrow \overbrace{P \text{ ktob } S} \\ (P, S) &\rightarrow (\text{ne}, \epsilon) \\ (P, S) &\rightarrow (\text{te}, \epsilon) \\ (P, S) &\rightarrow (\text{te}, \text{īn}) \\ &\vdots \\ (P, S) &\rightarrow (\text{te}, \text{ån}) \\ (P, S) &\rightarrow (\text{ne}, \epsilon) \end{aligned}$$

Table 5.1. *Syriac circumfixes of the imperfect verb*

Number	Person	Gender	Circumfix
Sing.	3rd	masc.	ne-
Sing.	3rd	fem.	te-
Sing.	2nd	masc.	te-
Sing.	2nd	fem.	te-īn
Sing.	1st	com.	ʔe-
Pl.	3rd	masc.	ne-ūn
Pl.	3rd	fem.	te-ån
Pl.	2nd	masc.	te-ūn
Pl.	2nd	fem.	te-ån
Pl.	1st	com.	ne-

It will be shown later on (see Section 7.4) that such operations are regular and can be compiled into finite-state machines.

5.4.2 Context-Free Morphotactics

The context-free approach to morphotactics provides a model whose expressiveness is beyond regular languages and that makes use of unification.

For the sake of presentation, it is assumed that the morphotactic component takes as input the categories associated with the morphemes realized from the lexicon and rewrite rules components. Suppose an analysis of English /unsuccessful/ produces the sequence of morphemes {un}, {success}, and {ful}, and suppose that these morphemes appear in some lexicon with the categories [prefix], [stem], and [suffix], respectively. The morphotactic component aims to find a parse for the sequence: [prefix][stem][suffix].

The lexical and rewrite rules components produce a tuple of sequences of lexical forms, one per lexical expression. For example, recall Arabic /wakatabat/, which consists of the prefix {wa} "and," the stem /katab/ "write – PERF ACT," and the suffix {at} "SING 3RD FEM" in this order. The stem /katab/ is further decomposed into the morphemes from which it is derived: the pattern {cvcvc}, the root {ktb}, and the vocalism {a}. An analysis of this word is given in Fig. 5.4(b). The analysis produces the lexical 3-tuple ⟨wa cvcvc at, ktb, a⟩, that is, the sequence of morphemes on each lexical element. The corresponding categories of these morphemes (based on the entries from p. 72) are

$$\left\langle \begin{bmatrix}\textsf{conj}\end{bmatrix} \begin{bmatrix}\begin{array}{l}\textsf{pattern}\\ \text{MEASURE} = 1\\ \text{VOICE} = \text{act}\end{array}\end{bmatrix} \begin{bmatrix}\begin{array}{l}\textsf{VIM}\\ \text{NUMBER} = \text{sing}\\ \text{PERSON} = \text{3rd}\\ \text{GENDER} = \text{fem}\end{array}\end{bmatrix}, \right.$$

$$\left. \begin{bmatrix}\begin{array}{l}\textsf{root}\\ \text{MEASURE} = \{1,2,3,4,5,6,7,8,10\}\end{array}\end{bmatrix}, \quad \begin{bmatrix}\textsf{vocalism}\end{bmatrix} \right\rangle$$

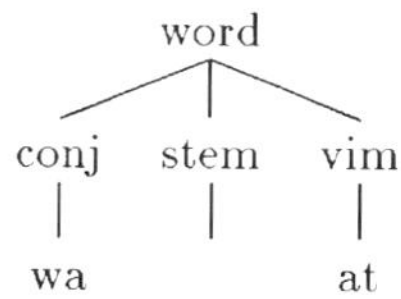

Fig. 5.6. A tentative parse tree for Arabic /wakatabat/. The lexical forms are shown in leaf nodes for clarity. Note that the parsing of the stem is still not known.

Parsing /wakatabat/ in a top-down manner, one can safely assume the parse in Fig. 5.6 to be valid since prefixation and suffixation are linear in Semitic. It is clear from the parse tree that there is linear precedence among the daughters of 'word' that can be expressed in a traditional manner with the production

$$\begin{bmatrix}\textsf{word}\end{bmatrix} \rightarrow \begin{bmatrix}\textsf{conj}\end{bmatrix} \begin{bmatrix}\textsf{stem}\end{bmatrix} \begin{bmatrix}\textsf{VIM} \\ \text{NUMBER} = \text{sing} \\ \text{PERSON} = \text{3rd} \\ \text{GENDER} = \text{fem}\end{bmatrix}$$

It only remains to find a way to express the derivation of $[\textsf{stem}]$ from the pattern {cvcvc}, root {ktb}, and vocalism {a}.

A production of the form

$$\begin{bmatrix}\textsf{stem}\end{bmatrix} \rightarrow \begin{bmatrix}\textsf{pattern} \\ \text{MEASURE} = 1 \\ \text{VOICE} = \text{act}\end{bmatrix} \begin{bmatrix}\textsf{root} \\ \text{MEASURE} = \{1,2,3,4,5,6,7,8,10\}\end{bmatrix} \begin{bmatrix}\textsf{vocalism}\end{bmatrix}$$

cannot capture the derivation at hand because in reality there is no ordering of the daughters (i.e., the categories of the right-hand side of the rule). One might be tempted to use immediate dominance rules (Gazdar et al., 1985) in which linear precedence is not specified. This would be acceptable had the input to the parser been a sequence of terminals (in any order); however, this is not the case here, as the diagram in Fig. 5.7 illustrates. The input is a tuple of terminals.

Kaplan and Kay (1994) note that context-free n-relations can be defined along the lines of context-free grammars in the same manner as regular relations are defined along the lines of regular languages (see Section 7.1.2 for the definition of regular relations). They state,

> . . . a system of context-free rewriting rules can be used to define a context-free n-relation simply by introducing n-tuples as the terminal symbols of the grammar. The standard context-free derivation procedure will produce tree structures with n-tuple leaves, and the relational yield of such a grammar is taken to be the set of n-way concatenations of these leaves.
>
> [p. 339]

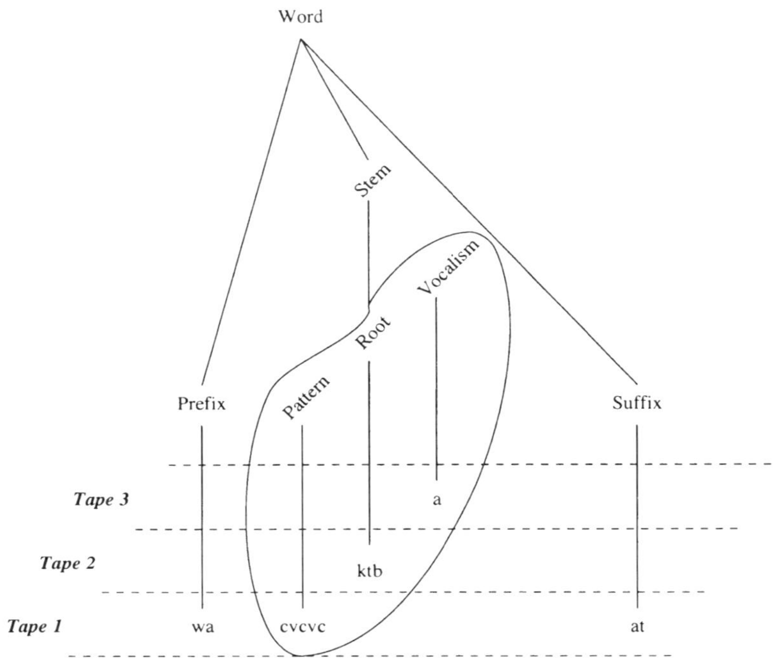

Fig. 5.7. Final parse tree for /wakatabat/. The terminal symbols are tuples of strings.

This model can be followed to resolve the issue at hand. One can write the following production to describe the daughters of the stem:

$$\begin{bmatrix} \text{stem} \\ \text{CATEGORY} = \text{verb} \\ \text{MEASURE} = \{1\} \\ \text{VOICE} = \text{act} \end{bmatrix} \rightarrow$$

$$\left\langle \begin{bmatrix} \text{pattern} \\ \text{MEASURE} = \{1\} \\ \text{VOICE} = \text{act} \end{bmatrix}, \begin{bmatrix} \text{root} \\ \text{MEASURE} = \{1,2,3,4,5,6,7,8,10\} \end{bmatrix}, \begin{bmatrix} \text{vocalism} \end{bmatrix} \right\rangle$$

Note that unification can be used for two purposes: first, to filter out undesired combinations (e.g., the unification of the values of MEASURE in the pattern and root morphemes); second, to propagate information to the mother category.

Recall from formal-language theory that a *context-free grammar* is a quadruple (V, T, P, S) where V is a finite-set set of *variables* (i.e., nonterminals) and T is a finite set of *terminals* (V and T are disjoint). Here P is a finite set of *productions*; each production is of the form $A \rightarrow \alpha$, where $A \in V$ and $\alpha \in (V \cup T)^*$. Finally, S is a special variable called the *start symbol* (Hopcroft and Ullman, 1979).

Assuming n-tuples of alphabets, out of which $n-1$ elements are lexical, a *context-free n-relation* is a context-free grammar but with T as a finite set of $(n-1)$ tuples of terminals. By convention, a terminal whose first element is the only nonempty expression can be shown without brackets; hence, x is a short-hand for $\langle x, \epsilon, \ldots, \epsilon \rangle$.

By way of illustration, consider a grammar $G = (V, T, P, S)$ where

$$
\begin{aligned}
V &= \{\,\mathrm{A, B, C, D, E}\,\} \\
T &= \{\,\mathrm{a}, \langle \mathrm{b, e, g}\rangle, \langle \mathrm{c, f, h}\rangle, \mathrm{d}\,\} \\
P &= \{\,\mathrm{A} \rightarrow \mathrm{a\ B\ E} \\
&\qquad \mathrm{B} \rightarrow \mathrm{C\ D} \\
&\qquad \mathrm{C} \rightarrow \langle \mathrm{b, e, g}\rangle \\
&\qquad \mathrm{D} \rightarrow \langle \mathrm{c, f, h}\rangle \\
&\qquad \mathrm{E} \rightarrow \mathrm{d}\,\} \\
S &= A
\end{aligned}
$$

A parse of the input ⟨a b c d, e f, g h⟩ is illustrated in Fig. 5.8. Note that the production B → C D puts a linear precedence constraint on the daughters of C and D. Since C precedes D, ⟨b, e, g⟩ must precede ⟨c, f, h⟩. This implies that there is a linear precedence among the elements of the daughters of C and D: b must precede c, e must precede f, and g must precede h, respectively.

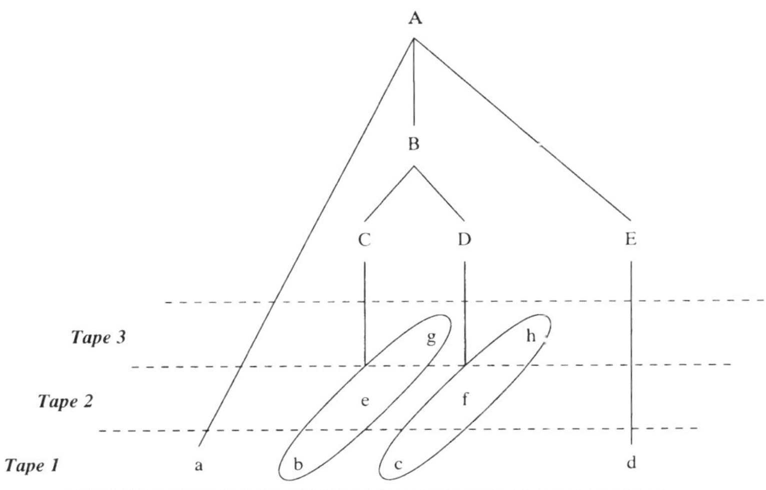

Fig. 5.8. Parse for ⟨a b c d, e f, g h⟩. There is a linear precedence constraint on the daughters of C and D since the former precedes the latter. This implies that b must precede c, e must precede f, and g must precede h.

Context-free n-relations can be extended to become unification-based context-free n-relations in the same manner as traditional context-free grammars are extended to become unification-based grammars.

5.5 Extensions to the Formalism

This final section briefly outlines some of the generalizations and extensions that may be applied to the rewrite rules formalism.

5.5.1 Other Formalisms and Notations

The work described here can be easily applied to other regular formalisms, such as the phonological formalism of Kaplan and Kay (1994), which already assumes tuples of symbols as its alphabet, and the two-level formalism of Koskenniemi (1983). The interpretation of such formalisms and notations need not be modified. Simply, their alphabet becomes a set of tuples of symbols. For example, R3 of Fig. 5.3 can be expressed in the formalism of Kaplan and Kay (1994) as

$$\langle \mathrm{v}, \epsilon, \epsilon \rangle \rightarrow \mathrm{X} \;/\; \langle \mathrm{v}, \epsilon, \mathrm{X} \rangle\, \Sigma^* \quad \_\_\_$$

and in Koskenniemi's formalism as

$$\mathrm{v{:}0{:}0{:}X} \Rightarrow \quad \mathrm{v{:}0{:}X{:}v}\ \Sigma^* \ \_\_\_$$

where the last element of the tuples represents surface symbols. (In both expressions Σ^* is the set of all valid tuples; in the latter, 0s replace ϵ.)

As is the case with other formalisms, the formalism adopted in this work may also allow expressions to make use of n-tuples of feature matrices as well as finite feature variables. Rules that make use of such expressions are still regular. (For a discussion on this, see Kaplan and Kay 1994, Section 5.6.)

Additionally, a rule may contain variables in different parts of the rule. For example, R3 in Fig. 5.3, repeated below,

$$\begin{array}{ccccccc} \langle \mathrm{v}, \varepsilon, \mathrm{X} \rangle\, * & - & \mathrm{v} & - & * & \Rightarrow \\ * & - & \mathrm{X} & - & * & \end{array}$$

has an X in LLC that must match the X in SURF. As long as such variables are defined over a finite set of possible values, such rules are equivalent to the set of rules where all variables are instantiated.

5.5.2 Grammatical Features

It has been proposed (see Section 3.2.1) that rewrite rules accommodate grammatical features that provide for finer and more elegant descriptions. Without such

Table 5.2. *Example of grammatical features*

Word	Category	Word	Category
abcd	l_1	j	l_4
ef	l_2	kl	l_5
ghi	l_3		
(a) Sublexicon 1		(b) Sublexicon 2	

Note: Each entry is associated with a category containing its features.

a mechanism, writing complex grammars for Semitic morphology would be extremely cumbersome.

5.5.2.1 *Intuitive Description*

Rewrite rules in the current formalism may be associated with categories similar to those in lexical entries (see p. 71). A rule that makes use of $n-1$ lexical expressions is associated with an $(n-1)$ tuple of categories, $\langle c_1, \ldots, c_{n-1} \rangle$. An uninstantiated category is denoted by an asterisk. When only the first category is given, the brackets can be ignored.

The following abstract example illustrates how categories work. Assume some set of rewrite rules over two lexical expressions, the entries in Table 5.2 and the analysis in Fig. 5.9(a). (We shall ignore the surface expression here.) The numbers between the lexical expressions and the surface expression denote some rules in the grammar that sanction the given lexical-surface subsequences. Let each rule k, $1 \leq k \leq 9$, in Fig. 5.9(a) be associated with a 2-tuple of categories $\langle r_{k_1}, r_{k_2} \rangle$, representing the category on each lexical element, respectively. For the analysis in Fig. 5.9(a) to be valid,

r_{1_1}, r_{2_1}, r_{3_1}, and r_{4_1}	must match l_1
r_{5_1} and r_{6_1}	must match l_2
r_{7_1}, r_{8_1}, and r_{9_1}	must match l_3
r_{3_2}	must match l_4
r_{6_2} and r_{8_2}	must match l_5

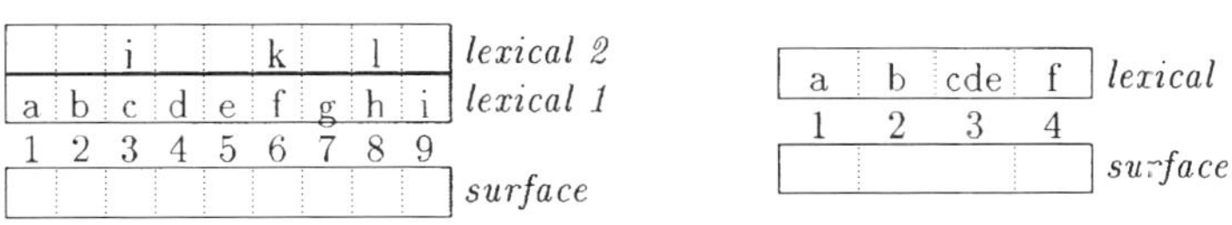

(a) (b)

Fig. 5.9. Analysis of feature example.

This version of rule category matching does not cater for rules whose centers span over two lexical forms. It is possible, of course, to avoid this limitation. Say that there is a rule whose center spans over two-lexical words as illustrated in the example in Fig. 5.9(b). In this case, the category associated with rule 3 must match both l_1, which is associated with {abcd} in the lexicon, and l_2, which is associated with {ef}.

Section 7.3.3 demonstrates how grammatical categories can be dealt with in a finite-state manner.

5.5.2.2 *Formal Description*

The following definitions assume a grammar with n expressions, out of which $n-1$ expressions are lexical.

> **Definition 5.5.1** A *category* becomes an $(n-1)$ tuple of categories (cf. Definition 5.2.1). □

The following definitions are variants of Definitions 5.3.13, 5.3.15, 5.3.16, and 5.3.18, respectively.

> **Definition 5.5.2** A *two-level rule* consists of a pair (C, LR), where C is a two-level tuple representing the center of the rule, and LR is a nonempty set of triples (λ, ρ, κ), with λ and ρ two-level tuples representing the left and right contexts, respectively, and κ a category tuple. □

> **Definition 5.5.3** Let
>
> (i) $S = \langle s, l_1, \ldots, l_{n-1} \rangle$ be a two-level tuple,
> (ii) $\mathcal{P} = (P^1, \ldots, P^{i-1}, P^i, P^{i+1}, \ldots, P^k)$, $1 \le i \le k$, be an n-way partition of S such that $P^t = \langle s^t, l_1^t, \ldots, l_{n-1}^t \rangle$, $1 \le t \le k$, and
> (iii) $\mathcal{L} = (L_1, \ldots, L_{n-1})$ be a tuple of lexical entry sequences from some lexicon where for each $1 \le h \le n-1$, there exist integers $m, p, q, \ldots, r$ with $1 \le p \le q \le \cdots \le r \le k$ such that $L_h = (W_{h_1}, C_{h_1}), \ldots, (W_{h_m}, C_{h_m})$ and
>
> $$W_{h_1} = l_h^1 \cdots l_h^p$$
> $$W_{h_2} = l_h^{p+1} \cdots l_h^q$$
> $$\vdots$$
> $$W_{h_m} = l_h^r \cdots l_h^k$$
>
> We say that a two-level rule (P^i, LR) *contextually allows* P^i *in* $\mathcal{P}$ *and* $\mathcal{L}$ if and only if LR contains a triple $(\lambda, \rho, \kappa = (c_1, \ldots, c_{n-1}))$ such that λ is an n-way suffix of $P^1 \cdots P^{i-1}$, ρ is an n-way prefix of $P^{i+1} \cdots P^k$, and
>
> $$c_h \text{ unifies with } \begin{cases} C_{h_1} & \text{if} \quad 1 \le i \le p \\ C_{h_2} & \text{if} \quad p+1 \le i \le q \\ \vdots & \\ C_{h_m} & \text{if} \quad r \le i \le k \end{cases}$$
>
> for all $1 \le h \le n-1$. □

Definition 5.5.4 Let

(i) $S = \langle s, l_1, \ldots, l_{n-1} \rangle$ be a two-level tuple,
(ii) $\mathcal{P} = (P^1, \ldots, P^{i-1}, P^i, \ldots, P^{j-1}, P^j, \ldots, P^k)$, $1 \leq i \leq j \leq k$, be an n-way partition of S such that $P^t = \langle s^t, l_1^t, \ldots, l_{n-1}^t \rangle$, $1 \leq t \leq k$, and
(iii) $\mathcal{L} = (L_1, \ldots, L_{n-1})$ be a tuple of lexical entry sequences from some lexicon where for each $1 \leq h \leq n-1$, there exist integers $m, p, q, \ldots, r$ with $1 \leq p \leq q \leq \cdots \leq r \leq k$ such that $L_h = (W_{h_1}, C_{h_1}), \ldots, (W_{h_m}, C_{h_m})$ and

$$\begin{aligned} W_{h_1} &= l_h^1 \cdots l_h^p \\ W_{h_2} &= l_h^{p+1} \cdots l_h^q \\ &\vdots \\ W_{h_m} &= l_h^r \cdots l_h^k \end{aligned}$$

We say that a two-level rule $(\langle s', l'_1, \ldots, l'_{n-1} \rangle, \mathrm{LR})$ *coercively disallows* $P^i \cdots P^{j-1}$ *in* $\mathcal{P}$ *and* $\mathcal{L}$ if and only if LR contains a triple $(\lambda, \rho, \kappa = (c_1, \ldots, c_{n-1}))$ such that λ is an n-way suffix of $P^1 \cdots P^{i-1}$, ρ is an n-way suffix of $P^j \cdots P^k$, $l'_h = l_h^i \cdots l_h^{j-1}$, $s' \neq s^i \cdots s^{j-1}$, and

$$c_h \text{ unifies with } \begin{cases} C_{h_1} & \text{if} \quad 1 \leq y \leq p \\ C_{h_2} & \text{if} \quad p+1 \leq y \leq q \\ \vdots & \\ C_{h_m} & \text{if} \quad r \leq y \leq k \end{cases}$$

for all $1 \leq h \leq n-1$ and all $i \leq y \leq j-1$. □

Definition 5.5.5 Let $G = (CR, SC)$ be a two-level grammar and S be a two-level tuple. We say that G *accepts* S if and only if there is an n-way partition $\mathcal{P} = (P_1, \ldots, P_k)$ of S and a tuple of lexical entry sequences from some lexicon $\mathcal{L}$ such that (i) for each P_i, $1 \leq i \leq k$, there is at least one rule in CR that contextually allows P_i in $\mathcal{P}$ and $\mathcal{L}$, and (ii) there is no i, j with $1 \leq i \leq j \leq k$ such that there is a rule in SC that coercively disallows $P_i \cdots P_j$ in $\mathcal{P}$ and $\mathcal{L}$. □

The quotation at the beginning of this book (on p. vi) comes now to mind!

6 Modeling Semitic Nonlinear Morphology

Just as vowels with consonants are the matter of syllables, so also syllables are the matter for the construction of nouns and verbs, and of the elements which are made out of them.

Antony the Rhetorician of Tagrit († *c.* 445?)
Knowledge of Rhetoric, Book Five, Canon One

Hebrew words are based on letters which make up their roots and foundation.

David ben Abraham (10th c.)
Kitâb ĵâmiʕ al-Alfâz

This chapter demonstrates how the model presented in the previous chapter can be applied to the various nonlinear morphological problems described in Chapter 2. For each section in Chapter 2, the corresponding section in this chapter provides sample lexica and rewrite rules. (It is recommended to review the material in Chapter 2 at this point.) An additional section at the end of this chapter discusses various issues that arise when Semitic lexica and grammars are developed.

Rewrite rule grammars in this chapter make use of the following identity rule:

$$\text{R0}\quad \begin{matrix} * & - & \text{X} & - & * & \Rightarrow \\ * & - & \text{X} & - & * & \end{matrix}$$

where X is any symbol from the alphabet. The rule states that any symbol from the *first* sublexicon – excluding symbols from the remaining sublexica – may surface. This rule is not hard coded in the implementations that are described in the next two chapters; it is given here in order to avoid repeating it in subsequent grammars.

In subsequent rules, the alphabets of root consonants and vocalism vowels are indicated by Σ_c and Σ_v, respectively. The scope of variables in rules is usually given in the following paragraphs, which describe the rule.

It must be stressed that for ease of presentation, the sample lexica and grammars presented here aim at showing how the data described in this work can be handled computationally. It is understood that when such lexica and grammars are part of a larger system, they may have to be altered in order to interact with the rest of the system.

Three linguistic models were presented for Semitic morphology in Chapter 2: CV, moraic, and affixational, in addition to the issue of the broken plural. Despite the CV analysis being superseded by the other models, it is given due attention here

Table 6.1. *Arabic verbal stems with the roots {ktb} and {dħrĵ}*

Measure	Active	Passive	Measure	Active	Passive
1	katab	kutib	8	ktatab	ktutib
2	kattab	kuttib	9	ktabab	
3	kaatab	kuutib	10	staktab	stuktib
4	ʔaktab	ʔuktib	11	ktaabab	
5	takattab	tukuttib	12	ktawtab	
6	takaatab	tukuutib	13	ktawwab	
7	nkatab	nkutib	14	ktanbab	
			15	ktanbay	
Q1	daħraĵ	duħriĵ	Q3	dħanraĵ	dħunriĵ
Q2	tadaħraĵ	tuduħriĵ	Q4	dħarĵaĵ	dħurĵiĵ

for a number of reasons. First, it serves as a good introduction to Semitic nonlinear morphology and to McCarthy's original findings (McCarthy, 1981). Second, it facilitates the comparison of the current work with other computational proposals that tend to adopt the CV analysis as basis. Third, the nonlinguist user writing a grammar of Semitic morphology may prefer to base the grammar on the CV model because of its ease of implementation and accessibility in the grammatical literature.

6.1 The CV Approach

Recall the Arabic data from Table 2.1, repeated for convenience in Table 6.1. Verbal stems are classified under 15 triliteral and four quadriliteral measures. Each stem is derived from at least three morphemes: the root morpheme (e.g., {ktb} for measures 1–15 and {dħrĵ} for measures Q1–Q4), the vocalism morpheme (e.g., {ad} for the active stems and {ui} for the passive ones), and the pattern morpheme, which dictates how the consonants and vowels are arranged on the surface. The simplest autosegmental analysis is when there is a one-to-one mapping between root segments and C segments of the pattern, as well as a one-to-one mapping between vowel segments and V segments of the pattern. This is illustrated in the analysis of /kutib/ (measure 1 – PASS) in Fig. 6.1(a). The analyses of other stems, however, cause a number of complications:

(i) *Conventional spreading.* Active stems spread the active vowel {a} as in /katab/ (measure 1 – ACT), depicted in Fig. 6.1(b), following the Association Convention (see p. 4).

(ii) *Language-specific spreading.* Passive stems spread the first vocalic segment [u] of the vocalism morpheme – instead of the last [i] segment – against the Association Convention as in /kuutib/ (measure 3 – PASS), depicted in Fig. 6.1(c).

(iii) *Affix linking.* Affixes must be linked to templates before root and vocalism segments as [ʔ] in /ʔaktab/ (measure 4 – ACT), depicted in Fig. 6.1(d). Additionally, measures 12–15 require that affixes are prelinked to the template in the initial configuration (see Fig. 2.3).

(iv) *Language-specific rules.* The gemination of the middle [t] of the root {ktb} in measures 2 and 5 requires a special rule to derive these measures, for example, /kattab/ and /takattab/ (see Fig. 2.4). The same holds for measure 8, where the infix {t} morpheme appears after the [k] of the root, for example, /ktatab/ (see Fig. 2.5).

To resolve such complications, the CV model in Section 2.1 can be simplified (for computational purposes) by incorporating affixes into the pattern morpheme and by indexing CV segments. For example, the template CVCCVC, which describes measures 2, 4, and Q1, becomes $c_1v_1c_2c_2v_1c_3$ for measure 2, $ʔv_1c_1c_2v_1c_3$ for measure 4, and $c_1v_1c_2c_3v_1c_4$ for measure Q1. (Because capital-initial strings denote variables, we present CV segments in small letters.) Note that the Vs also have to be indexed to cater for language-specific spreading in passive stems, for example, $c_1v_1v_1c_2v_2c_3$ for /kuutib/ (measure 3 – PASS). This implies that there should be two pattern specifications for each measure: one for the active and one for the passive.

Additionally, recall that in measure 1, the value of the second active vowel changes from one root to another and is lexically encoded with each root, for example, [a] in /katab/ "to write," [u] in /samuħ/ "to be generous," and [i] in /samiʕ/ "to hear," from the roots {ktb}, {smħ}, and {smʕ}, respectively. Such vowels will be encoded by means of categories in the lexicon.

6.1.1 Lexicon

A sample CV-based lexicon for the data at hand consists of three sublexica. The first sublexicon contains patterns and affixes. The second sublexicon contains root entries. The third sublexicon provides the various vocalisms.

Sublexicon 1 lists entries for CV patterns. Each pattern entry is associated with a category that indicates the measure in question and its voice. For example, the

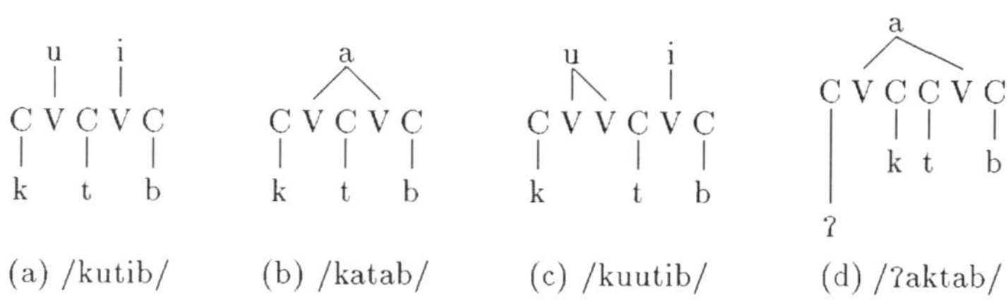

Fig. 6.1. Sample derivations: (a) with one-to-one mapping between root segments and C segments, and between vowel segments and V segments; (b) with the conventional spreading of [a]; (c) with the language-specific spreading of [u]; (d) with linking affix material before root and vocalism segments.

active pattern of measure 2, /kattab/, is

$$c_1v_1c_2c_2v_1c_3 \begin{bmatrix} \textsf{pattern} \\ \text{MEASURE} = 2 \\ \text{VOICE} = \text{act} \end{bmatrix}$$

and the passive pattern of measure 6, /tukuutib/, is

$$tv_1c_1v_1v_1c_2v_2c_3 \begin{bmatrix} \textsf{pattern} \\ \text{MEASURE} = 6 \\ \text{VOICE} = \text{pass} \end{bmatrix}$$

Note that since segments are indexed, each measure requires a pattern entry for the perfect active (with all [v]s having the same subscript denoting the spreading of the active vowel as in /kattab/) and another for the perfect passive (with all but the last [v] having the same subscript to denote the spreading of the first vowel of the vocalism as in /tukuutib/).

Since the vocalism morpheme for the active of measure 1 differs from one root to another, two patterns for the active of this measure are given. In the first one,

$$c_1v_1c_2v_1c_3 \begin{bmatrix} \textsf{pattern} \\ \text{MEASURE} = 1 \\ \text{VOICE} = \text{act} \\ \text{VOWEL} = \text{a} \end{bmatrix}$$

the [v]s have the same subscript; the first vowel spreads as in /katab/. In the second,

$$c_1v_1c_2v_2c_3 \begin{bmatrix} \textsf{pattern} \\ \text{MEASURE} = 1 \\ \text{VOICE} = \text{act} \\ \text{VOWEL} = \{\text{u,i}\} \end{bmatrix}$$

the [v]s having different subscripts; the vowel does not spread as in /samuħ/ and /samiʕ/. The attribute VOWEL indicates that the former only applies when the first active vowel for measure 1 is [a], and the latter when the vowel is either an [u] or an [i].

Additionally, in this and subsequent models, unless otherwise specified, all lexical morphemes that fall out of the domain of root-and-pattern morphology (e.g., prefixes, suffixes, particles, prepositions, etc.) are placed in sublexicon 1. This is exemplified by two verbal inflexional markers,

$$\text{a} \begin{bmatrix} \textsf{VIM} \\ \text{NUMBER} = \text{sing} \\ \text{PERSON} = \text{3rd} \\ \text{GENDER} = \text{masc} \end{bmatrix}$$

as in /kutiba/, and

$$\text{at} \begin{bmatrix} \textsf{VIM} \\ \text{NUMBER} = \text{sing} \\ \text{PERSON} = \text{3rd} \\ \text{GENDER} = \text{fem} \end{bmatrix}$$

as in /kutibat/, with the attributes for number, person, and gender.

Sublexicon 2 lists root morphemes. Recall (see p. 28) that each root does not occur in all measures, but in a subset of the measures. The category of each root gives the disjunction of this subset based on Wehr (1971). It also specifies the vocalism morpheme for the active of measure 1 with the VOWEL attribute. For example, the entry for {ktb} is

$$\text{ktb}\begin{bmatrix}\textsf{root}\\ \text{MEASURE} = \{1,2,3,4,6,7,8,10\}\\ \text{VOWEL} = \text{a}\end{bmatrix}$$

whereas the entry for {smħ} is

$$\text{sm}\hbar\begin{bmatrix}\textsf{root}\\ \text{MEASURE} = \{1,2,3,6,10\}\\ \text{VOWEL} = \text{u}\end{bmatrix}$$

Finally, sublexicon 3 provides for various vocalisms. For example, the passive vocalism is

$$\text{ui}\begin{bmatrix}\textsf{vocalism}\\ \text{VOICE} = \text{pass}\end{bmatrix}$$

while the active one is

$$\text{a}\begin{bmatrix}\textsf{vocalism}\\ \text{VOICE} = \text{act}\\ \text{VOWEL} = \text{a}\end{bmatrix}$$

Again, since the vocalism for the active of measure 1 varies, the attribute VOWEL distinguishes the above active vocalism from the two other active vocalisms,

$$\text{au}\begin{bmatrix}\textsf{vocalism}\\ \text{MEASURE} = 1\\ \text{VOICE} = \text{act}\\ \text{VOWEL} = \text{u}\end{bmatrix}$$

which applies to stems like /samuħ/, and

$$\text{ai}\begin{bmatrix}\textsf{vocalism}\\ \text{MEASURE} = 1\\ \text{VOICE} = \text{act}\\ \text{VOWEL} = \text{i}\end{bmatrix}$$

which applies to stems like /samiʕ/. Note that since the active vocalism {a} applies to all measures, it does not contain the attribute MEASURE.

6.1.2 *Rewrite Rules*

Since the lexicon makes use of three sublexica, each lexical expression in the rewrite rules grammar must be a triple, where the *i*th element refers to symbols from the *i*th sublexicon. For example, the rules that sanction stem segments,

$$\text{R1}\quad \begin{array}{ccccccc} * & - & \langle \mathrm{P}_c,\mathrm{C},\varepsilon\rangle & - & * & \Rightarrow \\ * & - & \mathrm{C} & - & * & \end{array}$$

$$\text{R2}\quad \begin{array}{ccccccc} * & - & \langle \mathrm{P}_v,\varepsilon,\mathrm{V}\rangle & - & * & \Rightarrow \\ * & - & \mathrm{V} & - & * & \end{array}$$

map pattern, root, and vocalism segments, respectively, to surface segments. R1 states that any $\mathrm{P}_c \in \{\, c_1, c_2, c_3, c_4 \,\}$ from the first (pattern) sublexicon and a consonant $\mathrm{C} \in \Sigma_c$ from the second (root) sublexicon – excluding any symbol from the third (vocalism) sublexicon – map the same consonant C to the surface; that is, lexical $\langle \mathrm{P}_c,\mathrm{C},\varepsilon\rangle$ maps to surface C. This rule sanctions stem consonants. Similarly, R2 states that any $\mathrm{P}_v \in \{\, v_1, v_2 \,\}$ from the pattern sublexicon and a vowel $\mathrm{V} \in \Sigma_v$ from the vocalism sublexicon – excluding any symbol from the root sublexicon – map the same vowel V to the surface; that is, lexical $\langle \mathrm{P}_v,\varepsilon,\mathrm{V}\rangle$ maps to V. This rule sanctions stem vowels. Both rules are optional. Figure 6.2(a) shows the lexical-surface analysis of /kutiba/ "it (MASC) was written," from the stem /kutib/ (measure 1 – PASS) and the suffix {a}. The numbers between the surface expression and the lexical expressions indicate the rules that sanction the subsequences. (R0, as before, is the default identity rule.)

Grammars and lexica usually employ a boundary symbol, here denoted by β, as a morpheme separator. Such symbols are deleted in surface forms; their deletion

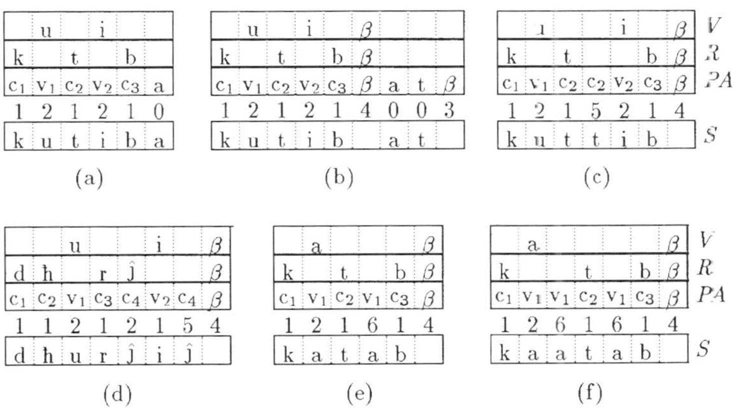

Fig. 6.2. Examples of lexical-surface mappings using CV templates. (a) /kutiba/; (b) /kutibat/; (c) /kuttib/; (d) /dħurjiĵ/; (e) /katab/; (f) /kaatab/. From bottom to top, S = surface, PA = pattern and affixes, R = root, and V = vocalism. Numbers indicate the rules that sanction the subsequences.

may be expressed by the following two rules:

$$\text{R3} \quad \begin{array}{ccccccc} X & - & \beta & - & * & \Leftrightarrow \\ * & - & \varepsilon & - & * & \end{array}$$

$$\text{R4} \quad \begin{array}{ccccccc} \langle P_c,C,*\rangle & - & \langle \beta,\beta,\beta\rangle & - & * & \Leftrightarrow \\ C & - & \varepsilon & - & * & \end{array}$$

where $X \neq \beta$. R3 is used for the boundary symbols of nonstem morphemes, for example, prefixes and suffixes, while R4 applies to boundary symbols in stems, deleting three boundary symbols simultaneously that mark the end of a stem. Both rules are obligatory. The left contexts in both rules ensure that the correct boundary rule is invoked at the right time. Figure 6.2(b) shows the analysis of /kutibat/ "it (FEM) was written," that is, /kutib/ followed by the suffix {at}, with the deletion of boundary symbols.

The spreading (and gemination) of consonants is sanctioned by the following rule:

$$\text{R5} \quad \begin{array}{ccccccc} \langle P_s,C,*\rangle\ * & - & P_s & - & * & \Rightarrow \\ * & - & C & - & * & \end{array}$$

It maps a pattern symbol $P_s \in \{c_2, c_3, c_4\}$[1] – excluding any symbols from the root or vocalism sublexica – to a consonant C on the surface. The value of C is determined from the left-lexical context (LLC), "$\langle P_s,C,*\rangle$ *." The asterisk after the tuple indicates that there could be intervening tuples between the LLC and the center as in the spreading of [b] in /ktabab/ (measure 9 – ACT). R5 is illustrated in the analysis of /kuttib/ (measure 2 – PASS) and /dħurĵiĵ/ (measure Q4 – PASS) in Fig. 6.2(c) and (d).

Finally, the following rule sanctions the spreading of the first vowel in passive stems:

$$\text{R6} \quad \begin{array}{ccccccc} \langle v_1,*,V\rangle\ * & - & v_1 & - & * & \Rightarrow \\ * & - & V & - & * & \end{array}$$

The rule maps a v_1 on the pattern sublexicon to a vowel V on the surface. As in R5, the value of the vowel is determined from LLC. Spreading examples appear in Fig. 6.2(e) and (f).

As a final example, consider the derivation of /dħunriĵa/ (measure Q3 – PASS), from the three morphemes $\{c_1c_2v_1nc_3v_2c_4\}$, {dħrĵ}, and {ui}, and the suffix {a}. This example illustrates how affix material, [n] in this case, is mapped by the default identity rule R0 as illustrated in Fig. 6.3.

[1] The first consonant never spreads. The second consonant is geminated in /kattab/ (measure 2) and /takattab/ (measure 5), and it spreads in /ktawtab/ (measure 12). The third consonant spreads in /ktabab/ (measure 9), /ktaabab/ (measure 11), and /ktanbab/ (measure 14). The fourth consonant in quadriliteral forms spreads in /dħarĵaĵ/ (measure Q4).

		u			i		β			*VT*
d	ħ			r		ĵ	β			*RT*
c_1	c_2	v_1	n	c_3	v_2	c_4	β	a	β	*PT*
1	1	2	0	1	2	1	4	0	3	
d	ħ	u	n	r	i	ĵ		a		*ST*

Fig. 6.3. Lexical-surface analysis of measure Q3 followed by the suffix {a}. Note that the default rule R0 maps stem infixes such as [n].

6.2 The Moraic Approach

Recall (Section 2.2) that while the CV approach describes pattern morphemes in terms of Cs and Vs, the moraic approach argues for a different vocabulary motivated by prosody, namely, syllables and morae. Consider the Arabic nominal stems in Table 2.2, shown again in Table 6.2 with moraic patterns.

As with the CV approach, stems are derived from patterns, roots, and vocalisms. In the moraic approach, the pattern is a sequence of symbols from the set $\{\sigma_x, \sigma_\mu, \sigma_{\mu\mu}\}$. The extrametrical syllable, denoted by σ_x, always corresponds to the final consonant in a stem, usually to be syllabified with case suffixes or with the next word. While a monomoraic syllable, denoted by σ_μ, corresponds to CV as in Fig. 6.4(b), a bimoraic syllable, denoted by $\sigma_{\mu\mu}$, may correspond to either CVV or to CVC as follows.

(i) In initial bimoraic syllables, $\sigma_{\mu\mu}$ is realized as CVV in triliteral roots as in Fig. 6.4(d), and CVC in quadriliteral roots as in Fig. 6.4(e).

(ii) In final bimoraic syllables, $\sigma_{\mu\mu}$ is realized as CVC in monosyllabic stems as in /nafs/ "soul," depicted in Fig. 6.4(a), and CVV in bisyllabic stems as in /ĵaziir/ "island," depicted in Fig. 6.4(c).

Recall (Section 2.2) that the moraic analysis argues that HL patterns do not exist. Hence, the stems in Table 6.2(f) and (g) are atemplatic and are entered as is in the lexicon.

Table 6.2. *Arabic nominal stems*

	CV Pattern	Moraic Pattern	Noun	Gloss
(a)	CVCC	$\sigma_\mu\sigma_x$	nafs	soul
(b)	CVCVC	$\sigma_\mu\sigma_\mu\sigma_x$	raĵul	man
			ʔasad	lion
(c)	CVCVVC + at	$\sigma_\mu\sigma_{\mu\mu}\sigma_x$	ĵaziir	island
(d)	CVVCVVC	$\sigma_{\mu\mu}\sigma_{\mu\mu}\sigma_x$	ĵaamuus	buffalo
(e)	CVCCVVC	$\sigma_{\mu\mu}\sigma_{\mu\mu}\sigma_x$	sulṭaan	sultan
			ĵumhuur	multitude
(f)	CVVCVC	N/A	xaatam	signet ring
(g)	CVCCVC	N/A	ĵundub	locust

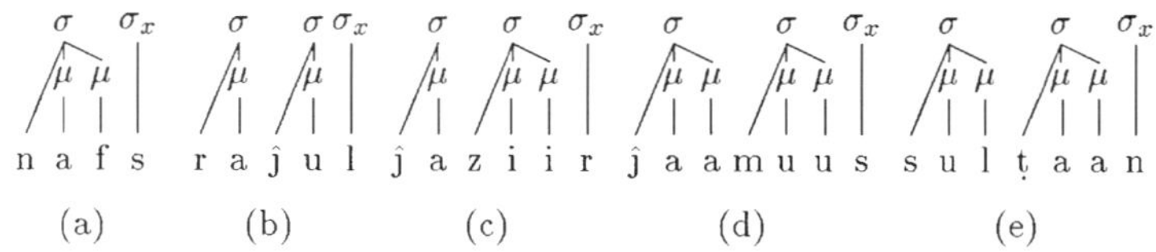

Fig. 6.4. Moraic analysis of nominal stems.

6.2.1 Lexicon

Similar to the CV model, the moraic lexicon makes use of three sublexica for patterns (and atemplatic stems in this case), roots, and vocalisms.

Sublexicon 1 lists the four prosodic patterns (namely, heavy, light–light, light–heavy and heavy–heavy). For example, the light–light pattern entry is

$$\sigma_\mu \sigma_\mu \sigma_x \begin{bmatrix} \textsf{pattern} \\ \text{MEASURE} = \text{light–light} \end{bmatrix}$$

where $[\sigma_\mu]$ is a symbol denoting a monomoraic syllable and $[\sigma_x]$ is another symbol denoting an extraprosodic syllable. Similarly, the light–heavy entry is

$$\sigma_\mu \sigma_{\mu\mu} \sigma_x \begin{bmatrix} \textsf{pattern} \\ \text{MEASURE} = \text{light–heavy} \end{bmatrix}$$

Here, $[\sigma_{\mu\mu}]$ is a symbol denoting a bimoraic syllable. Additionally, sublexicon 1 lists atemplatic stems such as

$$\text{xaatam} \begin{bmatrix} \textsf{stem} \\ \text{MEASURE} = \text{atemplatic} \end{bmatrix}$$

and

$$\text{ĵundub} \begin{bmatrix} \textsf{stem} \\ \text{MEASURE} = \text{atemplatic} \end{bmatrix}$$

Sublexicon 2 provides root entries. For example, the entry for the root {nfs} is

$$\text{nfs} \begin{bmatrix} \textsf{root} \\ \text{MEASURE} = \text{heavy} \\ \text{VOCALISM} = \text{a} \end{bmatrix}$$

and the entry for the root {slṭn} is

$$\text{slṭn} \begin{bmatrix} \textsf{root} \\ \text{MEASURE} = \text{heavy–heavy} \\ \text{VOCALISM} = \text{ua} \end{bmatrix}$$

The category indicates the root's measure[2] and its vocalism.

[2] As in verbs, roots may occur in a number of nominal measures. In reality, the value associated with the attribute MEASURE is a disjunction of the measures in which the root occurs (see the verb root entries in Section 6.1.1 for an example).

Sublexicon 3 lists the various nominal vocalisms, each associated with a category that indicates the vocalism quality. Two examples of such entries are

$$\text{a}\begin{bmatrix}\textsf{vocalism}\\ \text{VOCALISM} = \text{a}\end{bmatrix}$$

and

$$\text{ua}\begin{bmatrix}\textsf{vocalism}\\ \text{VOCALISM} = \text{ua}\end{bmatrix}$$

6.2.2 Rewrite Rules

The lexical expressions of the rewrite rules grammar employ triples to account for the three sublexica. For example, the rule that sanctions an extrametrical segment,

$$\text{R1}\quad \begin{matrix} * & - & \langle\sigma_x,\text{C},\varepsilon\rangle & - & \langle\beta,\beta,\beta\rangle & \Leftrightarrow \\ * & - & \text{C} & - & * & \end{matrix}$$

maps pattern, root, and vocalic segments, respectively, to a surface segment along the previous CV grammar. Here, the rule maps σ_x from the first (pattern) sublexicon and a consonant $\text{C} \in \Sigma_c$ from the second (root) sublexicon – excluding any symbols from the third (vocalism) sublexicon – to the same consonant C on the surface; that is, it maps lexical $\langle\sigma_x,\text{C},\varepsilon\rangle$ to surface C. This rule accounts for the obligatory final σ_x that must be followed by lexical boundary symbols, that is, the right-lexical context is $\langle\beta,\beta,\beta\rangle$.

The following rule is used to sanction monomoraic syllables:

$$\text{R2}\quad \begin{matrix} * & - & \langle\sigma_\mu,\text{C},\text{V}\rangle & - & * & \Rightarrow \\ * & - & \text{CV} & - & * & \end{matrix}$$

It maps a σ_μ from the first sublexicon, a consonant C from the second sublexicon, and a vowel $\text{V} \in \Sigma_v$ from the third sublexicon to the sequence CV on the surface; that is, it maps lexical $\langle\sigma_\mu,\text{C},\text{V}\rangle$ to surface CV. Ignoring the boundary symbols, β, for the moment, Fig. 6.5(a) illustrates the use of the above two rules in the analysis of /raĵul/ "man," depicted in Fig. 6.4(b).

Two rules are required to sanction final bimoraic syllables. One allows $\sigma_{\mu\mu}$ to be realized as CVC in monosyllabic stems as in /nafs/ "soul," depicted in Fig. 6.4(a), and the other allows $\sigma_{\mu\mu}$ to be realized as CVV in bisyllabic stems as in /ĵaziir/ "island," depicted in Fig. 6.4(c):

$$\text{R3}\quad \begin{matrix} * & - & \langle\sigma_{\mu\mu},\text{C}_1\text{C}_2,\text{V}\rangle & - & \sigma_x & \Leftrightarrow \\ * & - & \text{C}_1\text{VC}_2 & - & * & \end{matrix}$$

$$\text{R4}\quad \begin{matrix} \text{S} & - & \langle\sigma_{\mu\mu},\text{C},\text{V}\rangle & - & \sigma_x & \Leftrightarrow \\ * & - & \text{CVV} & - & * & \end{matrix}$$

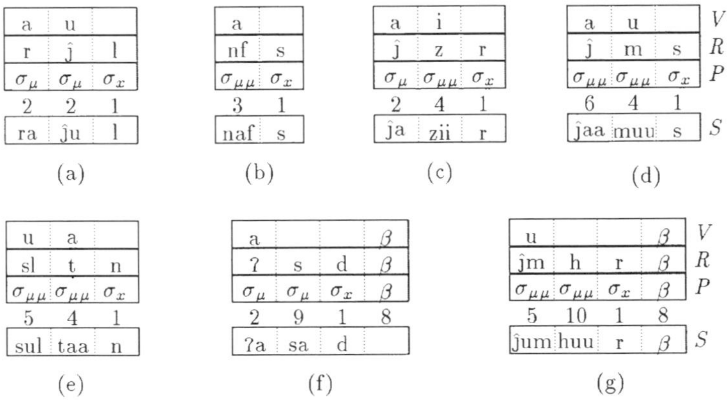

Fig. 6.5. Lexical-surface examples of the moraic approach (a) /raĵul/; (b) /nafs/; (c) /ĵaziir/; (d) /ĵaamuus/; (e) /sulṭaan/; (f) /ʔasad/; (g) /ĵumhuur/. From bottom to top, S = surface, P = pattern, R = root, V = vocalism.

R3 handles the former case by mapping a $\sigma_{\mu\mu}$ from the first sublexicon, two consonants C_1C_2 from the second sublexicon, and a vowel V from the third sublexicon to C_1VC_2 on the surface; that is, it maps $\langle\sigma_{\mu\mu},C_1C_2,V\rangle$ to C_1VC_2 (the subscripts merely indicate two distinct variables with $C_1,C_2 \in \Sigma_c$). The right-lexical context, σ_x, ensures that the rule only applies to the final syllable of a stem. This is enforced further by making the rule obligatory. The application of R3 is illustrated in the analysis of /nafs/ "soul" in Fig. 6.5(b).

R4 takes care of the latter case, in which a final bimoraic syllable is realized as CVV in bisyllabic stems. It maps a $\sigma_{\mu\mu}$ from the first sublexicon, a consonant C from the second sublexicon, and a vowel V from the third sublexicon to CVV on the surface; that is, it maps $\langle\sigma_{\mu\mu},C,V\rangle$ to CVV. The left-lexical context, $S \in \{\sigma_\mu,\sigma_{\mu\mu}\}$, ensures that this only applies in bisyllabic stems. Additionally, as in R3 the right-lexical context and the obligatoriness of the rule ensure that the rule only applies to final syllables. R4 is illustrated in the analysis of /ĵaziir/ "island" in Fig. 6.5(c).

Initial bimoraic syllables are sanctioned by the following two rules along the lines of R3 and R4, respectively:

$$\text{R5} \quad \begin{array}{ccccccc} * & - & \langle\sigma_{\mu\mu},C_1C_2,V\rangle & - & \sigma_{\mu\mu} & \Leftrightarrow \\ * & - & C_1VC_2 & - & * & \end{array}$$

$$\text{R6} \quad \begin{array}{ccccccc} * & - & \langle\sigma_{\mu\mu},C,V\rangle & - & \sigma_{\mu\mu} & \Leftrightarrow \\ * & - & CVV & - & * & \end{array}$$

The difference here lies in the right-lexical context, which ensures that the rules are only applied to initial syllables. The rules are illustrated in Fig. 6.5(d) and (e).

Recall that an initial bimoraic syllable is realized as CVV in triliteral roots as in /ĵaamuus/ "buffalo," depicted in Fig. 6.4(d), and CVC in quadriliteral roots as

a	
ĵm	
$\sigma_{\mu\mu}$	$\sigma_{\mu\mu}$
5	RLC
ĵam	

(a)

a	u	
ĵm	s	
$\sigma_{\mu\mu}$	$\sigma_{\mu\mu}$	σ_x
5	4	RLC
ĵam	suu	

(b)

a	u		V
ĵm	s	?	R
$\sigma_{\mu\mu}$	$\sigma_{\mu\mu}$	σ_x	P
5	4	1	
ĵam	suu	?	S

(c)

Fig. 6.6. Example showing the wrong application of a rule in bimoraic nouns: (a) R5 wrongly applied to the first subsequence and its right-lexical context requires that the next symbol from the pattern is $\sigma_{\mu\mu}$; (b) R4 applies to the second bimoraic syllable and its right-lexical context dictates that what follows must have σ_x in the pattern tape; (c) R1 is the only candidate now, but it will fail because there are no more consonants in the root.

in /sulṭaan/ "sultan," depicted in Fig. 6.4(e). In fact, there is no need to code this in rules: if a rule applies to the wrong root, the analysis will fail since there will be one extra (or one less) symbol in the lexical root entry. For example, in the analysis of /ĵaamuus/ in Fig. 6.5(d), assume that R5 wrongly applied to the first subsequence yielding the analysis in Fig. 6.6(a). The right-lexical context of R5 requires that the next symbol in the pattern should be $\sigma_{\mu\mu}$. R4 then applies to the second bimoraic syllable, yielding Fig. 6.6(b). By virtue of the right-lexical context of R4, what follows must have σ_x in the pattern that is only sanctioned by R1 as in Fig. 6.6(c). However, R1 will fail since it cannot find a consonant in the root; all the consonants of /ĵaamuus/ have been exhausted.

It is worth noting that by setting the lexical contexts in R3–R6 as shown above, the rules implicitly ensure that (i) HL templates are not allowed, and (ii) the minimal and maximal constraints are respected (see Section 2.2).

So far the boundary symbol, β, has been ignored. Rules R7 and R8 (below) fulfill this task. The former applies to atemplatic stems; the latter applies to templatic ones.

$$\text{R7}\quad \begin{array}{ccccccc} \text{X} & - & \beta & - & * & \Rightarrow \\ * & - & \varepsilon & - & * & \end{array}$$

$$\text{R8}\quad \begin{array}{ccccccc} \langle \sigma_x,\text{C},* \rangle & - & \langle \beta,\beta,\beta \rangle & - & * & \Rightarrow \\ \text{C} & - & \varepsilon & - & * & \end{array}$$

where X $\neq \beta$ as before.

As for spreading, note that intrasyllabic spreading is dealt with implicitly in R4 and R6 above. Intersyllabic spreading requires additional rules:

$$\text{R9}\quad \begin{array}{ccccccc} \langle \text{S},*,\text{V} \rangle & - & \langle \sigma_{\mu},\text{C},\varepsilon \rangle & - & * & \Rightarrow \\ * & - & \text{CV} & - & * & \end{array}$$

$$\text{R10}\quad \begin{array}{ccccccc} \langle \text{S},*,\text{V} \rangle & - & \langle \sigma_{\mu\mu},\text{C},\varepsilon \rangle & - & * & \Rightarrow \\ * & - & \text{CVV} & - & * & \end{array}$$

x	a	a	t	a	m	β	L
0	0	0	0	0	0	7	
x	a	a	t	a	m		S

(a)

ĵ	u	n	d	u	b	β	L
0	0	0	0	0	0	7	
ĵ	u	n	d	u	b		S

(b)

Fig. 6.7. Lexical-surface analyses of atemplatic stems: (a) /xaatam/; (b) /ĵundub/. Segments are usually mapped onto the surface by the identity rule R0. S = surface, L = lexical.

R9 takes care of spreading in monomoraic syllables mapping lexical $\langle\sigma_\mu$,C,$\varepsilon\rangle$ to surface CV. Similarly, R10 handles spreading in bimoraic syllables mapping lexical $\langle\sigma_{\mu\mu}$,C,$\varepsilon\rangle$ to surface CVV. In both rules, the value of the vowel V is determined from the left-lexical context. Note that since the maximal constraint states that Arabic nominals are at most two syllables, no asterisk is required after the tuple in the left-lexical context, unlike the case of spreading rules in CV grammars (see R5 and R6 on p. 96). Examples of spreading and the deletion of the boundary symbol β are given in Fig. 6.5(f) and (g).

Atemplatic stems are simply entered in sublexicon 1. They surface by means of the identity rule R0 as depicted in Fig. 6.7.

6.3 The Affixational Approach

Contrary to the previous two models, the affixational approach (see Section 2.3) argues for a different analysis of Arabic morphology. This will be exemplified by analyzing the Arabic perfect verb per Table 6.1.

Recall (Section 2.3) that the affixational approach assumes that Arabic measure 1, /katab/, has the moraic template in Fig. 6.8. The rest of the measures are derived from this template by means of affixation, for example, {n} + measure 1 $\rightarrow$ /nkatab/ (measure 7). The syncope rule

$$V \rightarrow \epsilon \ / \ \#CVC\_\_\_ \ CVC\#$$

applies to measures 4 and 10: {ʔa} + /katab/ $\rightarrow$ */ʔakatab/ $\rightarrow$ /ʔaktab/ (measure 4); similarly, {sta} + /katab/ $\rightarrow$ */stakatab/ $\rightarrow$ /staktab/ (measure 10).

Measure-specific rules are required for deriving the remaining measures. For instance, /ktatab/ (measure 8) is derived by the affixation of a {t} to the passive base template /katab/ under negative prosodic circumscription (see Section 2.3),

Fig. 6.8. Arabic measure 1 base template from which other measures are derived.

whereas /kattab/ (measure 2) is derived by prefixing a mora to the base template under negative prosodic circumscription. The form /kaatab/ (measure 3) is derived by prefixing the base template with μ. Finally, measures 5 and 6 are derived by prefixing {ta} to measures 2 and 3, respectively. Rare measures are considered atemplatic and are entered in the lexicon.

6.3.1 Lexicon

The sample affixational lexicon maintains four sublexica. Sublexicon 1 gives the base template

$$\sigma_\mu \sigma_\mu \sigma_x \begin{bmatrix} \textsf{pattern} \\ \text{MEASURE} = \{1,2,3,4,5,6,7,8,10\} \end{bmatrix}$$

which applies to all but rare measures. Verbs belonging to rare measures are entered in this sublexicon as well:

$$\text{swadad} \begin{bmatrix} \textsf{verb} \\ \text{MEASURE} = 9 \\ \text{VOICE} = \text{act} \end{bmatrix}$$

and

$$\text{ħmuurir} \begin{bmatrix} \textsf{verb} \\ \text{MEASURE} = 11 \\ \text{VOICE} = \text{pass} \end{bmatrix}$$

from the roots {swd} "notion of black" and {ħmr} "notion of red," respectively (Wright, 1988).[3]

Sublexica 2 and 3 maintain roots and vocalisms as in previous models. Sublexicon 4 provides the verbal affix morphemes. For example, the measure 7 affix is

$$\text{n} \begin{bmatrix} \textsf{affix} \\ \text{MEASURE} = 7 \end{bmatrix}$$

Vowels in affixes are entered as variables to account for active and passive stems. For example, having the affix of measure 4 in the form

$$\text{ʔV} \begin{bmatrix} \textsf{affix} \\ \text{MEASURE} = 4 \end{bmatrix}$$

allows for active /ʔaktab/ and passive /ʔuktib/. The same applies to the affixes of measures 4, 5, 6, and 10. (The value of [V] will be instantiated from rewrite rules, as will be shown shortly.)

Although it would have been possible to place such affixational morphemes in sublexicon 1, they were given in their own sublexicon to illustrate that the number of sublexica is not language dependent; rather, it is grammar dependent.

3 All rare forms surface with prosthetic ʔV; in measures 9 and 11, final CVC# $\rightarrow$ CC.

6.3.2 *Rewrite Rules*

Each lexical expression in the affixational rewrite rules is a quadruple that maps pattern, root, vocalism, and affix segments, respectively, to surface segments. For example, the rules

$$\text{R1}\quad \begin{array}{ccccc} * & - & \langle \sigma_x,\mathrm{C},\varepsilon,\varepsilon\rangle & - & \langle \beta,\beta,\beta,\beta\rangle \\ * & - & \mathrm{C} & - & * \end{array} \quad \Rightarrow$$

$$\text{R2}\quad \begin{array}{ccccc} * & - & \langle \sigma_\mu,\mathrm{C},\mathrm{V},\varepsilon\rangle & - & * \\ * & - & \mathrm{CV} & - & * \end{array} \quad \Rightarrow$$

sanction extrametrical consonants and monomoraic syllables, respectively, along the lines of their counterparts in Section 6.2.2. Similarly, boundary symbol segments are handled by rule R3 (cf. R8 on p. 101),

$$\text{R3}\quad \begin{array}{ccccc} \langle \sigma_x,\mathrm{C},*,*\rangle & - & \langle \beta,\beta,\beta,\beta\rangle & - & * \\ \mathrm{C} & - & \varepsilon & - & * \end{array} \quad \Rightarrow$$

while spreading is handled by R4 (cf. R9 on p. 101),

$$\text{R4}\quad \begin{array}{ccccc} \langle \sigma_\mu,*,\mathrm{V},*\rangle\ * & - & \langle \sigma_\mu,\mathrm{C},\varepsilon,\varepsilon\rangle & - & \sigma_x \\ * & - & \mathrm{CV} & - & * \end{array} \quad \Rightarrow$$

The only difference between the above rules and those in Section 6.2.2 is the use of the fourth affix lexical expression here. Such affix segments are mapped to the surface by rule R5:

$$\text{R5}\quad \begin{array}{ccccc} * & - & \langle \varepsilon,\varepsilon,\varepsilon,\mathrm{A}\rangle & - & * \\ * & - & \mathrm{A} & - & * \end{array} \quad \Rightarrow$$

The rule maps an affix character from the fourth sublexicon to the surface, where $\mathrm{A} \in \Sigma_a$ denotes the affix alphabet. The first five rules are illustrated in the analysis of /nkatab/ (measure 7) in Fig. 6.9(a).

The syncope used in the derivation of /ʔaktab/ (measure 4) and /staktab/ (measure 10) is represented by rule R6:

$$\text{R6}\quad \begin{array}{ccccc} * & - & \langle \sigma_\mu,\mathrm{C},\mathrm{V},\varepsilon\rangle & - & * \\ \mathrm{C}_1\mathrm{V} & - & \mathrm{C} & - & \mathrm{C}_2\mathrm{V}_1\mathrm{C}_3 \end{array} \quad \Leftrightarrow$$

(Here again, the subscripts denote distinct variables, with the Cs in Σ_c and the Vs in Σ_v.) The center of the rule is similar to that of R2 above, except that the vowel is deleted on the surface in the given context. Note that the [V] segment in the left-surface context must match with the [V] segment in LEX, ensuring that the vowel of the affix has the same quality as that of the stem. For example, after R5 is applied on the affix of measure 4, the analysis in Fig. 6.9(b) is obtained, with the value of the [V] segment uninstantiated. When R6 is applied, the value of [V] gets instantiated from the stem vowel: [a] in case of /ʔaktab/ and [u] in case of /ʔuktib/ as depicted in Fig. 6.9(c) and (d).

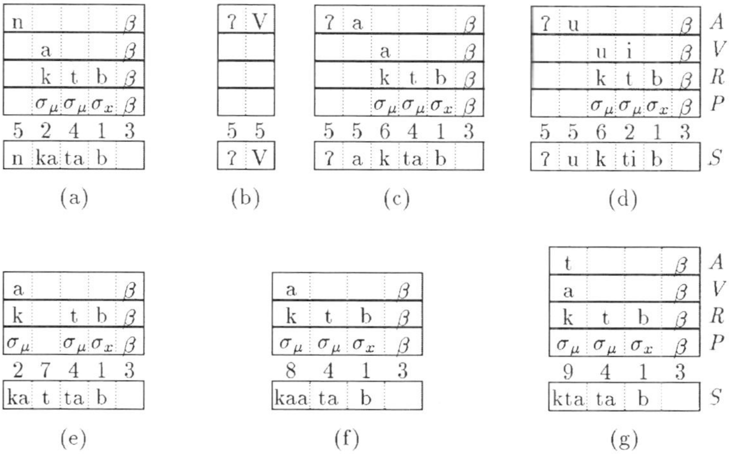

Fig. 6.9. Examples of surface-lexical analyses in the affixational model: (a) /nkatab/; (c) /ʔaktab/; (d) /ʔuktib/; (e) /kattab/; (f) /kaatab/; (g) /ktatab/. *S* = surface, *P* = pattern, *R* = root, *V* = vocalism, *A* = affix.

The rest of the rules are measure specific and illustrate the use of categories to constrain the usage of rules. Each rule is associated with a category that ensures that the rule is applied only to the proper measure. For example, the following rule handles passive /kuttib/ (measure 2) and /tukuttib/ (measure 5):

$$\text{R7}\quad \begin{array}{lllllll} \langle\sigma_\mu, \mathrm{C}_1, \mathrm{V}_1, *\rangle & - & \varepsilon & - & \langle\sigma_\mu, \mathrm{C}, *, *\rangle & \Rightarrow \\ \quad * & - & \mathrm{C} & - & \quad * & \\ \multicolumn{6}{l}{\text{Cat: } \left[\begin{array}{l} \texttt{pattern} \\ \text{MEASURE} = \{2,5\} \end{array}\right]} \end{array}$$

Recall (see p. 41) that measure 2 is derived by the doubling of the [t] and is handled by prefixing a mora to the base template under negative prosodic circumscription. The operation is 'prefix μ' and the parsing function is $\Phi_{(\sigma_\mu,\texttt{left})}$. The rule above represents the operation 'prefix μ' and the parsing function by placing the kernel /ku/ in the left-lexical context and the residue /tib/ in the right-lexical context, and inserting a consonant [C] (representing μ) on the surface. The filling of μ by the spreading of the adjacent consonant is achieved by the matching of [C] in SURF and the right-lexical context. The analysis of measure 2 is depicted in Fig. 6.9(e).

Forms /kuutib/ (measure 3) and /takaatab/ (measure 6) are sanctioned by the rule

$$\text{R8}\quad \begin{array}{lllllll} * & - & \langle\sigma_\mu, \mathrm{C}, \mathrm{V}, \varepsilon\rangle & - & \sigma_\mu & \Rightarrow \\ * & - & \mathrm{CVV} & - & * & \\ \multicolumn{6}{l}{\text{Cat: } \left[\begin{array}{l} \texttt{pattern} \\ \text{MEASURE} = \{3,6\} \end{array}\right]} \end{array}$$

Recall (see p. 41) that measure 3 is derived by prefixing the base template with μ. The rule above models the prefixation of a μ by spreading the vowel [V] in the lexical expression into VV in the surface expression. The right-lexical context ensures that this applies only to the first syllable of the template. The analysis of measure 3 is illustrated in Fig. 6.9(f).

Finally, /ktutib/ (measure 8) is derived by the rule

$$\text{R9}\quad \begin{array}{llllll} * & - & \langle\sigma_\mu,\text{C,V,A}\rangle & - & \sigma_\mu & \Rightarrow \\ * & - & \text{CAV} & - & * & \\ \multicolumn{6}{l}{\text{Cat: } \left[\begin{array}{l}\text{pattern} \\ \text{MEASURE} = 8\end{array}\right]} \end{array}$$

Recall (see p. 41) that /ktutib/ is derived by the affixation of a {t} to the passive base template /kutib/ under negative prosodic circumscription. The operation here is 'prefix {t}' and the parsing function is $\Phi_{(\texttt{C,left})}$, where C stands for consonant. The rule above represents the operation 'prefix {t}' and the parsing function. Since the [t] is inserted within the syllable CV, the rule sanctions the syllable and inserts the [t] at the same time, as depicted in Fig. 6.9(g).

6.4 The Broken Plural

Recall (Section 2.4) that the broken plural is derived from singular stems. This is supported by the following two observations. First, the length of the final syllable vowel (shown in boldface type in the following examples) is carried from the singular to the plural, for example, /ĵund**u**b/ → /ĵanaad**i**b/, /ṣulṭ**aa**n/ → /ṣalaaṭ**ii**n/. Second, the number of syllables in the plural depends on the number of morae in the singular; bimoraic stems form bisyllabic plurals, and longer stems form trisyllabic plurals. Additionally, recall that triconsonantal singulars with a long vowel require the insertion of [w], realized as [ʔ] under certain phonological conditions (McCarthy and Prince, 1990a, p. 218). Because singular forms are derived from

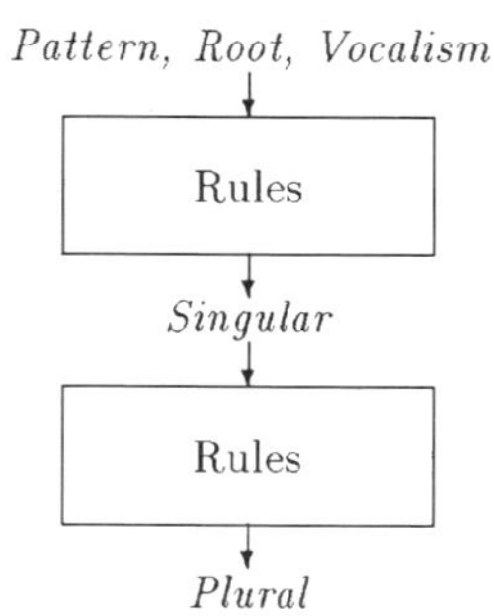

Fig. 6.10. Cascade model for handling the broken plurals. The first set of rules maps patterns, roots, and vocalisms into singular stems. The second set of rules maps singular stems into their plural counterparts.

Fig. 6.11. Iambic template for the broken plural.

pattern, root, and vocalism morphemes, the derivation of the broken plural is performed in two stages. The first stage maps lexical entries (i.e., patterns, roots, and vocalisms) into singular forms. The second stage maps singular stems into plurals. This is illustrated in Fig. 6.10. In the following discussion, plurals are derived from the singular nominal forms derived above, using the moraic approach as in Section 6.2.

Also recall (Section 2.4) that the broken plural is derived by means of positive prosodic circumscription. A singular noun is parsed into kernel that consists of the first two morae, and a residue (the remainder of the singular form). The kernel maps onto the plural iambic template, repeated in Fig. 6.11. The residue is then added and the plural melody {ai} overwrites the singular one.

The analysis of the data at hand is given in Table 6.3. The plus sign in the final column separates the kernel (after applying it to the iambic template) from the residue (after applying the plural vowel melody on it).

6.4.1 *Trisyllabic Plurals*

Trisyllabic plurals are derived from singular stems that consist of more than two morae. This is achieved by devoting one rule for the kernel and another for the residue. The rules must account for three types of kernels: CVC, CVV, and CVCV.

When the kernel is a CVC sequence (e.g., /ĵun/ of /ĵundub/), the following rule is applied:

$$\text{R1} \quad \begin{array}{ccccccc} * & - & C_1V_1C_2 & - & CV_2 & \Leftrightarrow \\ * & - & C_1aC_2aa & - & * & \end{array}$$

Table 6.3. *Parsing of the singular into kernel and residue, from which the plural is derived*

	Singular	Kernel	Residue	Plural
(a)	nafs	naf	s	nufuu + s
(b)	raĵul	raĵu	l	riĵaa + l
	ʔasad	ʔasa	d	ʔusuu + d
(c)	ĵaziir	ĵazi	ir	ĵazaa + ʔir
(d)	ĵaamuus	ĵaa	muus	ĵawaa + miis
(e)	sulṭaan	sul	ṭaan	salaa + ṭiin
(f)	xaatam	xaa	tam	xawaa + tim
(g)	ĵundub	ĵun	dub	ĵanaa + dib

ĵun	d	u	b	*S*
1	0	2	0	
ĵanaa	d	i	b	*P*

(a)

sul	ṭ	a	a	n	*S*
1	0	2	2	0	
salaa	ṭ	i	i	n	*P*

(b)

xaa	t	a	m	*S*
3	0	2	0	
xawaa	t	i	m	*P*

(c)

ĵaa	m	u	u	s	*S*
3	0	2	2	0	
ĵawaa	m	i	i	s	*P*

(d)

ĵazi		i	r	*S*
4	5	2	0	
ĵazaa	ʔ	i	r	*P*

(e)

Fig. 6.12. Singular–plural mapping of Arabic trisyllabic nominals, using the broken plural paradigm; *S* = singular, *P* = plural: (a) /ĵanaadib/; (b) /salaaṭiin/; (c) /xawaatim/; (d) /ĵawaamiis/; (e) /ĵazaaʔir/.

The rule maps the kernel to the iambic template /CaCaa/. By virtue of the right-lexical context, this only takes place at the first syllable (i.e., kernel) of the stem since singulars are maximally bisyllabic. (As before, subscripts are used to denote distinct variables, with the Cs in Σ_c and the Vs in Σ_v.)

The consonantal segments of the residue (e.g., /dub/ of /ĵundub/) surface without any modification by the identity rule. The vowels, however, have to be mapped onto the plural vowel melody, that is, the second segment of {ai}, since the first segment appears in the plural iambic template of R1. This is achieved by the rule

$$\text{R2}\quad \begin{array}{ccccccc} * & - & \mathrm{V} & - & * & \Leftrightarrow \\ \mathrm{C_1aC_2aa}\ * & - & \mathrm{i} & - & * & \end{array}$$

which maps any vowel in the residue to the plural vowel [i]. The left-surface context ensures that this only takes place following the iambic result of R1. This is illustrated in the analysis of /ĵanaadib/ in Fig. 6.12(a). The asterisk in the left-surface context states that there may be intervening material between the iambic result and the vowel of the residue (e.g., [d] in this case). Additionally, the asterisk allows a second vowel, if present, to undergo this rule as well. This is the case, for example, in the derivation of /salaaṭiin/ in Fig. 6.12(b).

When the kernel consists of a CVV sequence (e.g., /xaa/ in /xaatam/), the following rule applies:

$$\text{R3}\quad \begin{array}{cccccc} * & - & \mathrm{C_1V_1V_1} & - & \mathrm{CV_2} & \Leftrightarrow \\ * & - & \mathrm{C_1awaa} & - & * & \end{array}$$

It maps the CVV sequence to the iambic template and takes care of inserting the default [w]. This is illustrated for /xawaatim/ and /ĵawaamiis/ in Fig. 6.12(c) and (d).

Finally, when the kernel consists of a CVCV sequence (e.g., /ĵazi/ in /ĵaziir/), the following rule applies:

$$\text{R4}\quad \begin{array}{ccccccc} * & - & C_1V_1C_2V_2 & - & V_2 & \Leftrightarrow \\ * & - & C_1aC_2aa & - & * & \end{array}$$

The rule maps the kernel segments to the iambic template as illustrated in Fig. 6.12(e). In this example, the residue requires the insertion of the default [w], which (in this context) becomes [ʔ]. This is achieved by the following rule:

$$\text{R5}\quad \begin{array}{ccccccc} * & - & \epsilon & - & * & \Leftrightarrow \\ C_1aC_2aa & - & ʔ & - & VC & \end{array}$$

The surface contexts ensure that this mapping only takes place in the proper place.

6.4.2 Bisyllabic Plurals

Bisyllabic plurals are derived from bimoraic singular stems. These differ from the above in that the vowel melody of the plural is encoded in the lexicon with each singular entry. In the current analysis, we assume a lexicon that consists of two sublexica. Sublexicon 1 contains singular stems where each entry is associated with a category that indicates the relevant plural vowel melody. For example, /raĵul/ "man" has the plural melody {ia} as in /riĵaal/ "men"; its entry in the lexicon would be

$$\text{raĵul}\begin{bmatrix} \text{noun} \\ \text{PLURAL VOWEL} = \text{ia} \end{bmatrix}$$

The vowel melody itself is entered in sublexicon 2:

$$\text{ia}\begin{bmatrix} \text{vocalism} \\ \text{PLURAL VOWEL} = \text{ia} \end{bmatrix}$$

There are two types of plural vocalisms: those that consist of two segments as {ia} above, and those that consist of only one segment as

$$\text{u}\begin{bmatrix} \text{vocalism} \\ \text{PLURAL VOWEL} = \text{u} \end{bmatrix}$$

which spread in the plurals as in /ʔusuud/ "lions."

The first rule (below) applies to CVC kernels (e.g., /qad/ cf /qadħ/) with two-segment vocalisms (e.g., {ia} in /qidaaħ/):

$$\text{R1}\quad \begin{array}{ccccccc} * & - & \langle C_1V_sC_2, V_1V_2\rangle & - & C_3 & \Leftrightarrow \\ * & - & C_1V_1C_2V_2V_2 & - & * & \end{array}$$

(a)		(b)		(c)		(d)		
ia		u		ia		u		*V*
qad	ħ	naf	s	raĵu	l	ʔasa	d	*S*
1	0	2	0	3	0	4	0	
qidaa	ħ	nufuu	s	riĵaa	l	ʔusuu	d	*P*

Fig. 6.13. Singular–plural analyses of the bisyllabic broken plurals: (a) /qidaah/; (b) /nufuus/; (c) /riĵaal/; (d) /ʔusuud/. The upper expression gives the plural melody of the singular form in question; P = plural, S = singular, V = plural vocalism.

It maps the kernel to the plural iambic template, taking the values of the vowels from the vocalism sublexicon as illustrated in Fig 6.13(a). V_s in Σ_v denotes a singular vowel that is ignored on the surface, for example, [a] of /qadħ/.

The second rule applies to the same kernel, but with one-segment vocalisms (e.g., {u} in /nufuus/):

$$\text{R2} \quad \begin{array}{ccccccc} * & - & \langle C_1 V_s C_2, V_1 \rangle & - & C_3 & \Leftrightarrow \\ * & - & C_1 V_1 C_2 V_1 V_1 & - & * & \end{array}$$

It spreads the vocalism segment throughout the iambic template as in Fig 6.13(b).

CVCV kernels (e.g. /raĵu/ in /raĵul/) require two similar rules:

$$\text{R3} \quad \begin{array}{ccccccc} * & - & \langle C_1 V_{s_1} C_{2 s_2} V_{s_2}, V_1 V_2 \rangle & - & C_3 & \Leftrightarrow \\ * & - & C_1 V_1 C_2 V_2 V_2 & - & * & \end{array}$$

$$\text{R4} \quad \begin{array}{ccccccc} * & - & \langle C_1 V_{s_1} C_{2 s_3} V_{s_2}, V_1 \rangle & - & C_3 & \Leftrightarrow \\ * & - & C_1 V_1 C_2 V_1 V_1 & - & * & \end{array}$$

R3 applies to two-segment vocalisms (e.g., {ia} in /riĵaal/), whereas R4 applies to one-segment vocalisms (e.g., {u} in /ʔusuud/). Examples appear in Fig 6.13(c) and (d).

6.5 Issues in Developing Semitic Systems

When developing Semitic grammars, one comes across various issues and problems that normally do not arise with linear grammars. This section aims at pointing out some of these issues.

6.5.1 Linear versus Nonlinear Grammars

Nonlinearity in Semitic occurs mainly in the stem. Consider the Arabic stem /katab/ "to write." Unlike the nonlinear process of deriving it from lexical forms (pattern, root, and vocalism), prefixation and suffixation applies to it in a linear fashion. Hence, the prefix {wa} "and" is applied, resulting in /wakatab/ in a straightforward manner.

Using the nonlinear model is crucial for developing Semitic systems, as has been shown. Not only does it accurately represent the linguistic insights about the templatic nonlinear nature of these languages, it also allows the computational linguist to compile efficient, relatively small morphological lexica. However, maintaining a nonlinear lexical representation in rewrite rules has its own inconveniences and computational complexities. First, the grammar writer must keep track of multiple lexical representations (three in the case of Semitic as opposed to one for English), which makes writing grammars an arduous task. Second, rules that describe one phonological–orthographic phenomenon must be duplicated in order to account for the nonlinear nature of the stem, as well as the linear nature of segments present in prefixes and suffixes. Third, there is the issue of space complexity once rewrite rules are compiled into multitape automata, as will be described in the next chapter: although the space complexity for transitions of an automaton with respect to the number of tapes is linear, space can become costly for huge machines, especially those whose number of transitions exceeds by far the number of states, a typical characteristic of rule automata.

What is desired is a schema with which one can maintain the nonlinear lexical representation in templatic stems, yet allow for a linear model for representing phonological–orthographic and other script-related rules. Such rules are in fact linear and need not be made complex on the account of the nonlinear templatic phenomenon of stems.

In what follows, a description of the inconveniences that arise when nonlinear grammars are used to describe linear phenomena is outlined, followed by a solution based on linearization.

6.5.1.1 *Inconveniences of Nonlinear Grammar in Describing Linear Operations*

Surface-to-lexical mappings must account for phonological and orthographic processes. In fact, for many languages, the phonological and orthographic rules tend to be more numerous than the morphological rules. This applies to Semitic as well. For example, the Syriac grammar reported by Kiraz (1996b) contains approximately 50 rules. Only six rules (a mere 12.5%) are motivated by templatic morphology. The rest are phonological and orthographic. Had the grammar been more exhaustive, the percentage would be much smaller because most additions to the rules would be in the domain of phonology–orthography, rather than templatic morphology.

Consider the derivation of Syriac /ktab/ from the morphemes {cvcvc} (in some sublexicon 1), {ktb} (in some sublexicon 2), and {aa}[4] (in some sublexicon 3). The three morphemes produce the underlying form */katab/, which surfaces as /ktab/ because short vowels in open unstressed syllables are deleted in Syriac. The process of derivation is shown schematically in Fig. 6.14.

[4] For simplicity, we will not deal with issues of spreading here. The vocalism is entered as {aa}. For describing spreading, see Section 6.1.2.

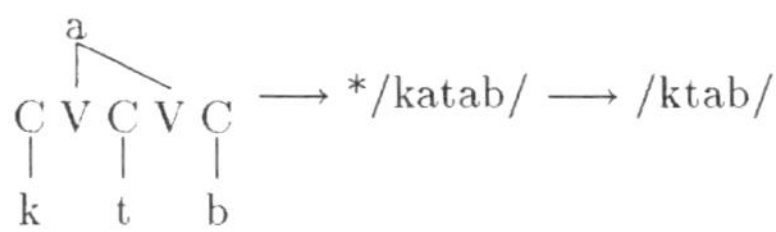

Fig. 6.14. Derivation of Syriac /ktab/. The nonlinear autosegmental configuration produces the underlying stem */katab/. The first vowel [a] is then deleted to produce the surface form. The latter operation is linear.

The following two rules make use of three lexical expressions and sanction stem consonants and vowels:

$$\begin{array}{lccccccc} & * & - & \langle \mathrm{c,C,}\varepsilon \rangle & - & * & \Rightarrow \\ \mathrm{R1} & * & - & \mathrm{C} & - & * & \\ & \multicolumn{6}{l}{\text{where } \mathrm{C} \in \{\mathrm{k,t,b}\}} \end{array}$$

$$\begin{array}{lcccccc} \multirow{2}{*}{R2} & * & - & \langle \mathrm{v,}\varepsilon\mathrm{,a} \rangle & - & * & \Rightarrow \\ & * & - & \mathrm{a} & - & * & \end{array}$$

The obligatory deletion of the first [a] in the stem is given in the following rule:

$$\begin{array}{lcccccc} & * & - & \langle \mathrm{v,}\varepsilon\mathrm{,a} \rangle & - & \langle \mathrm{cv,C,a} \rangle & \Leftrightarrow \\ \mathrm{R3} & * & - & \epsilon & - & * & \\ & \multicolumn{6}{l}{\text{where } \mathrm{C} \in \{\mathrm{k,t,b}\}} \end{array}$$

The right context of the above rule ensures that this takes place only in open syllables that are also nonfinal.[5]

The rules applies right to left; hence, when the object pronominal suffix {eh} "MASC 3RD SING" is added, the second vowel is deleted; */katabeh/ → /katbeh/. Similarly, prefixing the conjunction morpheme {wa} results in */wakatab/ → /waktab/ (first stem vowel is deleted), and */wakatabeh/ → /wkatbeh/ (prefix vowel and second stem vowel are deleted).

By virtue of its right-lexical context ⟨cv,C,a⟩, R3 can only apply to the *first* stem vowel, as illustrated in the derivation of /ktab/ from the underlying */katab/ by the deletion of the first vowel in Fig. 6.15(a).

Another rule (R4 below) is required for deriving → /katbeh/ from */katab/ and the suffix {eh}, where the *second* stem vowel is deleted by the same phonological phenomenon.

$$\begin{array}{lcccccc} \multirow{2}{*}{R4} & * & - & \langle \mathrm{v,}\varepsilon\mathrm{,a} \rangle & - & \langle \mathrm{cV,C,}\varepsilon \rangle & \Leftrightarrow \\ & * & - & \epsilon & - & * & \end{array}$$

where C is a consonant and V is a vowel as before. The centers of R3 and R4 are identical. The difference lies in the right-lexical context expression ⟨cV,C,ε⟩,

[5] This is a simplification of the actual phonological rule; it assumes that no suffixes follow the stem. For exceptions to this rule, see Section 6.5.3.

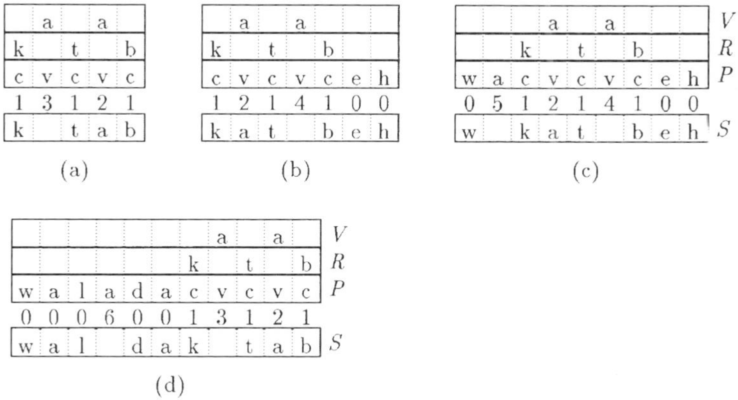

Fig. 6.15. Examples of the Syriac vowel deletion rule: (a) the deleted vowel and the right context segments belong to the stem; (b) the deleted vowel belongs to the stem, while the context segments belong to the suffix; (c) the first deleted vowel belongs to the prefix while the context belongs to the stem; (d) the first deleted vowel as well as the context belong to the prefix.

where the suffix vowel [V] appears in the first lexical expression. The analysis is illustrated in Fig. 6.15(b).

This does not resolve the entire problem. Both R3 and R4 fail when the deleted vowel itself appears in the prefix, for example, /wakatbeh/ → /wkatbeh/ (with the prefix {wa}). Yet another rule (R5 below) is required to handles this case:

$$\text{R5} \quad \begin{array}{ccccccc} * & - & \text{a} & - & \langle \text{cv,C,a} \rangle & \Leftrightarrow \\ * & - & \epsilon & - & * & \end{array}$$

Here, the right context ⟨cv,C,a⟩ belongs to the nonlinear stem as shown in Fig. 6.15(c). Still, one needs another rule (R6 below) in order to delete prefix vowels when the right context belongs to a (possibly another) linear prefix, for example, prefixing the sequence {wa} "and," {la} "to," and {da} "of" to the stem */katab/ giving /waldaktab/ (the [a] of {la} and the first stem vowel are deleted), as illustrated in Fig. 6.15(d).

$$\text{R6} \quad \begin{array}{cccccc} * & - & \text{a} & - & \text{CV} & \Leftrightarrow \\ * & - & \epsilon & - & * & \end{array}$$

The above examples clearly illustrate the proliferation that would result in maintaining large nonlinear grammars. It is worth noting that such phonological rules do not depend on the nonlinear lexical structure of the stem. They actually apply on the morphologically derived stem (e.g., Syriac */katab/). Semitic, then, maintains at least the following strata: lexical-morphological (where the lexical representation is nonlinear) and morphological-surface (where both representations are linear).

w	a	l	a	d	a	k	a	t	a	b
0	0	0	7	0	0	0	7	0	0	0
w	a	l		d	a	k		t	a	b

(a)

w	a	l	a	d	a	k	a	t	a	b	e	h
0	7	0	0	0	7	0	0	0	7	0	0	0
w		l	a	d		k	a	t		b	e	h

(b)

Fig. 6.16. Mapping from a linearized lexical form (the upper expression) to the surface (the lower expression): (a) /waldaktab/ and (b) /wladkatbeh/.

6.5.1.2 *The Best of Both Worlds: Linearization*

A better framework for computational Semitic morphology divides the lexical-surface mappings into two separate problems. The first handles the templatic nature of morphology, mapping the multiple lexical representation into a *linearized lexical form*. This linearized form maintains the same linguistic information of the original lexical representation, and it somewhat corresponds to McCarthy's notion of tier conflation (see p. 70).

The second takes care of phonological–orthographic–graphemic mappings between the linearized lexical form and the actual surface. Its input is the output of the first grammar, that is, the linearized lexical form such as Syriac */katab/, */waladakatab/, and so on. When compiled into finite-state machinary (described in the next chapter), the combined effect is mathematically the composition of the two machines representing the two sets of rules.

Since R3–R6 above represent one phonological phenomenon, namely, the deletion of a short vowel in a nonfinal open syllable, they can be combined into the following rule:

R7	*	–	a	–	CV	⇔
	*	_		_	*	

Applying this rule on linearized lexical forms is illustrated in Fig. 6.16. (Recall that R0 is the identity rule.)

6.5.2 *Vocalization*

Recall (see Section 1.3.3) that Semitic texts appear in three forms: consonantal texts that do not incorporate any vowels but *matres lectionis*, partially vocalized texts that incorporate some vowels to clarify ambiguity, and vocalized texts that incorporate full vocalization.

Handling all such forms can be resolved in line with the previous discussion on linearization. The grammar writer should assume that the surface text is fully vocalized when writing grammars. This will not only get rid of the duplicated rules for the same phonological–orthographic phenomenon, but it will also make understanding and debugging rules an easier task. Once a lexical-surface rewrite system has been achieved, a set of rules that optionally delete vowel segments can be specified and composed with the entire system.

w	a	l	d	a	k	t	a	b	*Vocalized Form*
0	8	0	0	0	0	0	8	0	
w		l	d	a	k	t		b	*Optionally Vocalized From*

Fig. 6.17. Optional deletion of short vowels (and other diacritic marks). In this example, the second [a] is retained while the rest are deleted.

Building on the previous example, the following optional rule allows for the deletion of short vowels:

$$\text{R8} \quad \begin{matrix} * & - & V_{sh} & - & * \\ * & - & \varepsilon & - & * \end{matrix} \quad \Leftrightarrow$$

where V_{sh} denotes short vowels (and in practical applications other diacritic symbols). The application of the rule to the output of Fig. 6.16 is illustrated in Fig. 6.17.

6.5.3 Diachronic Exceptions

The grammar writer may wish to express rules for diachronic phenomena that contradict the synchronic description of a language. The Syriac vowel deletion rule (R3 above), for example, does not apply to plural forms in early Syriac texts. Thus, one can find the forms /ktabūn/ "to write – PERF PL 3RD MASC" and /ktabēyn/ "to write – PERF PL 3RD FEM" (which retain the [a]).

Such problems can be handled by using rule categories in the following manner. The deletion rule is associated with a category such as

$$\begin{bmatrix} \text{pattern} \\ \vdots \\ \text{DIACHRONIC} = \text{no} \end{bmatrix}$$

Diachronic patterns in the lexicon are associated with the category

$$\begin{bmatrix} \text{pattern} \\ \vdots \\ \text{DIACHRONIC} = \text{yes} \end{bmatrix}$$

Since the feature values contradict each other, the deletion will not apply to diachronic patterns allowing /ktabūn/ to surface. The grammar writer, of course, may wish to place the constraints on other lexical morphemes.

In some cases, a diachronic phenomenon may be still present synchronically. Consider, for example, the shift in quality of the vowel in Syriac */katab/ followed by the suffix {et} $\longrightarrow$ */katabet/ $\longrightarrow$ /ketbet/ (where the first [a] is shifted to [e] and the second [a] is deleted according to the vowel deletion rule mentioned earlier). This can also be achieved by rule features. Building on the previous rules, one can add the rule

$$\begin{array}{ccccccc} \text{c} & - & \langle \text{v},\varepsilon,\text{a} \rangle & - & \text{cvc} & \Leftrightarrow \\ * & - & \text{e} & - & * & \end{array}$$

$$\text{Cat: } \begin{bmatrix} \texttt{pattern} & & \\ \text{NUM} & = & \texttt{sing} \\ \text{PER} & = & \texttt{1st} \\ \text{GEN} & = & \texttt{com} \end{bmatrix}$$

Clearly, the rest of the description (e.g., lexicon, morphosyntax) must be modified to cater to this change.

6.5.4 Script-Related Issues

The nature of the Semitic script adds complications to computational models. Under some of the recent platforms such as the Unicode-compliant Windows 2000 and Windows XP, the operating system takes care of text input–output operations and the whole issue need not be addressed. Under most other platforms, however, the computational morphophonology system has to handle script problems.

(Shortly, the rewrite rules component will be used to resolve script problems. As Semitic is written from right to left, the left context in a rewrite rule actually indicates what precedes the affected segment on the *right* in the script. Similarly, the right context in a rewrite rule refers to what follows the affected segment on the *left*. As a way to avoid such confusion, the terms *preceding context* and *following context* will be used instead.)

Syriac and Arabic are the most challenging in the Semitic family in terms of glyph shaping. Both languages use up to four glyph shapes per letter, which are called, in traditional grammars, stand alone, initial, medial, and final. An initial glyph, for example, appears when it is connected to the following letter, but not to the preceding one. Following Unicode terminology, glyphs are classified into the following types (The Unicode Consortium, 1991). The *nominal* glyph, denoted by X_n, is the basic form and does not join on either side. A *right-joining* glyph, denoted by X_r, is used when the character in question joins with the preceding character and usually has a line that extends to the right. A *left-joining* glyph, denoted by X_l, is the counterpart of the right-joining glyph in that it connects to the following character. The *dual-joining* glyph, denoted by X_d, combines right-joining and left-joining in that it connects to both neighboring characters.

To confuse matters further, letters of the alphabet fall into two classes: *dual-joining letters* employ all of the above four glyphs; *right-joining letters* only join to the right. Hence, the latter do not have the forms X_l and X_d. Figure 6.18 gives a sample from the Syriac alphabet.

Contextual analysis refers to the mechanism by which the appropriate glyph is chosen based on context. Syriac and Arabic make use of the following rules.

NAME	CLASS	LETTER	X_r X_d X_l X_n
Alaph	right-joining	?	
Beth	dual-joining	b	
Dalath	right-joining	d	
Nun	dual-joining	n	

Fig. 6.18. Examples of Syriac letters with their glyph variants. Note that Syriac is written right to left. Glyph X_n is the nominal one and is used when the character is not connected to its neighboring characters; glyph X_l connects to the following character; glyph X_d connects to both neighboring characters; and glyph X_r connects to the preceding character. Right-joining glyphs, for example, [?] and [d], connect only to the right; hence, they lack the forms X_l and X_d.

(i) A dual-joining letter X assumes the form X_r if its is preceded by another dual-joining letter and is at the end of the string. For example, in the string ⟨bn⟩ below, [n] takes an $[\text{n}]_r$ form because it is preceded by [b] (a dual-joining letter):

$\text{n} + \text{b} \quad \rightarrow \text{n}_r + \text{b}_l$

For the $[\text{b}]_l$ form, see rule (ii) below. (Because of typographical difficulties, it was not always possible to align the script line with the following transcription line.)

A right-joining letter assumes the same regardless of what follows. For example, in the string ⟨bdn⟩ below, [d] takes a $[\text{d}]_r$ form even though it is followed by another letter.

$\text{n} + \text{d} + \text{b} \rightarrow \text{n}_n + \text{d}_r + \text{b}_l$

Note that since [n] is no longer preceded by a dual-joining letter (this is so since [d] is a right-joining letter), it does not take the $[\text{n}]_r$ form in this case.

(ii) A dual-joining letter X assumes the form X_l if it is either at the beginning of the string or preceded by a right-joining letter within the string, and it is followed by another letter of either class. In the following example of the string ⟨bdn?⟩, the [b] takes a $[\text{b}]_l$ form since it is at the beginning of the string and is followed by another letter. Similarly, [n] takes the form

$[\text{n}]_l$ since it is preceded by the right-joining letter [d] and is followed by another letter.

$? + \text{n} + \text{d} + \text{b} \rightarrow\ ?_r + \text{n}_l + \text{d}_r + \text{b}_l$

Note that right-joining letters do not take the X_l form at all.

(iii) A dual-joining letter X assumes the form X_d if it is preceded by another dual-joining letter and is followed by another letter of either class. In the string ⟨bn?⟩, for example, [n] takes the form $[\text{n}]_d$.

$? + \text{n} + \text{b} \quad \rightarrow\ ?_r + \text{n}_d + \text{b}_l$

Note that right-joining letters do not take the X_d form at all.

(iv) Otherwise, a letter X assumes its default X_n form as in the string ⟨?b⟩ below.

$\text{b} +\ ? = \text{b}_n +\ ?_n$

The above rules can be modeled with a set of rewrite rules. Let Σ represent the letters of the alphabet, with $D \subset \Sigma$ representing dual-joining letters and $R \subset \Sigma$ representing right-joining letters. Further, let X_n, X_r, X_l, X_d denote the nominal, right-joining, left-joining, and dual-joining glyph versions of a letter X. The, rules for handling right-joining glyphs – that is, case (i) above – take the form

$$\text{R1} \quad \begin{array}{ccccc} D' & - & D & - & \# \\ * & - & D_r & - & * \end{array} \ \Leftrightarrow$$

$$\text{R2} \quad \begin{array}{ccccc} D' & - & R & - & * \\ * & - & R_r & - & * \end{array} \ \Leftrightarrow$$

R1 maps a dual-joining letter D to its right-joining counterpart D_r if it is preceded by another dual-joining letter D' and followed by the word boundary, #. R2 is similar but handles right-joining letters; here, anything may follow the segment in question.

The following rule takes care of left-joining glyphs – that is, case (ii) above (recall that only dual-joining letters have this form):

$$\text{R3} \quad \begin{array}{ccccc} \# \cup R & - & D & - & \Sigma \\ * & - & D_l & - & * \end{array} \ \Leftrightarrow$$

R3 maps a dual-joining letter D to its left-joining glyph D_l if it is preceded by # or a right-joining letter from R, and if it is followed by any letter (but not #).

Another rule is required to handle dual-joining glyphs – that is, case (iii) above (recall that only dual-joining letters have this form):

$$\text{R4} \quad \begin{array}{ccccc} D' & - & D & - & \Sigma \\ * & - & D_d & - & * \end{array} \ \Leftrightarrow$$

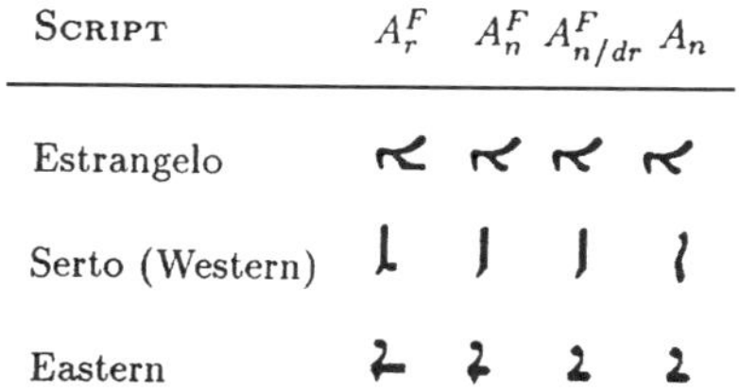

Fig. 6.19. Various forms of final ʔ in Syriac. Glyph A_n is the usual nominal form and is given here for comparison purposes. The final ʔ glyphs are as follows: $A_{n/dr}^F$ is the nominal form that follows a *Dalath* or *Rish*, A_n^F is the nominal form in all other cases, and A_r^F is the right-joining form.

R4 maps a dual-joining letter D to its dual-joining counterpart D_d if the preceding context of R1 and the following context of R3 are satisfied.

Finally, the following two rules handle nominal glyphs – that is, case (iv) above:

$$\text{R5} \quad \begin{matrix} \# \cup R & - & D & - & \# & \Leftrightarrow \\ * & - & D_n & - & * & \end{matrix}$$

$$\text{R6} \quad \begin{matrix} \# \cup R' & - & R & - & * & \Leftrightarrow \\ * & - & R_n & - & * & \end{matrix}$$

R5 (and R6) map a letter to its nominal glyph if the preceding context of R3 and the following context of R1 (and R2) are satisfied. (Note that R' is used in the preceding context of R6 merely to distinguish it from R in the center of the rule.)

Syriac poses an additional complication that is amplified by the fact that the language employs three scripts, all of which are in use: *Estrangelo* (the oldest), *Serto* (or West Syriac), and *Eastern* (i.e., East Syriac). The problem is concerned with the shape of the letter *Alaph* [ʔ] when it occurs at the end of a string. In the Serto script, a variant form appears when *Alaph* is preceded by a right-joining letter (this is the non-cursive vertical form under the A_n^F and $A_{n/dr}^F$ columns in Fig. 6.19). In the Eastern script, *Alaph* has a variant form when it is not preceded by the letters *Dalath* [d] or *Rish* [r], both of which are right joining (this is the form with the little "tail" on the bottom under the A_r^F and A_n^F columns in Fig. 6.19). The Estrangelo script does not employ a variant form at all.

In order to model this in a script-independent manner, Nelson, Kiraz, and Hasso (1988) proposed definitions for the following three classes of the final *Alaph* glyph, denoted here by A^F (in addition to the usual nominal and right-joining forms), for all three scripts:

(i) *Final post Dalath/Rish nominal*, denoted by $A_{n/dr}^F$, is the nominal form when preceded by either a *Dalath* or *Rish*.

(ii) *Final nominal*, denoted by A_n^F, is the nominal form when preceded by any right-joining letter except *Dalath* or *Rish*.

(iii) *Final right-joining*, denoted by A_r^F, is the final right-joining glyph. (Note that since *Dalath* and *Rish* are right-joining letters, they do not precede this glyph anyway.)

Case (i) above can be modeled with the following rule:

$$\text{R7} \quad \begin{matrix} \mathrm{d} \cup \mathrm{r} & - & ? & - & \# & \Leftrightarrow \\ * & - & ?^F_{n/dr} & - & * & \end{matrix}$$

The rule maps an *Alaph* to its $?^F_{n/dr}$ form when it is preceded by either [d] or [r]. The following context, that is, #, ensures that this takes place at the end of a string. In a similar manner, the R8,

$$\text{R8} \quad \begin{matrix} (R\text{-}\{\mathrm{r,d}\}) & - & ? & - & \# & \Leftrightarrow \\ * & - & ?^F_{n} & - & * & \end{matrix}$$

takes care of case (ii) above. Finally, rule R9,

$$\text{R9} \quad \begin{matrix} D & - & ? & - & \# & \Leftrightarrow \\ * & - & ?^F_{r} & - & * & \end{matrix}$$

takes care of the right-joining case (iii) above.

In order to get the desired behavior from the above rules, R7–R9 must apply before R1–R6.

This section touched upon the primary technical issues involved in developing Semitic grammars. Obviously, there are also numerous linguistic issues that have to be resolved as well before a large linguistically motivated system of any Semitic language can be implemented efficiently. Our interest here, and in the rest of this book, has been in linguistic issues that pose technical computing difficulties for handling Semitic morphology with finite-state techniques, the formal details of which are discussed in the next chapter.

7 Compilation into Multitape Automata

SIGMA STAR MUSTARD. Ingredients: Water, Distilled Vinegar, Mustard Seed, Salt, Turmeric.

From a label on a mustard product by
Sigma Star Food Corp. (New York, NY)

One must know that for the Syriac nouns there are no rigid rules, from which one can learn to form from singular and masculine nouns, plural and feminine ones. On the contrary, one must learn to understand the inflection of almost all, through means of tradition.

Elia of Ṣobha († 1049)
Syriac Grammar

Traditional rule compilers (Koskenniemi, 1986; Karttunen and Beesley, 1992; Mohri and Sproat, 1996, inter alia) compile rules into two-tape transducers. As Semitic morphology employs a complex lexical representation for pattern, root, and vocalism morphemes, the compiler presented here compiles rewrite rules into multitape automata.

The algorithms presented here assume the existence of a library of functions for creating and manipulating multitape automata with all the basic regular operators. For an example of such a library, see Kiraz and Grimley-Evans (1997), the library with which the present algorithms were implemented.

Section 7.1 introduces multitape machines and the various operations that are necessary for the compilation of rules and lexica into automata. The following three sections describe how the three components of the multitiered model of Chapter 5 are compiled into multitape automata. Finally, Section 7.5 goes through an example showing various stages of the compilation process.

7.1 Mathematical Preliminaries

The compilation of lexica and rewrite rules into finite-state automata is made possible by the mathematical concepts and tools presented by Kaplan and Kay (1994). This section introduces multitape automata, regular relations, and some necessary operations.

7.1.1 Multitape Finite-State Automata

Rabin and Scott (1959) describe a multitape finite-state automaton as follows: an n-tape automaton M has n scanning heads reading n tapes $(t_1, \ldots, t_n)$. The automaton reads for a while on one tape, then changes control and reads on another tape, and so on until all the tapes are exhausted. At this point M stops and accepts the n tapes if and only if M is in a designated final state. The change of control from one tape to another is designated by splitting the states of the automaton into n classes: the first class contains those states in which the first tape t_1 is being read, the second class contains those states in which the second tape t_2 is being read, and so on till the nth class.

Elgot and Mezei (1965) extend this notion to permit the automaton to read simultaneously from all tapes. In this version, each tape has a string over some alphabet Σ written on it, followed by an infinite succession of blanks. Starting from a designated start state, the automaton reads simultaneously the first symbol of each tape, changes state, reads simultaneously the second symbol of each tape, changes state, and so on, until it reads blank on each tape. If the automaton at this point is in a designated final state, it accepts the tuple of strings.

The multitape finite-state automata model used in the current work follows the automata described in Elgot and Mezei (1965). More formally, an *n-tape finite-state automaton* (FSA) is a 5-tuple $M = (Q, \Sigma, \delta, q_0, F)$, where Q is a finite set of *states*, Σ is a finite *input alphabet*, δ is a *transition function* mapping $Q \times (\Sigma^{\epsilon})^n$ to Q (where $\Sigma^{\epsilon} = \Sigma \cup \{\epsilon\}$ and ϵ is the empty string), $q_0 \in Q$ is the *initial state*, and $F \subseteq Q$ is a set of *final states*. An n-tape FSA accepts an n tuple of strings if and only if, starting from the initial state q_0, it can simultaneously scan all the symbols on every tape i, $1 \leq i \leq n$, and end up in a final state $q \in F$.

An *n-tape finite-state transducer* (FST) is simply an n-tape finite-state automaton but with each tape marked as to whether it belongs to the domain or range of the transduction; note, however, that transducers are bidirectional. By convention, domain tapes are written after range tapes.[1] Graphically, domain tapes are represented on top of range tapes. More formally, an n-tape finite-state transducer is a 6-tuple $M = (Q, \Sigma, \delta, q_0, F, d)$, where Q, Σ, δ, q_0 and F are as before and d, $1 \leq d < n$, is the number of *domain tapes*. The number of *range tapes* is simply $n - d$. An ϵ-free FST is an FST that does not have any ϵ-containing transitions. In other words, the transition function δ maps $Q \times \Sigma^n$ to Q.

There are two methods for interpreting transducers. When interpreted as acceptors with n tuples of symbols on each transition, their behavior is similar to multitape FSAs. When interpreted as a transduction, each of the n tuples of symbols on each transition belongs to either the domain or range of the transduction. In this sense, the transducer computes a mathematical (regular) relation.

[1] In what follows, we consider lexical symbols to be in the domain and surface symbols to be in the range of the lexical-surface relation. Since there is always only one surface symbol mapping to multiple lexical symbols in the case of Semitic, it is more convenient to write the surface symbol first.

7.1.2 Regular Relations

Parallel to regular languages in formal language theory, regular relations[2] are families of string relations over some alphabet. A *string relation* in turn is a particular collection of ordered tuples of strings over some alphabet Σ, that is, subset of $\Sigma^* \times \cdots \times \Sigma^*$.

Regular n-relations are defined along the lines of the recursive definition of regular languages (cf. p. 10) in terms of n-way concatenation over an alphabet Σ (the superscript i denotes concatenation repeated i times):

(i) The empty set and $\{a\}$ for all $a \in (\Sigma^\epsilon)^n$ are regular n relations.
(ii) If R_1, R_2, and R are regular n relations, then so are
$R_1 R_2 = \{xy \mid x \in R_1, y \in R_2\}$ (n-way concatenation)
$R_1 \cup R_2 = \{x \mid x \in R_1 \text{ or } x \in R_2\}$ (union)
$R^* = \bigcup_{i=0}^{\infty} R^i$ (Kleene closure)
(iii) There are no other regular n relations.

In this vein, the notion of regular expressions extends to the n-dimensional case. An *n-way regular expression* is a regular expression whose terms are n tuples of alphabetic symbols or the empty string ϵ. (For clarity, the elements of the n tuple are separated by colons: e.g., $a{:}b{:}c^*\ q{:}r{:}s$ describes the 3-relation $\{\langle a^k q, b^k r, c^k s\rangle \mid k \geq 0\}$.) The Kleene correspondence theorem that shows the equivalence between regular n relations, n way regular expressions, and n-tape finite-state transducers is as follows (cf. p. 18):

(i) Every n-way regular expression describes a regular n relation.
(ii) Every regular n relation is described by an n-way regular expression.
(iii) Every n-tape finite-state transducer accepts a regular n relation.
(iv) Every regular n relation is accepted by an n-tape finite-state transducer.

A *same-length regular n relation* is a regular n relation that contains only same-length n tuples of strings. Kaplan and Kay (1994) show that R is a same-length regular n relation if and only if it is accepted by an ϵ-free FST. Further, they demonstrate that regular n relations are closed under composition, while the subclass of same-length regular n relations is closed under intersection and complementation.

From now on, unless otherwise specified, "n relations" and "n tuples" are simply called "relations" and "tuples," respectively. An "n-way regular expression" is called "regular expression" if the value of n is implicit from the context. When "n-" is shown in italic, it denotes a specific integer (e.g., n-way concatenation is the concatenation of tuples of strings where each tuple consists of exactly n elements), whereas a roman "n-" simply denotes a multidimensional case

[2] Also called "transductions" by Elgot and Mezei (1965) and by Nivat (1968) and "rational" relations by Eilenberg (1974) and other earlier writers. The computational linguistics community uses the term "regular" relations (Kaplan and Kay, 1994). In what follows, we base the discussion on Kaplan and Kay (1994).

(e.g., n-way concatenation denotes concatenation over tuples of strings without a reference to how many elements the tuples contain).

7.1.3 n-Way Operations

A number of operations that will be used in the compilation of rewrite rules and lexica into automata are defined below. When an operator $\mathtt{Op}$ takes a number of arguments $(a_1, \ldots, a_k)$, the arguments are shown as a subscript, for example, $\mathtt{Op}_{(a_1,\ldots,a_k)}$; the parentheses are ignored if there is only one argument. When the operator is mentioned without reference to arguments, it appears on its own, for example, $\mathtt{Op}$.

Unless otherwise specified, operations that are defined on tuples of strings can be extended to sets of tuples and relations. For example, if S is a tuple of strings and $\mathtt{Op}(S)$ is an operator defined on S, the operator can be extended to a relation R in the following manner:

$$\mathtt{Op}(R) = \{ \mathtt{Op}(S) | S \in R \}$$

7.1.3.1 *Identity*

The identity operator is a generalization of the $\mathtt{Id}$ operation in Kaplan and Kay (1994).

Definition 7.1.1 Let L be a regular language. $\mathtt{Id}_n(L) = \{ X \mid X$ is an n tuple of the form $\langle x, \ldots, x\rangle, x \in L \}$ is the n-way identity of L. □

Construction 7.1.1 Let L be a regular language and let $M = (Q, \Sigma, \delta, q_0, F)$ be a one-tape FSA that accepts L. We can construct an n-tape FSA that accepts $\mathtt{Id}_n(L)$, $M' = (Q, \Sigma, \delta', q_0, F)$, where

$$\delta'(q, \langle a, \ldots, a\rangle) = \delta(q, a) \quad \text{for all } q \in Q \text{ and } a \in \Sigma$$

and $\langle a, \ldots, a\rangle$ is an n tuple. □

Example 7.1.1 Let $\Sigma = \{ a, b, c \}$ and L be a regular language described by the regular expression ab^*c. $\mathtt{Id}_3(L)$ is a 3-relation described by the regular expression $a{:}a{:}a\ b{:}b{:}b^*\ c{:}c{:}c$. The automata for both expressions are given in Fig. 7.1. □

Remark 7.1.1 If $\mathtt{Id}$ is applied to a string s, we simply write $\mathtt{Id}_n(s)$ to denote the n tuple $\langle s, \ldots, s\rangle$. □

7.1.3.2 *Insertion and Removal*

The following $\mathtt{Insert}$ operator is the n-way version of the subscript operator in Kaplan and Kay (1994). It inserts symbols freely throughout a relation.

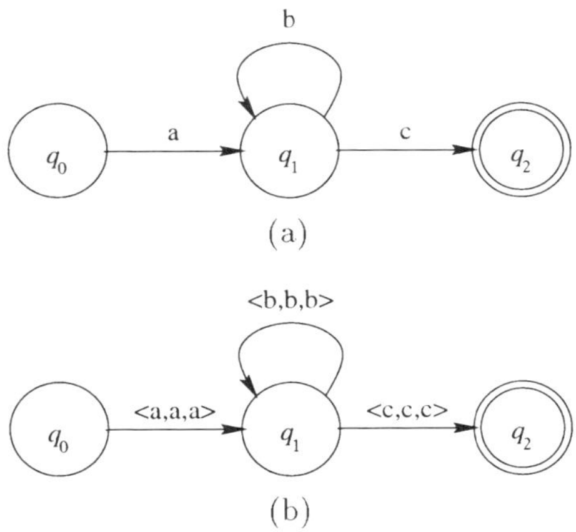

Fig. 7.1. Id operator. Each symbol in (a), ab^*c, is mapped onto itself n times in (b), $a{:}a{:}a\ b{:}b{:}b^*\ c{:}c{:}c$.

Definition 7.1.2 Let R be a regular relation over the alphabet Σ and let m be a set of symbols not necessarily in Σ. $\mathtt{Insert}_m(R)$ inserts the relation $\mathtt{Id}_n(a)$ for all $a \in m$ freely throughout R. □

Remark 7.1.2 $\mathtt{Insert}_m^{-1}$ (with $\mathtt{Insert}_m^{-1} \circ \mathtt{Insert}_m(R) = R$) removes all such instances if and only if m is disjoint from Σ. □

Construction 7.1.2 Let $M = (Q, \Sigma, \delta, q_0, F)$ be an n-tape FSA that accepts the relation R, and m be a set of symbols; further, let $I_a = \mathtt{Id}_n(a)$ for all $a \in m$. We can construct an n-tape FSA that accepts $\mathtt{Insert}_m(R)$, $M' = (Q, \Sigma \cup m, \delta', q_0, F)$, where

(i) $\delta'(q, a) = \delta(q, a)$ for all $q \in Q$ and $a \in \Sigma^n$
(ii) $\delta'(q, I_a) = q$ for all $q \in Q$ and $a \in m$

Conversely, one can construct an FSA for $\mathtt{Insert}^{-1}$. □

Example 7.1.2 Let R be a 2-relation described by the regular expression $a{:}b\ b{:}c$. $R' = \mathtt{Insert}_{\{\alpha,\beta\}}(R)$ is a 2-relation described by the regular expression $(\alpha{:}\alpha \cup \beta{:}\beta)^*\ a{:}b\ (\alpha{:}\alpha \cup \beta{:}\beta)^*\ b{:}c\ (\alpha{:}\alpha \cup \beta{:}\beta)^*$. In a similar manner, $R = \mathtt{Insert}_{\{\alpha,\beta\}}^{-1}(R')$ if and only if $\{\alpha, \beta\}$ is disjoint from the alphabet of R. The automata for both expressions are given in Fig. 7.2. □

Remark 7.1.3 We can define another form of Insert where the elements in m are tuples of symbols as follows: Let R be a regular n relation over the alphabet Σ; further, let m be a set of n tuples of symbols not

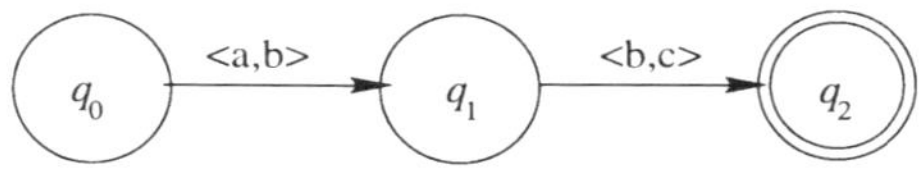

(a) $R = a{:}b\ b{:}c$

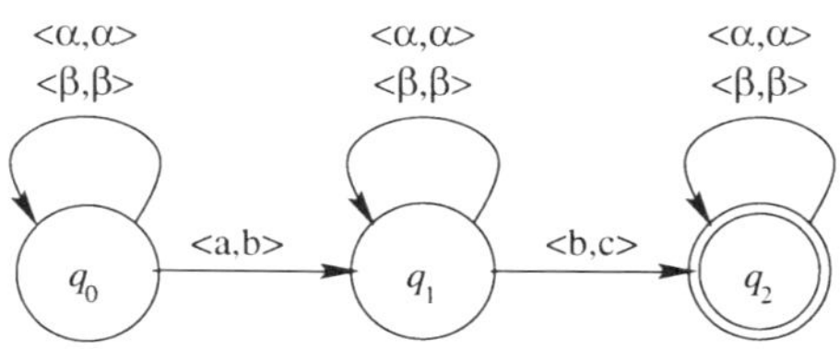

(b) $R' = \texttt{Insert}_{\{\alpha,\beta\}}(R)$

Fig. 7.2. Insert operator. Each state in the resulting machine in (b) has an arc that goes to the same state. The label on the arc is the inserted symbol mapped onto itself n times.

necessarily in Σ. $\texttt{Insert}_m(R)$ inserts a, for all $a \in m$, freely throughout R. □

Remark 7.1.4 If Insert is applied to a string s, we simply write $\texttt{Insert}_m(s)$ to denote $\texttt{Insert}_m(\{\langle s\rangle\})$. In a similar manner, we simply write $\texttt{Insert}_m(S)$ instead of $\texttt{Insert}_m(\{S\})$ if S is a tuple of strings. □

7.1.3.3 Substitution

Definition 7.1.3 Let S and S' be same-length n tuples of strings over some alphabet Σ, $I = \texttt{Id}_n(a)$ for some $a \in \Sigma$, and $S = S_1 I S_2 I \cdots S_k$, $k \geq 1$, such that S_i does not contain I; that is, $S_i \in (\Sigma^n - \{\, I\, \})^*$. We say that $\texttt{Substitute}_{(S',I)}(S) = S_1 S' S_2 S' \cdots S_k$ substitutes every occurrence of I in S with S'. □

An algorithm for constructing an FSA for substitution is given in Hopcroft and Ullman (1979).

Example 7.1.3 Let R_1 be a 2-relation described by the regular expression $a{:}b\ \alpha{:}\alpha\ b{:}c$ and R_2 be a 2-relation described by the regular expression $x{:}x\ y{:}y$. $\texttt{Substitute}_{(R_2,\alpha:\alpha)}(R_1)$ is a 2-relation described by the regular expression $a{:}b\ x{:}x\ y{:}y\ b{:}c$. The automata for the above expressions are given in Fig. 7.3. □

7.1.3.4 Cross Product

The following operation takes two same-length regular relations and returns their cross product.

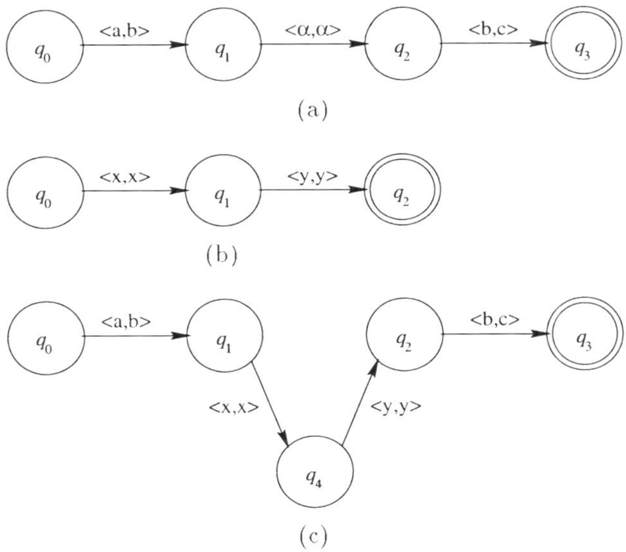

Fig. 7.3. `Substitute` operator. The arc with the label $\langle \alpha, \alpha \rangle$ in (a), $R_1 = a{:}b\ \alpha{:}\alpha\ b{:}c$, is removed and the machine in (b), $R_2 = x{:}x\ y{:}y$, is substitute for it as shown in (c), $\texttt{Substitute}_{(R_2, \alpha:\alpha)}\ (R_1)$.

Definition 7.1.4 Let R_1 be a same-length regular m relation and R_2 be a same-length regular n relation. $R_1 \times R_2$ is the same-length regular $(m+n)$ relation

$$
\begin{aligned}
R = \{ \langle a_1, \ldots, a_m, b_1, \ldots, b_n \rangle \mid \langle a_1, \ldots, a_m \rangle \\
\in R_1, \langle b_1, \ldots, b_n \rangle \in R_2, |a_1| = |b_1| \}
\end{aligned}
$$
□

Remark 7.1.5 The last condition above, namely $|a_1| = |b_1|$, ensures that the outcome is also a same-length relation. □

Construction 7.1.3 Let $M_1 = (Q_1, \Sigma_1, \delta_1, q_1, F_1)$ be an m-tape FSA that accepts a same-length relation, and $M_2 = (Q_2, \Sigma_2, \delta_2, q_2, F_2)$ be an n-tape FSA that accepts a same-length relation. We can construct an $(m+n)$ tape FSA that accepts $M_1 \times M_2$,

$$M = (Q_1 \times Q_2, \Sigma_1 \cup \Sigma_2, \delta, [q_1, q_2], F_1 \times F_2)$$

where for all $p_1 \in Q_1$, $p_2 \in Q_2$, $\langle a_1, \ldots, a_m \rangle \in (\Sigma_1)^m$, and $\langle b_1, \ldots, b_n \rangle \in (\Sigma_2)^n$,

$$
\begin{aligned}
&\delta([p_1, p_2], a_1 : \cdots : a_m : b_1 : \cdots : b_n) \\
&\quad = [\delta_1(p_1, a_1 : \cdots : a_m), \delta_2(p_2, b_1 : \cdots : b_n)]
\end{aligned}
$$
□

Example 7.1.4 Let R_1 be a same-length 2-relation described by the regular expression $a{:}b\ v{:}w$, and let R_2 be a same-length 3-relation described by the

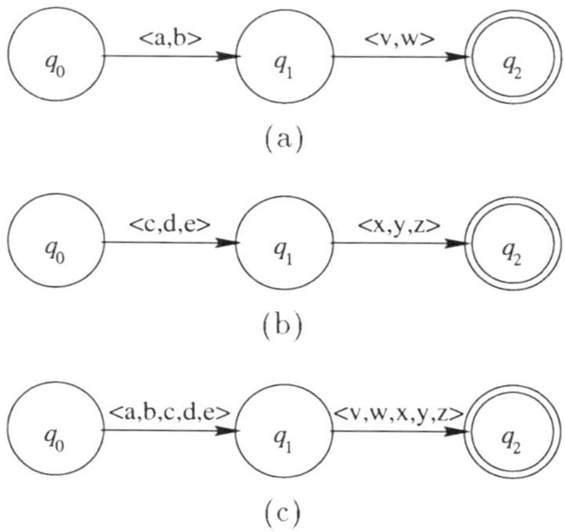

Fig. 7.4. Cross product operator. The two tapes of machine (a), $R_1 = a{:}b\ v{:}w$, and the three tapes of machine (b), $R_2 = c{:}d{:}e\ x{:}y{:}z$, are combined in machine in (c), $R_1 \times R_2$.

regular expression *c:d:e x:y:z*. $R_1 \times R_2$ is a 5-relation described by the regular expression *a:b:c:d:e v:w:x:y:z*. The automata for the above expressions are given in Fig. 7.4. □

7.1.3.5 *Production of Same-Length Tuples*

The following operator takes a (possibly unequal-length) tuple of strings and turns it into a same-length tuple of strings.

Definition 7.1.5 Let $S = \langle s_1, \ldots, s_n \rangle$ be a tuple of strings and a be a symbol. $\texttt{EqStr}_a(S)$ produces a same-length tuple of strings,

$$S' = \langle s_1 a^{l_1}, \ldots, s_n a^{l_n} \rangle$$

where $l_i = k - |s_i|$ and $k = \max_{1 \le i \le n}\{\, |s_i| \,\}$. □

Remark 7.1.6 The operator $\texttt{EqStr}_a$ suffixes a string of as to all the strings in S to make them as long as the longest string in S. □

Example 7.1.5 Let $S = \langle \text{a,bcd,ef} \rangle$, the operation $\texttt{EqStr}_0(S)$ produces $\langle \text{a00,bcd,ef0} \rangle$. □

Remark 7.1.7 The operator $\texttt{EqStr}_a$ cannot be extended to relations. Consider the relation $R = \{\, \langle a^n, a^{2n} \rangle \mid n \ge 0 \,\}$. If EqStr was defined on relations, then we get $\texttt{EqStr}_b(R) = \{\, \langle a^n b^n, a^{2n} \rangle \mid n \ge 0 \,\}$ where the first element may be projected (see Definition 7.1.6 below) into a context-free language. □

7.1.3.6 Projection

Definition 7.1.6 Let $S = \langle s_1, \ldots, s_n \rangle$ be a tuple of strings. The operator $\texttt{Project}_i(S)$, for some $i \in \{1, \ldots, n\}$, denotes the tuple element s_i. $\texttt{Project}_i^{-1}(S)$, for some $i \in \{1, \ldots, n\}$, denotes the $(n-1)$ tuple $\langle s_1, \ldots, s_{i-1}, s_{i+1}, \ldots, s_n \rangle$. □

Example 7.1.6 Let $S = \langle \text{a,b,c} \rangle$. Then $\texttt{Project}_1(S) = \text{a}$, $\texttt{Project}_2(S) = \text{b}$, and $\texttt{Project}_3^{-1}(S) = \langle \text{a,b} \rangle$. □

Constructing an FSA for `Project` and $\texttt{Project}^{-1}$ can be achieved by modifying the labels on transitions in a straightforward manner.

7.1.3.7 Composition

Although the algorithms that follow shortly do not make use of composition per se, it is customary in rewrite rules systems to divide a grammar into sets of rules that operate in a cascade form by using composition (see the cascade model on p. 47 ff.).

The composition of two transducers A and B is a generalization of the intersection of the same two machines in that each state in the resulting transducer is a pair drawn from one state in A and the other from B, and each transition corresponds to a pair of transitions, one from A and the other from B, with compatible labels. The composition of two binary transducers is straightforward since one tape is taken for input and the other for output. The composition of multitape transducers, however, is ambiguous. Which tapes are input and which are output?

Consider the transducer that accepts the regular 3-relation $a{:}b{:}b^*$ and a second transducer that accepts the regular 3-relation $b{:}b{:}c^*$. The composition of the two machines be either the transducer accepting the regular 2-relation $a{:}c^*$ (where $a{:}b{:}b^*$ is taken to map a^* into $b{:}b^*$, and $b{:}b{:}c^*$ is taken to map $b{:}b^*$ into c^*), or the transducer accepting $a{:}b{:}b{:}c^*$ (where $a{:}b{:}b^*$ is taken to map $a{:}b^*$ into b^*, and $b{:}b{:}c^*$ is taken to map b^* into $b{:}c^*$).

However, when tapes are marked as belonging to the domain or range of the transduction, the ambiguity is resolved. Hence, a composition of two multitape transducers is possible if and only if the number of range tapes in the first transducer is equal to the number of domain tapes in the second.

Construction 7.1.4 Recalling the definition of n tape finite-state transducer (Section 7.1.1), let A and B be two multitape transducers over n_1 and n_2 tapes, respectively, such that $A = (Q_1, \Sigma_1, \delta_1, q_1, F_1, d_1)$ and $B = (Q_2, \Sigma_2, \delta_2, q_2, F_2, d_2)$. Further, let s_i denote the symbol on the ith tape. There is a composition of A and B, denoted by $A \circ B$, if and only if $d_2 = n_1 - d_1$ with

$$A \circ B = (Q_1 \times Q_2, \Sigma_1 \cup \Sigma_2, \delta, [q_1, q_2], F_1 \times F_2, d_1)$$

where for all $p_1 \in Q_1$ and $p_2 \in Q_2$,

$$\begin{aligned}\delta([p_1, p_2], s_1 : \cdots : s_{d_1} : s'_{d_2+1} : \cdots : s'_{n_2}) = \\ [\delta_1(p_1, s_1 : \cdots : s_{d_1} : s_{d_1+1} : \cdots : s_{n_1}), \\ \delta_2(p_2, s'_1 : \cdots : s'_{d_2} : s'_{d_2+1} : \cdots : s'_{n_2})]\end{aligned}$$

if and only if

$$s_{d_1+1} = s'_1, \ldots, s_{n_1} = s'_{d_2}$$ □

Remark 7.1.8 The resulting automaton is a k-tape automaton, where $k = d_1 - d_2 + n_2$. □

7.1.3.8 *Summary of Operators*

The above operators are given in Table 7.1. The last two columns give the domain and range types of each operator.

7.2 Compiling the Lexicon Component

Recall (see Section 5.2) that the lexicon in the current model consists of multiple sublexica, with each sublexicon containing entries for one particular lexical representation. Further, recall that each entry in a sublexicon is associated with a

Table 7.1. *Summary of n-way operators*

Operator	Description	Domain Type	Range Type
$\circ$	composition	relation	relation
$\times$	cross product	same length relation	same length relation
`EqStr`	same length tuple of strings	tuple of strings	same length tuple of strings
`Id`	n way identity	language	relation
`Insert`	insertion	relation	relation
`Insert`$^{-1}$	removal	relation	relation
`Project`	projection	tuple of strings	string
`Project`$^{-1}$	inverse projection	tuple of strings	tuple of strings/string
`Substitute`	substitution	relation	relation

category of the form

$$\begin{bmatrix} \text{cat} \\ \text{ATTRIBUTE}_1 = \text{value}_1 \\ \text{ATTRIBUTE}_2 = \text{value}_2 \\ \vdots \end{bmatrix}$$

where *cat* is an atom representing a (grammatical) category followed by an unordered list of *attribute* = *value* pairs. An *attribute* is an atomic label. A *value* can be an atom or a variable drawn from a predefined finite set of possible values. The formal definition of the lexical component, upon which the compilation process relies, is given in Section 5.2.2. (It is recommended that the reader reviews this material at this point.)

The compilation process builds a one-tape automaton for each sublexicon. The sublexica are then put together by using the cross product operator with the effect that the resulting machine accepts entries from the ith sublexicon on its ith tape.

Recall that a lexical entry is a pair (W, C), where W is the word (e.g., morpheme) in question and C is its category. The entry is simply expressed by the expression $WC\beta$, where β is a boundary symbol (which is not in the alphabet of the lexicon) marking the end of the entry. Representing W in an automaton is achieved by concatenating the symbols of W one after the other. Compiling C, however, is more involved.

It is assumed that the grammar writer declares for each category a finite set of the attributes it can take. Likewise, he or she declares for each attribute a finite set of possible values. An implementation would expect such declarations by using some notation. For purposes of presentation, assume the following notation:

```
Category  Cat  attribute₁  attribute₂...  attributeₙ
```

declares a category `Cat` with n attributes. Likewise,

```
Attribute  Attr  value₁  value₂...
```

specifies the finite set of possible values for an attribute `Attr`. A lexicon, for example, may use the following declarations:

```
Category verb number person gender
Attribute number sing pl
Attribute person 1st 2nd 3rd
Attribute gender masc fem
```

To compile categories into automata, the category symbol (`verb` in the above example) and value symbols become part of the machine's alphabet (there is no need to add the attribute symbols as will be shown shortly). A category

$$C = \begin{bmatrix} \mathsf{cat} \\ \text{ATTRIBUTE}_1 = \text{value}_1 \\ \text{ATTRIBUTE}_2 = \text{value}_2 \\ \vdots \end{bmatrix}$$

is built into a machine $M(C)$ by using the expression

$$M(C) = \mathsf{cat}\ \text{value}_1 \text{value}_2 \ldots \tag{7.1}$$

The first symbol in the expression is the category, followed by the values. By convention, the position of a specific value in the sequence is based on the position of its attribute in the `Attribute` declaration. If a category is underspecified, a disjunction of all the possible values of the unspecified attributes are used instead.

Now let $\mathcal{L}_i = \{ (W_1, C_1), (W_2, C_2), \ldots \}$ be the set of lexical entries in the ith sublexicon. The expression for the ith sublexicon becomes

$$L_i = \bigcup_{(W,C) \in \mathcal{L}_i} W\ M(C)\, \beta \tag{7.2}$$

that is, the disjunction of all entries in the ith sublexicon.

The overall lexicon can then be expressed by taking the cross product of all the sublexica. However, recall that the arguments of the cross product operator must be same-length relations. This is achieved by inserting [0]s in each sublexicon prior to applying the cross product operation as follows:

$$Lexicon = \prod_{i=1}^{n-1} \mathtt{Insert}_{\{0\}}(L_i) \tag{7.3}$$

The result of the cross product operation is also a same-length relation since, by definition, the operation discards any relation whose elements are not of equal length.

7.3 Compiling the Rewrite Rules Component

The compilation of rewrite rules is much more involved than compiling lexica and is performed in a number of steps. The algorithm presented in this section is based on collaborative work reported by Grimley-Evans, Kiraz, and Pulman (1996).

The formal definition of the rule formalism, upon which the compilation algorithm relies, was given in Section 5.3.2. (It is recommended that the reader review this material at this point.) In the following discussion, it is assumed that grammars employ n expressions: one surface and $n - 1$ lexical. For ease of reference, symbols that are used in later equations are shown in the outer margin next to the place of their original definition.

v	a	a	a	*lexical string*
0	1	2	2	
v	b	b	b	*surface string*

Fig. 7.5. Iterative application of R1 and R2. The second ⟨b,a⟩ pair serves as the center of the first application of R2 as well as the left context of the second application of the same rule.

The following rules will be used throughout the discussion for illustrative purposes:

$$
\begin{array}{lccccccc}
 & * & - & X & - & * & \Rightarrow \\
\text{R0} & * & - & X & - & * & \\
 & \multicolumn{6}{l}{\text{where } X \in \{\text{v,c,d}\}} \\
\text{R1} & \text{v} & - & \text{a} & - & * & \Rightarrow \\
 & \text{v} & - & \text{b} & - & * & \\
\text{R2} & \text{a} & - & \text{a} & - & * & \Rightarrow \\
 & \text{b} & - & \text{b} & - & * & \\
\text{R3} & \text{c} & - & \epsilon & - & \text{d} & \Leftrightarrow \\
 & \text{c} & - & \text{b} & - & \text{d} &
\end{array}
$$

R0 is the identity rule. R1 and R2 illustrate the iterative application of rules on strings. They sanction ⟨vbbb, vaaa⟩ as illustrated in Fig. 7.5. Notice that the second ⟨b,a⟩ pair serves as the center of the first application of R2 as well as the left context of the second application of the same rule. R3 is an epenthetic rule, which also demonstrates centers of unequal length. R3 is also an obligatory rule; hence, it has two components: optional and obligatory.

The compilation of rewrite rules requires a preprocessing stage before the actual compilation takes place. Preprocessing involves converting all expressions in rules into same-length relations and collecting information about the rules that is used in the actual compilation.

7.3.1 Preprocessing Rewrite Rules

The purpose behind preprocessing is twofold: first, to transform rewrite rules that may describe mappings of unequal lengths into same-length mappings; second, to compute the set of feasible tuples, that is, the set of all tuples that are sanctioned by the grammar regardless of context. Recall (see Section 5.3.2.4) that rules are defined over two-level tuples of the form $\langle s, l_1, l_2, \ldots, l_{n-1} \rangle$, where s is a surface symbol and l_i, $1 \leq i \leq n-1$, are the corresponding lexical symbols.

Preprocessing involves the following computations: (i) making all centers of equal length, (ii) computing feasible tuples, and (iii) making all contexts of equal length.

7.3.1.1 Equal-Length Centers

Recall (Definition 5.3.17) that a grammar is a pair $G = (CR, SC)$, where CR and SC are finite sets of optional and obligatory rules, respectively, and that each rule is a pair $R = (C, LR)$, with C representing the center of the rule and LR representing the left and right contexts (see Section 5.3.2.5).

Each center C of a rule $R = (C, LR) \in CR$ (i.e., optional rules only) C' is replaced by a corresponding center

$$C' = \texttt{EqStr}_0(C) \tag{7.4}$$

This makes every center a same-length two-level tuple. The reason this is not applied to obligatory rules is to allow for epenthetic rules, as will be described shortly (see p. 140).

> **Example 7.3.1** When applying Eq. (7.4) to the centers of the rules on p. 133, the center of R3, repeated below,
>
> | R3 | c | – | ϵ | – | d | $\Leftrightarrow$ |
> |---|---|---|---|---|---|---|
> | | c | – | b | – | d | |
>
> becomes ⟨b,0⟩; the rest of the centers are already of equal length. □

7.3.1.2 Feasible Tuples

Having all C's in hand, one computes the set of feasible tuples, π. For each $C' = \langle a_{11} \cdots a_{1k}, a_{21} \cdots a_{2k}, \ldots, a_{n1} \cdots a_{nk} \rangle$ of rule R (where a_{ij} is the jth symbol of the ith string), the set of *feasible tuples* for R is

$$\pi_R = \{ \langle a_{11}, \ldots, a_{n1} \rangle, \langle a_{12}, \ldots, a_{n2} \rangle, \ldots, \langle a_{1k}, \ldots, a_{nk} \rangle \} \tag{7.5}$$

The overall set of feasible tuples is the union of all such sets,

$$\pi = \bigcup_{R \in CR} \pi_R \tag{7.6}$$

In a similar manner, one computes the set of *feasible symbols* with respect to each element in the tuples: π_s, the set of feasible surface symbols, and π_i, $1 \le i \le n-1$, the set of feasible lexical symbols on the ith lexical expression as follows:

$$\pi_s = \{ \texttt{Project}_1(t) | t \in \pi \} \tag{7.7}$$

$$\pi_i = \{ \texttt{Project}_{i+1}(t) | t \in \pi \} \tag{7.8}$$

If a grammar makes use of only one lexical expression, the set of feasible lexical symbols is designated by π_l.

Example 7.3.2 The set of feasible tuples for the rules on p. 133 is from Eq. (7.6),

$\pi = \{ \langle \text{b,a} \rangle, \langle \text{b,0} \rangle, \langle \text{v,v} \rangle, \langle \text{c,c} \rangle, \langle \text{d,d} \rangle \}$

The tuple $\langle \text{b,a} \rangle$ is the center of R1 and R2, and $\langle \text{b,0} \rangle$ is the center of R3 (after applying $\texttt{EqStr}_0$); the rest of the tuples are the center of R0.

The sets of feasible surface and lexical symbols are $\pi_s = \{ \text{v,b,c,d} \}$, from Eq. (7.7), and $\pi_l = \{ \text{v,a,c,d,0} \}$, from Eq. (7.8). □

7.3.1.3 Equal-Length Contexts

Unlike the case of computing equal-length centers (see p. 134 above), computing equal-length contexts is applied to context restriction as well as obligatory rules.

Every set of context pairs LR of a rule $R = (C, LR) \in CR \cup SC$ is replaced by a corresponding set of context pairs LR' as follows.

Let $(\lambda, \rho) \in LR$ be a context pair with $\lambda = \langle l_s, l_1 \ldots, l_{n-1} \rangle$ and $\rho = \langle r_s, r_1 \ldots, r_{n-1} \rangle$. The set of contexts corresponding to λ, denoted by $\mathcal{L}_\lambda$, is

$$\mathcal{L}_\lambda = \left(\texttt{Insert}_{\{0\}}(\pi_s^* l_s) \times \prod_{i=1}^{n-1} \texttt{Insert}_{\{0\}}(\pi_i^* l_i) \right) \cap \pi^* \tag{7.9}$$

Here, l_s is prefixed with π^* to allow any surface symbols to precede the left-surface context. Similarly, each l_i, $1 \leq i < n$, is prefixed with π_i.

Since [0]s were appended to the centers in the computation of C' above, Eq. (7.4), the $\texttt{Insert}$ operation allows [0]s to appear anywhere in the contexts. The cross product operation joins the elements into a single same-length two-level tuple. The intersection with π^* eliminates the contexts that contain tuples other than the feasible ones.

Similarly, the set of contexts corresponding to ρ, denoted by $\mathcal{R}_\rho$, is

$$\mathcal{R}_\rho = \left(\texttt{Insert}_{\{0\}}(r_s \pi_s^*) \times \prod_{i=1}^{n-1} \texttt{Insert}_{\{0\}}(r_i \pi_i^*) \right) \cap \pi^* \tag{7.10}$$

The new set of context pairs LR' is constructed from the sets of context pairs drawn from $\mathcal{L}_\lambda$ and $\mathcal{R}_\rho$ for all $(\lambda, \rho) \in LR$,

$$LR' = \bigcup_{(\lambda,\rho) \in LR} \{ (\lambda', \rho') \mid \lambda' \in \mathcal{L}_\lambda, \rho' \in \mathcal{R}_\rho \} \tag{7.11}$$

Example 7.3.3 Completing the preprocessing phase of the rules on p. 133, one computes new left and right contexts as follows. Contexts marked with an asterisk (i.e., any context) become

$\texttt{Insert}_{\{0\}}(\pi_s^*) \times \texttt{Insert}_{\{0\}}(\pi_l^*)$

The right context of R3, repeated below,

$$\text{R3} \quad \begin{array}{ccccccc} \text{c} & - & \epsilon & - & \text{d} & \Leftrightarrow \\ \text{c} & - & \text{b} & - & \text{d} & \end{array}$$

becomes

$$\texttt{Insert}_{\{0\}}(\mathrm{d}\pi_s^*) \times \texttt{Insert}_{\{0\}}(\mathrm{d}\pi_l^*)$$

All other contexts are computed in a similar manner. □

Upon completion of the preprocessing phase, one ends up with a new grammar whose expressions (apart from obligatory rules' centers) are of equal length.

7.3.2 Compiling Rewrite Rules

The actual compiler takes as its input the rules that have been preprocessed. The algorithm is subtractive in nature: it starts off by creating an automaton that overgenerates (i.e., it accepts more strings than the rules would allow), and then starts subtracting strings that violate the rules. This subtractive approach is from Grimley-Evans, as outlined in Grimley-Evans, Kiraz, and Pulman (1996).

The algorithm consists of three phases. The first phase gathers all the centers of the rules, regardless of their context, and constructs an automaton that accepts any sequence of the centers. The second phase goes through the optional rules and removes (i.e., subtracts) from the automaton all sequences of centers that violate the rules. This makes the machine accept all (but not only) the sequences of tuples described by the grammar. Finally, the third phase goes through the obligatory rules and further removes from the automaton all sequences of tuples that violate the rules. This results in an automaton that accepts all and only the sequences of tuples described by the grammar.

7.3.2.1 *First Phase: Accepting Centers*

Let $G = (CR, SC)$ be a preprocessed grammar over n expressions, over some alphabets $(\Sigma_1, \ldots, \Sigma_n)$. Further, let σ be a special symbol (not σ in the mentioned alphabets) denoting a subsequence boundary within a partition, and let $\sigma' = \texttt{Id}_n(\sigma)$. The automaton that accepts the centers σ' of the grammar is described by the relation

$$Centers(CR) = \sigma'\Big(\Big(\bigcup_{(C,LR)\in CR} C\Big)\sigma'\Big)^* \tag{7.12}$$

Centers accepts the subsequence boundary symbols, σ', followed by zero or more centers, each (if any) followed by σ'. In other words, the automaton accepts any sequence of the centers described by the grammar (each center surrounded by σ')

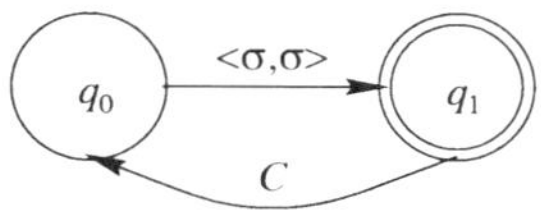

Fig. 7.6. Result of the first phase. The machine accepts any sequence of the centers $C = \{ \langle b,a \rangle, \langle b,0 \rangle, \langle v,v \rangle, \langle c,c \rangle, \langle d,d \rangle \}$, each (if any) surrounded by the subsequence boundary symbols, σ'.

irrespective of their contexts. Here, σ' is used to mark each partition following the definition of the formalism.

Example 7.3.4 Building on the previous example, the automaton for *Centers* is depicted in Fig. 7.6. This automaton accepts any sequence of the centers, each (if any) surrounded by the subsequence boundary symbols, σ'. □

7.3.2.2 Second Phase: Optional Rules

The second phase involves eliminating all the sequences accepted by *Centers* whose left and right contexts violate the grammar. For each rule $R = (C, LR) \in CR$, where $LR = \{ (\lambda_1, \rho_1), (\lambda_2, \rho_2), \dots \}$, the *invalid* contexts for C, denoted by the *Restrict*(C) relation, are expressed by

$$\begin{aligned} Restrict(C, LR) &= \pi^* C \pi^* - (\lambda_1 C \rho_1 \cup \lambda_2 C \rho_2 \cup \cdots) \\ &= \pi^* C \pi^* - \bigcup_{(\lambda,\rho) \in LR} \lambda C \rho \end{aligned} \tag{7.13}$$

The first component of Eq. (7.13) gives all the contexts for C. The second component gives all the valid contexts for C taken from the context-restriction rules. The subtraction results in all the invalid contexts for C.

However, because in Eq. (7.12) the subsequence boundary symbol σ appears freely, it has to be introduced in Eq. (7.13) as well. The *Restrict* relation becomes

$$Restrict(C, LR) = \mathtt{Insert}_{\{\sigma\}}\left(\pi^* C \pi^* - \bigcup_{(\lambda,\rho) \in LR} \lambda C \rho\right) \tag{7.14}$$

This expression works only if the center of the C consists of just one tuple. In order to allow C to be a sequence of such tuples, C must be: (i) surrounded by σ' on both sides marking it as one subsequence, and (ii) devoid of any σ'. The first condition is accomplished by simply placing σ' to the left and right of C,

$$Restrict(C, LR) = \mathtt{Insert}_{\{\sigma\}}\left(\pi^* \sigma' C \sigma' \pi^* - \bigcup_{(\lambda,\rho) \in LR} \lambda \sigma' C \sigma' \rho\right) \tag{7.15}$$

As for the second condition, an auxiliary symbol ω is used as a place-holder representing C in order to avoid inserting σ' in C by the `Insert` operator. One then introduces σ freely by using the `Insert` operator, and then substitutes C back in place of ω. This way, the `Insert` operator will not introduce σ between the tuples of C. More formally, let ω be an ω' auxiliary symbol (not in the grammar's alphabet), and let $\omega' = \mathtt{Id}_n(\omega)$ be a place-holder representing C. The above expression becomes

$$\mathit{Restrict}(C, LR) =$$
$$\mathtt{Substitute}_{(C,\omega')}\left(\mathtt{Insert}_{\{\sigma\}}\left(\pi^*\sigma'\omega'\sigma'\pi^* - \bigcup_{(\lambda,\rho)\in LR} \lambda\sigma'\omega'\sigma'\rho\right)\right) \quad (7.16)$$

Finally, one subtracts all such invalid relations from the *Centers* relation, Eq. (7.12), of the first phase, yielding the context-restriction relation,

$$\mathit{ContRest}(CR) = \mathit{Centers}(CR) - \bigcup_{(C,LR)\in CR} \mathit{Restrict}(C, LR) \quad (7.17)$$

ContRest now accepts all the sequences of tuples described by the grammar (including the subsequence boundary symbols σ'); however, it does not enforce obligatory constraints.

Example 7.3.5 Continuing the same example (see the rules on p. 133), there are two centers to process: ⟨b,a⟩ in R1 and R2, and ⟨b,0⟩ in R3. For each center, first one computes the set of *invalid* expressions in which the centers occur by using *Restrict*, and then one subtracts the union of all such expressions from the automaton in Fig. 7.6. However, for clarity we shall process one center at a time by using *Restrict*, subtracting the result from the automata under construction as follows.

Applying *Restrict* on the center ⟨b,a⟩ and its contexts per Eq. (7.16), and subtracting the result from *Centers* per Eq. (7.17), we obtain the automaton in Fig. 7.7. States q_0 and q_1 represent the automaton in Fig. 7.6 (except for the D

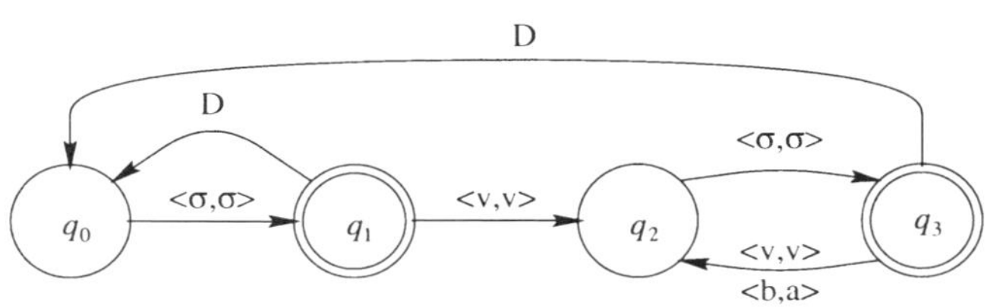

Fig. 7.7. Processing the center ⟨b,a⟩ of rules R1 and R2 (on p. 133). States q_0 and q_1 represent the automaton in Fig. 7.6 (except for the $D = \{ \langle b,0\rangle, \langle c,c\rangle, \langle d,d\rangle \}$ label). States q_2 and q_3 represent R1 and the iterative rule R2. Upon scanning ⟨v,v⟩, that is, the left context of R1 (q_2), the automaton reads $\langle\sigma,\sigma\rangle$ (q_3) and possibly scans the center of R1 (q_2), after which it can iterate between states q_2 and q_3 modeling rule R2.

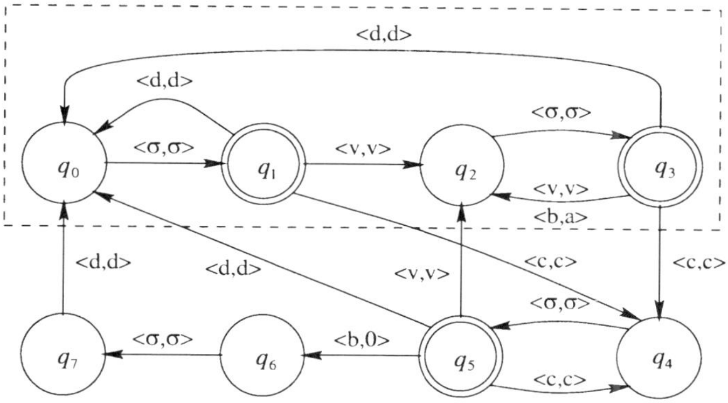

Fig. 7.8. Result of the second phase. The dashed box represents the automaton in Fig. 7.7 (except for the edges to q_0). States q_4–q_7 represent the optional portion of R3. Once the left context is scanned (q_4), the automaton scans $\langle\sigma,\sigma\rangle$ and optionally stops (q_5). If the center ⟨b,0⟩ is read (q_6), the automaton reads a $\langle\sigma,\sigma\rangle$ (q_7) and expects to find the right context ⟨d,d⟩ (q_0).

label). States q_2 and q_3 represent R1 and the iterative rule R2. Once a ⟨v, v⟩ is scanned satisfying the left context of R1 (q_2), the automaton reads a subsequence boundary symbol (q_3) and possibly scans the center of R1 (q_2), after which it can iterate between states q_2 and q_3 modeling rule R2.

The second center ⟨b,0⟩ is processed in a similar manner. The end result is the automaton in Fig. 7.8. The dashed box represents the automaton in Fig. 7.7 (except for the edges to q_0). States q_4–q_7 represent the context-restriction portion of the obligatory epenthesis rule, R3. Once the left context is scanned (q_4), the automaton scans the subsequence boundary symbol and optionally stops (q_5). If the center ⟨b,0⟩ is read (q_6), the automaton reads a subsequence boundary symbol (q_7) and expects to find the right context ⟨d,d⟩ (q_0).

Note that the automaton accepts the undesired input *⟨cd,cd⟩ as illustrated in Fig. 7.9, because the obligatory portion of R3 has yet to be processed. The numbers in the diagram indicate the current state in Fig. 7.8. □

7.3.2.3 *Third Phase: Obligatory Rules*

The third phase forces obligatory constraints. For each rule $R = (C, LR)$ in SC, let $\bar{C}$ represent the center of the rule with the *correct* lexical C expressions and the

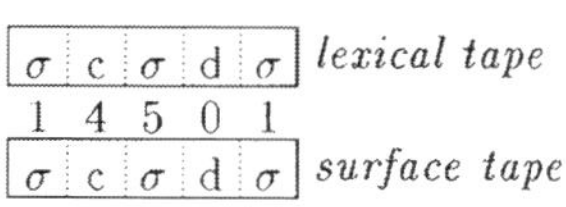

Fig. 7.9. Deriving the ill-formed mapping *⟨cd,cd⟩ (with σ interspersed). The numbers indicate the current state in Fig. 7.8.

incorrect surface expression with respect to R:

$$\mathcal{C} = \texttt{Insert}_{\{0\}}\left(\overline{\texttt{Project}_1(C)}\right) \times \prod_{i=2}^{n} \texttt{Insert}_{\{0\}}\left(\texttt{Project}_i(C)\right) \tag{7.18}$$

The operator $\texttt{Project}_i$ extracts the ith element in C, `Insert` allows [0]s to appear anywhere in the center, and the cross product turns the elements of all strings into same-length tuples. Note that $\overline{\texttt{Project}_1(C)} = \pi_s^* - \texttt{Project}_1(C)$.

Unlike optional rules, the centers are not padded with 0s by using `EqStr`; instead, the above expression is used to make the center of equal length in order to handle epenthetic rules.

The following *Coerce* relation describes all sequences of two-level tuples that contain an unlicensed segment:

$$\textit{Coerce}(\mathcal{C}, LR) = \bigcup_{(\lambda,\rho)\in LR} \texttt{Insert}_{\{\sigma\}}(\lambda\sigma'\mathcal{C}\sigma'\rho) \tag{7.19}$$

Recall that obligatory rules apply on a sequence of zero or more adjacent pairs of lexical-surface subsequences (see p. 73). The two σ's surrounding $\mathcal{C}$ in Eq. (7.19) ensure that coercion applies to at least one pair. The `Insert` operator inserts additional σ's through the contexts *and* the center. The insertion of σ' through the center allows *Coerce* to apply to a sequence of pairs. To handle the case of epenthetic rules, one needs to allow *Coerce* to apply on zero pairs of lexical-surface subsequences as well. In such a case, one takes the union of Eq. (7.19) with $\texttt{Insert}_{\{\sigma\}}(\lambda\sigma'\rho)$, that is, the empty subsequence.

Finally, for all obligatory rules, one subtracts $\textit{Coerce}(\mathcal{C}, LR)$ from the *ContRest* relation, Eq. (7.17), yielding the obligatory relation,

$$\textit{SurfCoer}(CR, SC) = \textit{ContRest}(CR) - \bigcup_{(\mathcal{C},LR)\in SC} \textit{Coerce}(\mathcal{C}, LR) \tag{7.20}$$

where $\mathcal{C}$ above is computed per Eq. (7.19). The *SurfCoer* relation accepts *all* and *only* the sequences of tuples described by the grammar (including the subsequence symbols σ').

Example 7.3.6 Completing the example at hand, this phase deals with the obligatory portion of R3 on p. 133. First, the set of strings in which R3 is violated is computed by using *Coerce*. Second, the result is subtracted from the automaton in Fig. 7.8, resulting in an automaton that only differs from the one in Fig. 7.8 in that the edge from q_5 to q_0 is removed. The automaton now does *not* accept the undesired input $*\langle$cd,cd$\rangle$ of Fig. 7.9. □

7.3.2.4 The Final Automaton

It remains only to remove all instances of the subsequence boundary symbol σ and the symbol [0] from Eq. (7.20). The whole expression for the automaton that accepts the grammar $G = (CR, SC)$ is expressed by

$$Rules(CR, SC) = \texttt{Insert}^{-1}_{\{\sigma,0\}}\Bigg(Centers(CR) - \bigcup_{(C_1, LR_1)\in CR} Restrict(C_1, LR_1) - \bigcup_{(C_2, LR_2)\in SC} Coerce(C_2, LR_2)\Bigg) \quad (7.21)$$

Finally, the constructed automaton is determinized and minimized. Recall that there are two methods for interpreting transducers. When interpreted as acceptors with tuples of symbols on each transition, they can be determinized by using standard algorithms Hopcroft and Ullman (1979). When interpreted as a transduction that maps an input to an output, they cannot always be turned into a deterministic form (see Mohri, 1994; Roche and Schabes, 1995; and Mohri, 1997 for quasi-determinization algorithms).

7.3.3 Incorporating Grammatical Features

This section shows how categories that are associated with rewrite rules can be incorporated into FSAs.

At first, one computes the set of feasible categories per sublexicon. Let $\mathcal{L}_i = \{ (W_1, C_1), (W_2, C_2), \dots \}$ be the set of lexical entries in the ith sublexicon; the set of categories for $\mathcal{L}_i$ is

$$\mathcal{F}_i = \{ C \mid \exists W : (W, C) \in \mathcal{L}_i \} \quad (7.22)$$

The expression for all *feasible categories*, that is, the possible combinations of categories from all the sublexica, becomes

$$F = 0^* \times \prod_{i=1}^{n-1} \bigcup_{f_i \in \mathcal{F}_i} M(f_i) \quad (7.23)$$

That is, 0^* on the first (surface) tape since categories are deleted on the surface, and any category from $\mathcal{F}_i$ on the ith lexical tapes. Here, $M(f_i)$ compiles a category into an automaton per Eq. (7.1).

During the preprocessing of rewrite rules, in addition to the computations presented in Section 7.3.1, for each rule $R = (C, LR) \in CR \cup SC$, let $LR = \{ (\lambda_1, \rho_1, \kappa_1), (\lambda_2, \rho_2, \kappa_2), \dots \}$. If κ_j does not specify a category on some tape i, the ith element of κ_j becomes $\mathcal{F}_i$, the set of categories for tape i. In addition, to allow feasible category-feature tuples to appear in the contexts, we simply perform $\texttt{Insert}_F(\lambda_i)$ and $\texttt{Insert}_F(\rho_i)$ – this is because we will be incorporating categories into the right contexts of rules shortly.

Further, the following modifications to the procedure given in Section 7.3.2 are required. In the first phase of the compilation process, Eq. (7.12), which expresses centers of the rules, becomes

$$Centers = \sigma' \left(\left(\left(\bigcup_{(C, LR) \in CR} C \right) \sigma' \right)^{+} F \sigma' \right)^{*} \tag{7.24}$$

This relation accepts the subsequence boundary symbols, σ', followed by zero or more occurrences of the following: (1) one or more centers, each followed by σ', and (2) a feasible category-feature tuple followed by σ'.

In the second phase of the compilation process, the first component in the *Restrict* relation, Eq. (7.13), that is, $\pi^* C \pi^*$, becomes

$$(\pi \cup \pi F)^* C (\pi \cup F)^* \tag{7.25}$$

The expression allows the insertion of F in the left and right contexts of C; note that $(\pi \cup \pi F)$ puts the restriction that the first tuple at the left end of C must be in π, not in F. The second component in the *Restrict* relation, Eq. (7.13), becomes

$$\bigcup_{(\lambda, \rho, \kappa) \in LR} \lambda C \left(\rho \cap \pi^* \kappa (\pi \cup F)^* \right) \tag{7.26}$$

The modification here is in what follows C: ρ in Eq. (7.13) is replaced by $(\rho \cap \pi^* \kappa (\pi \cup F)^*)$. The intersection with $\pi^* \kappa (\pi \cup F)^*$ ensures that the first category tuple to appear to the right of C is κ, with the possibility of π^* appearing between C and κ. The expression also allows any number of feasible tuples or feasible category tuple to follow κ. These modifications apply to the final *Restrict* relation in Eq. (7.16).

In the third phase of the compilation process, the *Coerce* relation, Eq. (7.19), becomes

$$Coerce(\mathcal{C}, LR) = \bigcup_{(\lambda, \rho) \in LR} \texttt{Insert}_{\{\sigma\}} \left(\lambda \sigma' C' \sigma' \left(\rho \cap \pi^* \kappa (\pi \cup F)^* \right) \right) \tag{7.27}$$

where ρ in Eq. (7.19) is replaced by $\left(\rho \cap \pi^* \kappa (\pi \cup F)^* \right)$.

7.4 Compiling the Morphotactic Component

Two methods for handling Semitic morphotactics were presented in Section 5.4: regular and context free. This section describes how the former can be compiled into finite-state devices.

Recall (see Section 5.4.1) that Semitic morphotactics is divided into templatic (which occurs when the pattern, root, vocalism, and possibly other morphemes join together in a nonlinear manner to form a stem) and nontemplatic (which takes place when the stem is combined with other morphemes to form larger morphological or syntactic units). The former is handled implicitly in the rewrite rules component.

The latter is divided into linear nontemplatic (which makes use of simple prefixation and suffixation) and nonlinear nontemplatic (which makes use of circumfixation). Prefixation and suffixation are simply modeled in automata terms by using the concatenation operator. As for handling circumfixation, the following rule formalism was introduced:

$$
\begin{aligned}
A &\rightarrow \widehat{P\,B\,S} \\
(P, S) &\rightarrow (p_1, s_1) \\
(P, S) &\rightarrow (p_2, s_2) \\
&\vdots \\
(P, S) &\rightarrow (p_n, s_n)
\end{aligned}
$$

Recall that a circumfix is a pair (P, S) where P represents the prefix portion of the circumfix and S represents the suffix portion. The circumfixation operation $\widehat{PBS}$ applies the circumfix (P, S) to B.

Let $(P, S) = \{\, (p_1, s_1), (p_2, s_2), \ldots, (p_n, s_n) \,\}$ be a set of circumfixes and let B be the domain of the circumfixation operation; a rule $A \rightarrow \widehat{PBS}$ is compiled into an automaton by using the expression

$$
A = \bigcup_{(p,s)\in(P,S)} pBs \tag{7.28}
$$

The expression ensures that the prefix and suffix portions of each circumfix are associated together.

7.5 Illustration from Syriac

The final section in this chapter demonstrates the algorithms discussed for the rewrite rules component by analyzing Syriac /ktab/ "to write" with inflected forms using circumfixation.

The rules for deriving Syriac /ktab/ from the above lexical elements were given on p. 112 and are repeated below:

$$
\begin{array}{llcccccl}
 & * & - & \langle \mathrm{c,C,}\varepsilon \rangle & - & * & \Rightarrow \\
\mathrm{R1} & * & - & \mathrm{C} & - & * & \\
 & \multicolumn{6}{l}{\text{where C} \in \{\,\mathrm{k,t,b}\,\}}
\end{array}
$$

$$
\begin{array}{llcccccl}
 & * & - & \langle \mathrm{v,}\varepsilon\mathrm{,a} \rangle & - & * & \Rightarrow \\
\mathrm{R2} & * & - & \mathrm{a} & - & * &
\end{array}
$$

$$
\begin{array}{llcccccl}
 & * & - & \langle \mathrm{v,}\varepsilon\mathrm{,a} \rangle & - & \langle \mathrm{cv,C,a} \rangle & \Leftrightarrow \\
\mathrm{R3} & * & - & \epsilon & - & * & \\
 & \multicolumn{6}{l}{\text{where C} \in \{\,\mathrm{k,t,b}\,\}}
\end{array}
$$

R1 and R2 sanction stem consonants and vowels; R3 deletes the first [a] in the stem.

7.5.1 Preprocessing

The preprocessing stage takes care of three tasks following the procedure in Sections 7.3.1.

First, $\texttt{EqStr}_0$ is applied to make all centers of same length, as shown in Eq. (7.4). The centers of R1–R4 become $\langle 0,\beta,\beta,\beta\rangle$, $\langle \mathrm{C,c,C}\ 0\rangle$, $\langle \mathrm{a,v,0,a}\rangle$, and $\langle \mathrm{0,v,0,a}\rangle$, respectively.

Second, the set of feasible tuples and the sets of feasible symbols per tape are computed – see Eqs. (7.6), (7.7), and (7.8) – as

$$\begin{aligned}
\pi &= \{\, \langle 0,\beta,\beta,\beta\rangle,\ \langle \mathrm{k,c,k,0}\rangle,\ \langle \mathrm{t,c,t,0}\rangle, \\
&\qquad \langle \mathrm{b,c,b,0}\rangle,\ \langle \mathrm{a,v,0,a}\rangle,\ \langle \mathrm{0,v,0,a}\rangle \,\} \\
\pi_s &= \{\, \mathrm{0,k,t,b,a} \,\} \\
\pi_1 &= \{\, \beta,\mathrm{c,v} \,\} \\
\pi_2 &= \{\, \beta,\mathrm{k,t,b,0} \,\} \\
\pi_3 &= \{\, \beta,\mathrm{0,a} \,\}
\end{aligned}$$

The set of feasible categories is computed as well – see Eq. (7.23) – as

$$F = \{\, \langle 0,\ \big[\ \text{pattern}\ \big],\ \big[\ \text{root}\ \big],\ \big[\ \text{vocalism}\ \big]\rangle \,\}$$

Third, the context expressions are computed, as shown in Eqs. (7.9) and (7.10). All contexts, apart from the right context of R4, become

$$\left(\texttt{Insert}_{\{0\}}(\pi_s^*) \times \prod_{i=1}^{3} \texttt{Insert}_{\{0\}}(\pi_i^*)\right) \cap \pi^*$$

The right context of R4 becomes

$$\Big(\texttt{Insert}_{\{0\}}(\pi_s^*) \times \texttt{Insert}_{\{0\}}(\mathrm{cv}\pi_1^*) \times \texttt{Insert}_{\{0\}}((\mathrm{k} \cup \mathrm{t} \cup \mathrm{b})\pi_2^*) \\ \times \texttt{Insert}_{\{0\}}(\mathrm{a}\pi_3^*)\Big) \cap \pi^*$$

7.5.2 First Phase: Accepting Centers

Let

$$C = \{\, \langle 0,\beta,\beta,\beta\rangle,\ \langle \mathrm{k,c,k,0}\rangle,\ \langle \mathrm{t,c,t,0}\rangle,\ \langle \mathrm{b,c,b,0}\rangle,\ \langle \mathrm{a,v,0,a}\rangle,\ \langle \mathrm{0,v,0,a}\rangle \,\}$$

be the set of all centers. The automaton that accepts all the centers, Eq. (7.24), is depicted in Fig. 7.10. It scans a tuple of subsequence boundary symbols, σs (q_1),

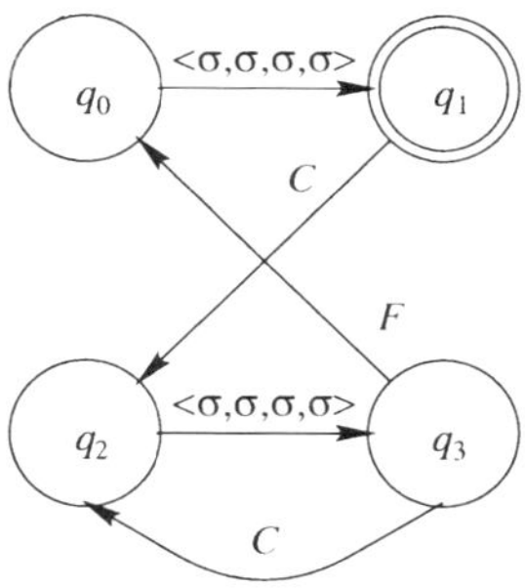

$$C = \{\ \langle 0,\beta,\beta,\beta\rangle,\ \langle \mathrm{C,c,C,0}\rangle,\ \langle \mathrm{a,v,0,a}\rangle,\ \langle \mathrm{0,v,0,a}\rangle\ \}$$

Fig. 7.10. Example: phase 1.

followed by zero or more of the following sequence: one or more centers (q_2), each followed by a tuple of σs (q_3); a category-feature tuple (q_0); and a tuple of σs (q_1).

This automaton does not force any context constraints. It will accept */katab/ (on the surface tape, with σ interspersed) as illustrated in Fig. 7.11. The numbers indicate the current state.

7.5.3 *Second Phase: Optional Rules*

The only rule that explicitly provides a context is R4. This rule is obligatory; that is, it states that: (a) if the center ⟨0,v,0,a⟩ is accepted, then it must be followed by the specified right context, and (b) if the lexical center and the specified contexts are satisfied, then the specified surface center must also be satisfied.

The second phase deals with condition (a). Applying the *Restrict* relation, Eq. (7.16) with Eqs. (7.25) and (7.26) incorporated, on R4 produces an automaton that describes the *invalid* expressions in which the center ⟨0,v,0,a⟩ occurs. Subtracting this automaton from the automaton of the first phase (Fig. 7.10) yields the automaton in Fig. 7.12. The portion in the dashed box represents the automaton

σ	0	σ	a	σ	0	σ	a	σ	0	σ	β	σ	C_v	σ	*Vocalism Tape*
σ	k	σ	0	σ	t	σ	0	σ	b	σ	β	σ	C_r	σ	*Root Tape*
σ	c	σ	v	σ	c	σ	v	σ	c	σ	β	σ	C_p	σ	*Pattern Tape*
1	2	3	2	3	2	3	2	3	2	3	2	3	0	1	
σ	k	σ	a	σ	t	σ	a	σ	b	σ	0	σ	0	σ	*Surface Tape*

Note. In the penultimate column, C_p, C_r and C_v represent transitions for pattern, root and vocalism categories, respectively.

Fig. 7.11. Path for */katab/.

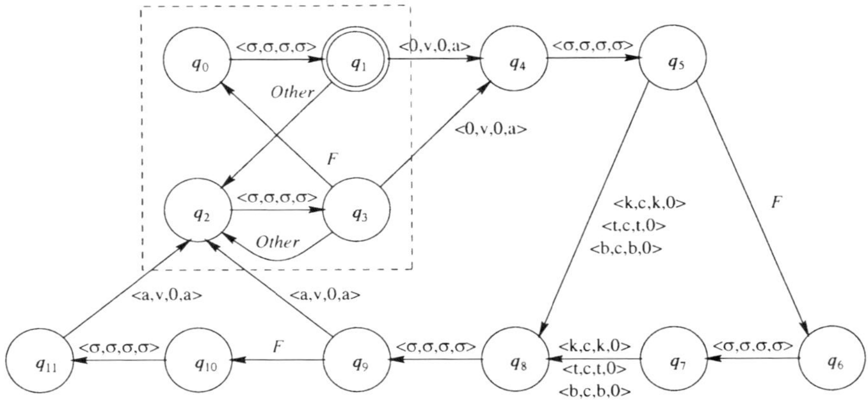

$Other = C - \{ \langle 0,\text{v},0,\text{a} \rangle \}$

Fig. 7.12. Example: phase 2.

in Fig. 7.10; the only difference is the label *Other*, which replaces the label *C* in Fig. 7.10. In other words, the boxed portion does not scan the center of R4.

Once the automaton scans the center of R4 (q_4), it expects to find the right context specified by the rule: a tuple of σs (q_5); the first tuple in the right context (q_8), which can be preceded by a category-feature tuple (q_6, q_7); a tuple of σs (q_9); the second tuple in the right context, namely, ⟨a,v,0,a⟩ (q_2), which can be preceded by a category-feature tuple (q_{10}, q_{11}). Once in q_2, the right context has been satisfied.

This automaton does not enforce R4. One can still get ill-formed */katab/ by following the same path described in Fig. 7.11.

7.5.4 *Third Phase: Obligatory Rules*

The third phase deals with condition (b), stated in the previous subsection: if the specified contexts and lexical center are satisfied, then the specified surface center must also be satisfied.

Applying *Coerce*, Eq. (7.27), on R4 produces an automaton that represents the centers with the *correct* lexical tuples and *incorrect* surface symbols with respect to R4. Subtracting this automaton from the one in Fig. 7.12 produces the automaton in Fig. 7.13. The portion in the small dashed box (states $q_0 - q_3$) represents the automaton from the first phase (Fig. 7.10) with the following difference: the edges to q_2 are marked with $\overline{Lex}$, which represents the centers with the *incorrect* lexical tuples with respect to R4.

If the automaton scans the *correct* lexical tuples, it will move to (a) state q_4 if it scans the *correct* surface symbol, or (b) state q_{12} if it scans the *incorrect* surface symbol.

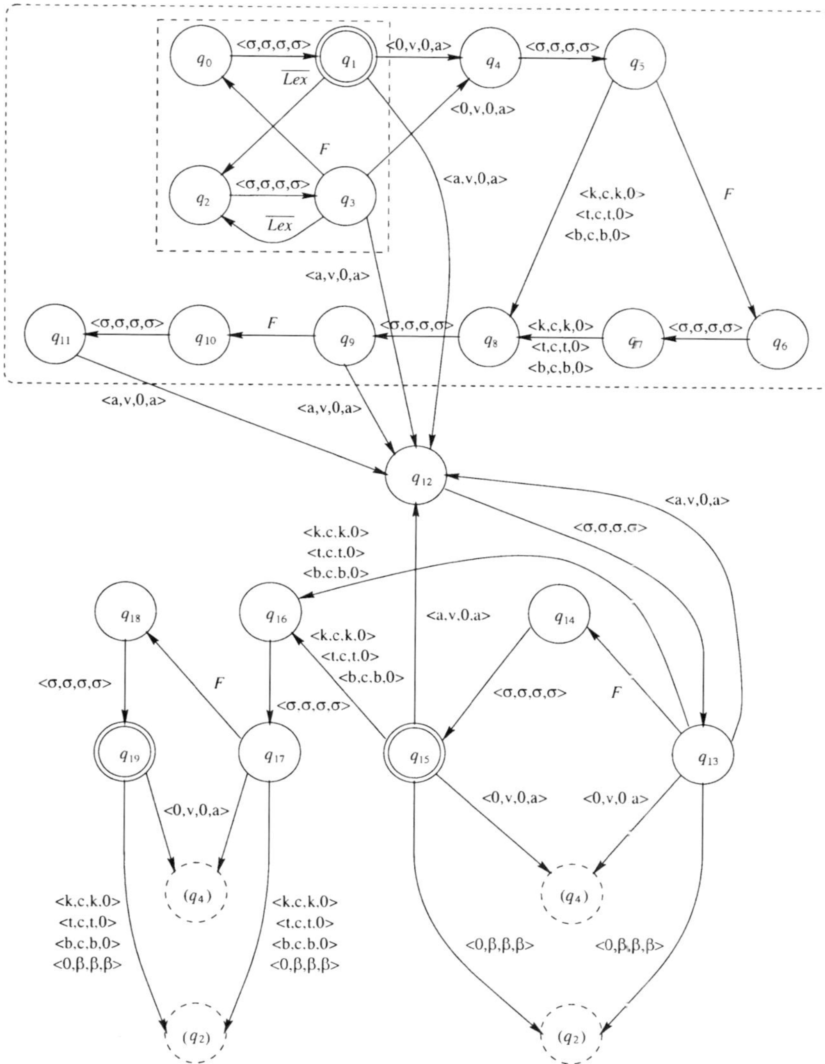

$\overline{Lex} = C - \{ \langle 0,\mathrm{v},0,\mathrm{a}\rangle, \langle \mathrm{a},\mathrm{v},0,\mathrm{a}\rangle \}$

Note. States q_2 and q_4 are repeated at the bottom of the automaton for clarity.

Fig. 7.13. Example: phase 3.

In case (a), the automaton will proceed within the large dashed box (states $q_0 - q_{11}$), which represents the automaton from the second phase (Fig. 7.12) with the following exception: the edges from states q_9 and q_{11} go to q_{12} rather than q_2; this is because the label on these arcs represents the *correct* lexical tuples with the *incorrect* surface symbol.

In case (b), the automaton will proceed to the lower portion of the automaton ($q_{12} - q_{19}$). Once the automaton is at q_{12}, it has to make sure that what follows is *not* the right context specified by the rule. Recall that the right context in this case is the tuple ⟨C,c,C,0⟩ followed by ⟨a,v,0,a⟩.

After reading a tuple of σs (q_{13}), the automaton can scan a category followed by a tuple of σs and optionally stop (q_{14}, q_{15}). Alternatively, it determines whether the first symbol after the center is ⟨C,c,C,0⟩ or not: if so, it moves to q_{16}; otherwise, it loops back to

(i) q_{12} on ⟨a,v,0,a⟩ (to make sure that the right context is not satisfied again);
(ii) q_4 on ⟨0,v,0,a⟩ (to enforce the right context of the rule);
(iii) q_2 on all other tuples (in this case the only remaining tuple is ⟨0,β,β,β⟩), after it is found that the right context is *not* satisfied.

Once a ⟨C,c,C,0⟩ has been scanned, the automaton will be in q_{16}. Now the automaton has to make sure that the rest of the right context, that is, ⟨a,v,0,a⟩, is *not* permitted. Once a tuple of σs is scanned (q_{17}), the automaton can either scan a category followed by a tuple of σs and optionally stop (q_{18}, q_{19}), or having satisfied that the right context does not occur, it loops back to the upper portion of the automaton (q_2 or q_4) as above. Note that once in q_{16} and the tuple ⟨a,v,0,a⟩ is found on the input satisfying the right context, the automaton will halt.

Finally, one removes all instances of the subsequence boundary symbols, σ, and σs from the automaton.

8 Conclusion

> I have discerned that no one writes a book on a certain day, but does not say in the next day, "if this were changed, it would be better; and if this were inserted, it would be commendable; and if this preceded, it would be preferable; and if this were deleted, it would be more beautiful." This is an excellent piece of advice, and indicative of the imperfection engraved in all mankind.
>
> al-Imâd al-Iṣfahânî (1125–1201)

This final chapter provides some concluding remarks. It presents the potential use of the current model in problems beyond Semitic, and it outlines directions for further research.

8.1 Beyond Semitic

The departure point of the formal linguistic descriptions of Semitic upon which this work is based is the autosegmental model. McCarthy's first findings demonstrated how autosegmental phonology can be applied to morphology as well. It is then expected that the computational model presented here be capable of handling general autosegmental problems. Although this has not been tested thoroughly, it is believed that this is the case, as the following example demonstrates.

Recall the Ngbaka example (see p. 3). Tense in Ngbaka is indicated by tone morphemes as shown in Fig. 1.1. Within the framework of the current model, the Ngbaka lexicon consists of two sublexica: sublexicon 1 contains verb morphemes such as {kpolo}. sublexicon 2 lists the tone morphemes {l}, {m}, {lh}, and {h} for low, mid, low–high, and high tones, respectively.

Because the lexicon makes use of two sublexica, each lexical expression in the rewrite rules must be a pair describing characters from the first and second sublexica, respectively. For example, rule R1 (below) handles low tones by mapping the segment [o] from the first sublexicon and the low tone morpheme segment [l] from the second sublexicon to [ò] on the surface:

$$\text{R1} \quad \begin{array}{ccccccc} * & - & \langle \text{o}, \text{l} \rangle & - & * & \Rightarrow \\ * & - & \grave{\text{o}} & - & * & \end{array}$$

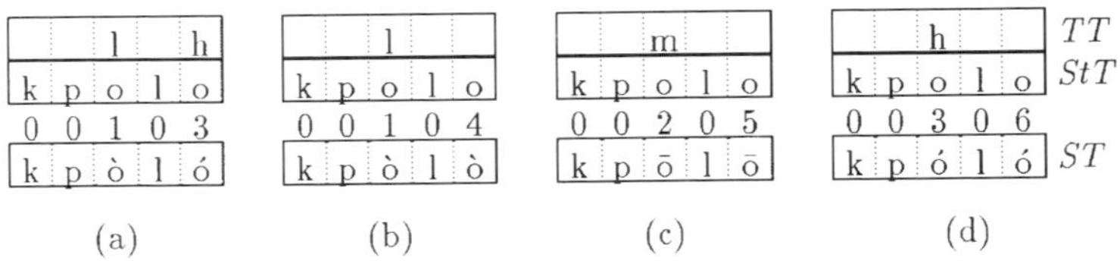

Fig. 8.1. Analyses of the Ngbaka verb: *ST* = surface tape, *StT* = stem tape, *TT* = tone tape.

Similarly, rules R2 and R3 handle mid and high tones, respectively, as follows:

$$\text{R2}\quad \begin{array}{ccccccc} * & - & \langle \text{o, m} \rangle & - & * & \Rightarrow \\ * & - & \bar{\text{o}} & - & * & \end{array}$$

$$\text{R3}\quad \begin{array}{ccccccc} * & - & \langle \text{o, h} \rangle & - & * & \Rightarrow \\ * & - & \acute{\text{o}} & - & * & \end{array}$$

The lexical-surface analysis of /kpòló/ appears in Fig. 8.1(a). The numbers between the surface and the lexical expressions indicate the above rules that sanction the subsequences. Recall that R0 is the identity rule as before.

Spreading is taken care of in the following rules.

$$\text{R4}\quad \begin{array}{ccccccc} \langle \text{o, l} \rangle\ * & - & \text{o} & - & * & \Rightarrow \\ * & - & \grave{\text{o}} & - & * & \end{array}$$

$$\text{R5}\quad \begin{array}{ccccccc} \langle \text{o, m} \rangle\ * & - & \text{o} & - & * & \Rightarrow \\ * & - & \bar{\text{o}} & - & * & \end{array}$$

$$\text{R6}\quad \begin{array}{ccccccc} \langle \text{o, h} \rangle\ * & - & \text{o} & - & * & \Rightarrow \\ * & - & \acute{\text{o}} & - & * & \end{array}$$

For example, R4 maps [o] from the first sublexicon to [ò] on the surface, as long as an ⟨o, l⟩ has already occurred in the left-lexical context. Note the use of an asterisk in left-lexical context to indicate that other segments may separate the two vowels in the lexical representation. Lexical-surface analyses with spreading appear in Fig. 8.1(b)–(d).

This demonstrates the possibility of modeling general autosegmental problems by using the framework described in this book.

8.2 Directions for Further Research

The field of Semitic computational morphology and phonology remains in its infancy. A substantial number of serious, and interesting, problems remain to be solved. This section briefly outlines some of these problems, with the aim of receiving some attention from the community.

8.2.1 Disambiguation

It is not uncommon that a morphophonological analysis of a word produces multiple results. The English word /can/, for example, can be either an auxiliary verb (e.g., /I can write/) or a noun (e.g., /a can of food/). This applies to Semitic languages as well, except that the ambiguity is notoriously large.

This ambiguity is due to a number of factors. First, and foremost, it is due to the absence of short vowels in the orthographic strings. Consider the Arabic string ⟨ktb⟩. It can be analyzed as: /kataba/ "he wrote – PERF ACT," /kutiba/ "it was written – PERF PASS," /kutub/ "books," /kutubu/ "books – NOMINATIVE," /kutuba/ "books – ACCUSATIVE," and /kutubi/ "books – GENITIVE."

When there are a number of morphemes in a word, some of the ambiguity may be resolved by ignoring ill-formed ones by morphotactic means. This, however, is not always the case. Syriac ⟨ktbt⟩, where the final {t} is a verbal inflexional marker, for example, may be /ketbat/ "she wrote," /ktabt/ "you (MASC) wrote," and /ketbet/ "I wrote." To complicate matters further, the verbal paradigm contains fully vocalized homographs such as Syriac /nektob/ for "he/we shall write," as well as /tektob/ for "she/you (SING MASC) shall write."

It is then necessary for a successful morphophonological system to look at the context of a given word syntactically and maybe semantically. If a sufficient corpus is available, some statistical method might prove useful. A naive corpus-based approach was performed by R. Sproat and Y. Meron at Bell Labs on a limited vocalized corpus of Hebrew (the Old Testament text) and Syriac (the New Testament text). For each orthographic word in the corpus, they chose its most frequent vocalization as the correct one. This approach resulted in 61–71% accuracy for Hebrew, depending on whether prefixes were included in the test or not; a better result for Syriac was obtained, probably because it employs a smaller set of vowels and patterns. This naive approach will not be suitable, nor was it intended to be so, for a real application.

8.2.2 Semantics in Semitic Morphology

What adds to the complexity of Semitic morphology is that some frequent morphemes have more than one morphological function. The Syriac prefix {la}, which occurs in 3.9% of the words of the New Testament, has at least two functions: a preposition meaning "to," as in /zel l-baytå/ "go to [the] house," and an object marker, as in /bnå l-baytå/ "[he] built [the] house" (the [a] of {la} is deleted in open syllables). It was mentioned earlier that the Syriac prefix {da} has 16 syntactic and semantic functions David (1896).

A large-scale implementation ought to employ semantic markings in the lexicon (and rules, if need be). Categories of the type used in this work can be expanded to cater for such markings. Although this might complicate matters in taking morphology into the realm of semantics, the ambiguity problem discussed above can make use of semantic knowledge.

8.2.3 Coinage and Neologism

The development of the Semitic languages that are still used today is a rapid process. Today, linguists speak of Modern Standard Arabic versus Classical Arabic, or Israeli Hebrew versus Biblical Hebrew. While the skeleton and structure of modern languages is still that of the classical ones, there has been noticeable development in the lexicon, syntax, and semantics of these languages. Less so is the impact on morphological structure.

Morphology, however, is still affected by this development in a number of ways. Although new patterns are not invented, using a pattern that hitherto has not been used with a specific root is one of the means of coining new words. The Arabic nominal patterns {miCCaC} and {miCCaaC}, for example, are used to coin instruments: /miĵhar/ "microscope" from the root {ĵhr} "notion of bringing to light, showing," /minðaar/ "telescope" from the root {nð̣r} "notion of eyesight, vision (Versteegh, 1997a).

Syriac has its own share of neologisms, albeit with the absence of the various language academies that Arabic enjoys. I recall seeing a sign in Lebanon above the Syriac Orthodox Co-op shop with the word /taʕdartå/ from the root {ʕdr} "notion of helping" with the nominal pattern {CVCVeCtå}. Had I not read on the same sign its Arabic counterpart, /taʕaawuniyya/ from the root {ʕwn} also "notion of helping," and had I not known that this particular pattern is used in other Syriac neologisms, I would not have guessed its meaning. The same pattern is used in /taħreztå/ "program" from the root {ħrz} "notion of arranging" and /takreztå/ "radio" from the root {krz} "notion of preaching."

Obviously, a good morphological system has to tackle such problems. Allowing each root to be analyzed in all plausible patterns, however, will be disastrous, as it will magnify the ambiguity issue discussed above. Here, weighted automata, in which each transition is associated with a weight, might come in handy. One can give higher costs to associating roots with patterns that are not used in the language's lexicon and corpora, but may possibly be used in neologisms.

8.2.4 Linguistic Research

One of the main obstacles in developing a *linguistically motivated* morphophonological system in Semitic is the lack of sufficient formal descriptions. While there has been some recent work in formal Semitic linguistics, the main bulk of the literature is still driven by the philological approach of traditional grammars.

Having said that, traditional grammars, and indeed classical ones, cannot be totally ignored. They tend to apply formal analyses implicitly which can be, with some effort, formalized to bring them up to date for computational purposes, especially when no other formal accounts are available.

8.3 Future of Semitic Computational Linguistics

While research in Semitic computational linguistics remains in its infancy (especially in the West), there has been recent efforts to remedy this, most notably the Semitic workshop held during COLING-ACL'98. It is hoped that such activities become more regular.

I would like to stress what I have already mentioned in the preface. Semitic is important for both commercial and academic research. Commercially, the Middle East market is tremendous, and personal computers are becoming more and more popular. Academically, Semitic languages exhibit interesting characteristics in their lexica, phonology, morphology, syntax, and semantics. Researching these characteristics would put current trends in computational linguistics to the test, as this work has done with two-level morphology.

It is hoped that this monograph will help in resolving one of the many challenges of Semitic languages, namely, their nonlinear morphology.

References

ܟܬ̈ܒܐ ܢܗܘܘܢ ܦܬܘܪܟ : ܘܒܗܘܢ ܬܣܒܥ ܒܘܣ̈ܡܐ

ܘܗܢܘܢ ܢܗܘܘܢ ܡܫܘܝܬܟ : ܘܬܕܡܟ ܫܢܬܐ ܕܢܝܚܐ

Let books be your dining table,
And you shall be full of delights
Let them be your mattress
And you shall sleep restful nights

St. Ephrem the Syrian (303–373)
Quoted in Bar Ebrōyô's *Ethicon*

Aho, A., R. Sethi, and J. Ullman. 1986. *Compilers, Principles, Techniques and Tools*. Addison-Wesley.

Antworth, E. 1990. *PC-KIMMO: A Two-Level Processor for Morphological Analysis*. Occasional Publications in Academic Computing 16. Summer Institute of Linguistics, Dallas.

Antworth, E. 1994. Morphological parsing with a unification-based word grammar. In *North Texas Natural Language Processing Workshop*. [`http://www.sil.org/pckimmo/ntnlp94.html`].

Aronoff, M. 1994. *Morphology by Itself. Stems and Inflectional Classes*. Linguistic Inquiry Monographs 22. The MIT Press.

Ballard, D. and E. Kohen. 1996. Microsoft truetype open specification. [`http://www.microsoft.com/opentype/tt/ch1.htm`].

Bat-El, O. 1989. *Phonology and Word Structure in Modern Hebrew*. Ph.D. thesis, University of California at Los Angeles.

Bear, J. 1986. A morphological recognizer with syntactic and phonological rules. In *COLING-86: Papers Presented to the 11th International Conference on Computational Linguistics*, pages 272–6.

Bear, J. 1988. Morphology with two-level rules and negative rule features. In *COLING-88: Papers Presented to the 12th International Conference on Computational Linguistics*, volume 1, pages 28–31.

Beesley, K. 1990. Finite-state description of Arabic morphology. In *Proceedings of the Second Cambridge Conference: Bilingual Computing in Arabic and English*, page n.p.

Beesley, K. 1991. Computer analysis of Arabic morphology: A two-level approach with detours. In B. Comrie and M. Eid, editors, *Perspectives on Arabic Linguistics III: Papers from the Third Annual Symposium on Arabic Linguistics*. Benjamins, Amsterdam, pages 155–72.

Beesley, K. 1996. Arabic finite-state morphological analysis and generation. In *COLING-96: Papers Presented to the 16th International Conference on Computational Linguistics*, pages 89–94.

Beesley, K. forthcoming. Arabic stem morphotactics via finite-state intersection. In E. Benmamoun, editor, *Perspectives on Arabic Linguistics XII: Papers from the Twelfth Annual Symposium on Arabic Linguistics*, Benjamins, Amsterdam, pages 85–100.

Beesley, K., T. Buckwalter, and S. Newton. 1989. Two-level finite-state analysis of Arabic morphology. In *Proceedings of the Seminar on Bilingual Computing in Arabic and English*, page n.p.

Bird, S. and T. Ellison. 1992. One-level phonology: Autosegmental representations and rules as finite-state automata. Technical report, University of Edinburgh, Research Paper EUCCS/RP-51.

Bird, S. and T. Ellison. 1994. One-level phonology. *Computational Linguistics*, 20(1): 55–90.

Bird, S. and E. Klein. 1994. Phonological analysis in typed feature systems. *Computational Linguistics*, 20(3):455–91.

Black, A., G. Ritchie, S. Pulman, and G. Russell. 1987. Formalisms for morphographemic description. In *Proceedings of the Third Conference of the European Chapter of the Association for Computational Linguistics*, pages 11–8.

Bowden, T. and G. Kiraz. 1995. A morphographemic model for error correction in nonconcatenative strings. In *Proceedings of the 33rd Annual Meeting of the Association for Computational Linguistics*, pages 24–30.

Budd, T. 1994. *Classic Data Structures in C++*. Addison-Wesley.

Carter, D. 1995. Rapid development of morphological descriptions for full language processing systems. In *Proceedings of the Seventh Conference of the European Chapter of the Association for Computational Linguistics*, pages 202–9.

Chomsky, N. 1951. Morphophonemics of modern Hebrew. Master's thesis, University of Pennsylvania. Later published by Garland Press, New York, 1979.

Chomsky, N. and M. Halle. 1968. *The Sound Pattern of English*. Harper and Row, New York.

Crystal, D. 1994. *An Encyclopedic Dictionary of Language and Linguistics*. Penguin.

Daniels, P. and W. Bright, editors. 1996. *The World's Writing Systems*. Oxford University Press.

David, C. 1896. *kitâb 'al-lum'ah al-šahiyyah fī naḥw 'al-luḡah 'al-suryâniyyah*. Dominican Press, Mossoul, 2nd edition.

Eilenberg, S. 1974. *Automata, Languages, and Machines*, volume A. Academic Press.

Elgot, C. and J. Mezei. 1965. On relations defined by generalized finite automata. *IBM Journal of Research and Development*, 9:47–68.

Gazdar, G., E. Klein, G. Pulum, and I. Sag. 1985. *Generalized Phrase Structure Grammar*. Basil Blackwell.

Gazdar, G. and C. Mellish. 1989. *Natural Language Processing in LISP: An Introduction to Computational Linguistics*. Addison-Wesley.

Goldsmith, J. 1976. *Autosegmental Phonology*. Ph.D. thesis, MIT. Published as *Autosegmental and Metrical Phonology*, Oxford, 1990.

Grimley-Evans, E., G. Kiraz, and S. Pulman. 1996. Compiling a partition-based two-level formalism. In *COLING-96: Papers Presented to the 16th International Conference on Computational Linguistics*, pages 454–9.

Harris, Z. 1941. Linguistic structure of Hebrew. *Journal of the American Oriental Society*, 62:143–67.

Holes, C. 1995. *Modern Arabic, Structures, Functions and Varieties*. Longman.

Hopcroft, J. and J. Ullman. 1979. *Introduction to Automata Theory, Languages, and Computation*. Addison-Wesley.

Johnson, C. 1972. *Formal Aspects of Phonological Description*. Mouton.

Kaplan, R. and M. Kay. 1994. Regular models of phonological rule systems. *Computational Linguistics*, 20(3):331–78.

Karttunen, L. 1983. Kimmo: A general morphological processor. *Texas Linguistic Forum*, 22:165–86.

Karttunen, L. 1993. Finite-state lexicon compiler. Technical report, Palo Alto Research Center, Xerox Corporation.

Karttunen, L. and K. Beesley. 1992. Two-level rule compiler. Technical report, Palo Alto Research Center, Xerox Corporation.

Kataja, L. and K. Koskenniemi. 1988. Finite state description of Semitic morphology. In *COLING-88: Papers Presented to the 12th International Conference on Computational Linguistics*, volume 1, pages 313–15.

Kay, M. 1987. Nonconcatenative finite-state morphology. In *Proceedings of the Third Conference of the European Chapter of the Association for Computational Linguistics*, pages 2–10.

Kay, M. and R. Kaplan. 1983. Word recognition. This paper was never published. The core ideas are published in Kaplan and Kay (1994).

Kiraz, G. 1994. Multi-tape two-level morphology: a case study in Semitic non-linear morphology. In *COLING-94: Papers Presented to the 15th International Conference on Computational Linguistics*, volume 1, pages 180–6.

Kiraz, G. 1995. *Introduction to Syriac Spirantization*. Bar Hebraeus Verlag, The Netherlands.

Kiraz, G. 1996a. Analysis of the Arabic broken plural and diminutive. In *Proceedings of the 5th International Conference and Exhibition on Multi-Lingual Computing*. Cambridge.

Kiraz, G. 1996b. Computational prosodic morphology. In *COLING-96: Papers Presented to the 16th International Conference on Computational Linguistics*, pages 454–9.

Kiraz, G. 1996c. ṢEMḤE: A generalised two-level system. In *Proceedings of the 34th Annual Meeting of the Association for Computational Linguistics*, pages 159–66.

Kiraz, G. 1996d. Syriac morphology: From a linguistic description to a computational implementation. In R. Lavenant, editor, *VI-Itum Symposium Syriacum 1996*, forthcoming in Orientalia Christiana Analecta. Pontificio Institutum Studiorum Orientalium.

Kiraz, G. 1997a. Compiling regular formalisms with rule features into finite-state automata. In *Proceedings of the 35th Annual Meeting of the Association for Computational Linguistics and 8th Conference of the European Chapter of the Association of Computational Linguistics*, pages 329–36.

Kiraz, G. 1997b. Linearization of nonlinear lexical representations. In J. Coleman editor, *Proceedings of the Third Meeting of the ACL Special Interest Group in Computational Phonology*, pages 57–62.

Kiraz, G. 1998. Arabic computational morphology in the West. In *Proceedings of the 6th International Conference and Exhibition on Multi-Lingual Computing*. Cambridge.

Kiraz, G. (2000). Multitiered Nonlinear Morphology Using Multitape Finite Automata: A Case Study on Syriac and Arabic. *Computational Linguistics* 26(1): 77–105.

Kiraz, G. and E. Grimley-Evans. 1997. Multi-tape automata for speech and language systems: A Prolog implementation. In *Proceedings of the Second International Workshop on Implementing Automata*. Forthcoming in Springer-Verlag Lecture Notes in Computer Science Series.

Kornai, A. 1991. *Formal Phonology*. Ph.D. thesis, Stanford University. Later published as Kornai, 1995.

Koskenniemi, K. 1983. *Two-Level Morphology*. Ph.D. thesis, University of Helsinki.

Koskenniemi, K. 1986. Compilation of automata from morphological two-level rules. In *Papers from the Fifth Scandinavian Conference of Computational Linguistics*. University of Helsinki.

Krist, J. 1998. New-age musicians singing to preserve an age-old language. *The Associated Press*. May 23 issue.

Lavie, A., A. Itai, and U. Ornan. 1990. On the applicability of two level morphology to the inflection of Hebrew verbs. In Y. Choueka, editor, *Literary and Linguistic Computing 1988: Proceedings of the 15th International Conference*, pages 246–60.

Liberman, M. and A. Prince. 1977. On stress and linguistic rhythm. *Linguistic Inquiry*, 8:249–336.

Linz, P. 1990. *An Introduction to Formal Languages and Automata*. D.C. Heath and Company.

Matthews, P. 1974. *Morphology*. Cambridge.

McCarthy, J. 1981. A prosodic theory of nonconcatenative morphology. *Linguistic Inquiry*, 12(3):373–418.

McCarthy, J. 1986. OCP effects: gemination and antigemination. *Linguistic Inquiry*, 17:207–63.

McCarthy, J. 1993. Template form in prosodic morphology. In Stvan, L. et al., editor, *Papers from the Third Annual Formal Linguistics Society of Midamerica Conference*, pages 187–218. Indiana University Linguistics Club, Bloomington.

McCarthy, J. and A. Prince. 1990a. Foot and word in prosodic morphology: The Arabic broken plural. *Natural Language and Linguistic Theory*, 8:209–83.

McCarthy, J. and A. Prince. 1990b. Prosodic morphology and templatic morphology. In M. Eid and J. McCarthy, editors, *Perspectives on Arabic Linguistics II: Papers from the Second Annual Symposium on Arabic Linguistics*. Benjamins, Amsterdam, pages 1–54.

McCarthy, M. 1991. Morphology. In K. Malmkjær, editor, *The Linguistics Encyclopedia*. Routledge, pages 314–23.

Mohri, M. 1994. On some applications of finite-state automata theory to natural language processing. Technical report, Institut Gaspard Monge.

Mohri, M. 1997. Finite-state transducers in language and speech processing. *Computational Linguistics*, 23(2):269–311.

Mohri, M. and R. Sproat. 1996. An efficient compiler for weighted rewrite rules. In *Proceedings of the 34th Annual Meeting of the Association for Computational Linguistics*, pages 231–8.

Moore, E. 1956. Gedanken experiments on sequential machines. In *Automata Studies*. Princeton, pages 129–53.

Moore, J. 1990. Doubled verbs in Modern Standard Arabic. In M. Eid and J. McCarthy, editors, *Perspectives on Arabic Linguistics II: Papers from the Second Annual Symposium on Arabic Linguistics*. Benjamins, Amsterdam, pages 55–93.

Moscati, S., A. Spitaler, E. Ullendorff, and W. von Soden. 1969. *An Introduction to the Comparative Grammar of the Semitic Languages: Phonology and Morphology*. Porta Linguarum Orientalium. Otto Harrassowitz, Wiesbaden, 2nd edition.

Muraoka, T. 1997. *Classical Syriac: A Basic Grammar. With a bibliography prepared by S.P. Brock*. Porta Linguarum Orientalium. Otto Harrassowits.

Murre-van den Berg, H. 1995. *From a Spoken to a Written Language: The Introduction and Development of Literary Urmia Aramaic in the Nineteenth Century*. Ph.D. thesis, Rijksuniversiteit, Leiden.

Narayanan, A. and L. Hashem. 1993. On abstract finite-state morphology. In *Proceedings of the Sixth Conference of the European Chapter of the Association for Computational Linguistics*, pages 297–304.

Nelson, P., G. Kiraz, and S. Hasso. 1998. Proposal to encode syriac in iso/iec 10646. Technical report, Unicode Technical Committee Web Site.

Nida, E. 1949. *Morphology: The Descriptive Analysis of Words*. University of Michigan Press.

Nivat, M. 1968. Transductions des languages de Chomsky. *Ann. Inst. Fourier (Grenoble)*, 18:339–455.

Partee, B., A. ter Meulen, and R. Wall. 1993. *Mathematical Methods in Linguistics*. Kluwer Academic.

Pulman, S. and M. Hepple. 1993. A feature-based formalism for two-level phonology: a description and implementation. *Computer Speech and Language*, 7:333–58.

Rabin, M. and D. Scott. 1959. Finite automata and their decision problems. *IBM Journal of Research and Development*, 3:114–25. Reprinted in Moore, E. (ed.) *Sequential Machines*. Addison-Wesley, 1964, pages 63-91.

Rayward-Smith, V. 1983. *A First Course in Formal Language Theory*. Blackwell Scientific.

Ritchie, G. 1992. Languages generated by two-level morphological rules. *Computational Linguistics*, 18(1):41–59.

Ritchie, G., A. Black, G. Russell, and S. Pulman. 1992. *Computational Morphology: Practical Mechanisms for the English Lexicon*. MIT Press.

Robins, R. 1979. *A Short History of Linguistics*. Longman, 2nd edition.

Robinson, T. 1978. *Paradigms and Exercises in Syriac Grammar*. The Clarendon Press, Oxford, 4th edition.

Roche, E. and Y. Schabes. 1995. Deterministic part-of-speech tagging with finite-state transducers. *Computational Linguistics*, 21(2):227–53.

Roche, E. and Y. Schabes, editors. 1997. *Finite-State Language Processing*. MIT Press.

Ruessink, H. 1989. Two level formalisms. Technical Report 5, Utrecht Working Papers in NLP.

Spencer, A. 1991. *Morphological Theory*. Basil Blackwell.

Sproat, R. 1992. *Morphology and Computation*. MIT Press.

Sproat, R., editor. 1997. *Multilingual Text-to-Speech Synthesis: The Bell Labs Approach*. Kluwer.

The Unicode Consortium. 1991. *The Unicode Standard: Worldwide Character Encoding*. Addison-Wesley.

The Unicode Consortium. 1997. *The Unicode Standard, Version 2.0*. Addison-Wesley.

The Unicode Consortium. 2000. *The Unicode Standard, Version 3.0*. Addison-Wesley.

Trask, R. 1993. *A Dictionary of Grammatical Terms in Linguistics*. Routledge.

Trost, H. 1990. The application of two-level morphology to non-concatenative German morphology. In H. Karlgren, editor, *COLING-90: Papers Presented to the 13th International Conference on Computational Linguistics*, volume 2, pages 371–6.

Versteegh, K. 1997a. *The Arabic Language*. Columbia University.

Versteegh, K. 1997b. *Landmarks in Linguistic Thought III: The Arabic Linguistic Tradition*. Routledge.

Wehr, H. 1971. *A Dictionary of Modern Written Arabic*. Spoken Language Services.

Wiebe, B. 1992. Modelling autosegmental phonology with multi-tape finite state transducers. Master's thesis, Simon Fraser University.

Wright, W. 1988. *A Grammar of the Arabic Language*. Cambridge University, 3rd edition.

Quotation Credits

Antony the Rhetorician of Tagrit (p. 90), Syriac. Text and translation from J. W. Watt (ed.), *The Fifth Book of Rhetoric of Antony of Tagrit.* Corpus Scriptorum Christianorum Orientalium 480/1, Scriptores Syri 203/4 (Louvain, 1986).

Bar Ebroyo (p. 69), Syriac. Text from A. Martin, *Œuvres grammaticales d'Abou 'lfaradj dit Bar Hebreus* (Paris, Lauvain, 1872). Translation from J. B. Segal, *The Diacritical Point and the Accent in Syriac* (Oxford, 1953).

David ben Abraham (p. 90), Hebrew. Translation kindly provided by Dr Geoffrey Khan.

Elia of Ṣobha (p. 121), Syriac. Text and translation from R. Gottheil (ed.), *A Treatise of Syriac Grammar by Mâr(i) Eliâ of Ṣôb*^{h}*â* (Berlin, 1887).

Ephrem the Syrian (in Bibliography), Syriac. Text quoted in P. Bedjan (ed.), *Ethicon, seu Moralia, Gregorii Barhebraei* (Paris, 1898).

Ḥunayn bar Isḥâq (p. 69), Syriac. Text from A. Merx, *Historia artis grammaticae apud Syros* (Leipzig, 1889).

Ibn Jinnî (p. 47), Arabic. Translation from (Versteegh, 1997b).

Isaac of Antioch (p. xx) Syriac. Translation from Burkitt, *Evangelion da-Mepharreshe, the Curetonian Version of the Four Gospels, with the readings of the Sinai Palimpsest and the early Syriac Patristic evidence* (Cambridge, 1904).

Job of Edessa (p. 32), Syriac. Text and Translation from A. Mingana (ed.), *Book of Treasures by Job of Edessa* (Cambridge, 1935).

Sîbawayhi (p. 32), Arabic. Translation taken from (Versteegh, 1997b).

ܐܝܟܢܐ ܕܚܕܐ ܡܠܚܐ : ܕܡܛܬ ܐܠܦܗ ܠܠܡܐܢܐ

ܗܟܢ ܚܕܐ ܟܬܘܒܐ : ܕܣܘܪܓܐ ܐܚܪܝܐ ܟܬܒ

As the seaman rejoices
When his ship reaches the port,
So does the writer rejoice
When he writes the final word.

Language, Word, and Morpheme Index

Name Index

Subject Index